MW00619522

The Hollywood Motion Picture Blacklist

The
Hollywood
Motion Picture
Blacklist

Seventy-Five Years Later

LARRY CEPLAIR

UNIVERSITY PRESS OF KENTUCKY

Copyright © 2022 by The University Press of Kentucky

Scholarly publisher for the Commonwealth,
serving Bellarmine University, Berea College, Centre
College of Kentucky, Eastern Kentucky University,
The Filson Historical Society, Georgetown College,
Kentucky Historical Society, Kentucky State University,
Morehead State University, Murray State University,
Northern Kentucky University, Spalding University,
Transylvania University, University of Kentucky, University
of Louisville, University of Pikeville, and Western Kentucky
University.
All rights reserved.

Editorial and Sales Offices: The University Press of Kentucky
663 South Limestone Street, Lexington, Kentucky 40508-4008
www.kentuckypress.com

The following chapters were published in slightly different form in the
publications listed below.

Chapter 5: "Isobel Lennart and the Dynamics of Informing in Hollywood."
Historical Journal of Film, Radio and Television 27, no. 4 (2007): 513–29.

Chapter 6: "Ring Lardner, Jr. and the Hollywood Blacklist: A New Perspective
on the Perennial Struggle against Thought Control in the United States."
Historical Journal of Film, Radio and Television 39, no. 1 (2019): 75–95.

Chapter 7: "Shedding Light on Darkness at High Noon." *Cineaste* 27, no. 4
(Fall 2002): 20–22.

Cataloging-in-Publication data is available from the Library of Congress.

ISBN 978-0-8131-9588-9 (hardcover)
ISBN 978-0-8131-9589-6 (pdf)
ISBN 978-0-8131-9590-2 (epub)

This book is printed on acid-free paper meeting
the requirements of the American National Standard
for Permanence in Paper for Printed Library Materials.

Manufactured in the United States of America

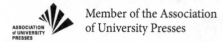

Member of the Association
of University Presses

To the memory of Albert Maltz. Steven Englund and I wanted to dedicate *The Inquisition in Hollywood* to him, in gratitude for his close reading and constructive critique of the manuscript. He declined, fearing that such a dedication would compromise the book in the eyes of many reviewers. Albert was a generous and caring man, whose fidelity to the historical record, while a pain in the ass to some, was an inspiration to me.

Contents

Preface

This year marks the seventy-fifth anniversary of the Hollywood motion picture blacklist and the forty-seventh anniversary of my first foray into the archives to write about it. Since then, I have coauthored *The Inquisition in Hollywood*, two biographies of blacklisted screenwriters, dozens of articles and book and film reviews on the subject, conducted many oral histories, and curated an exhibit at the Academy of Motion Picture Arts and Sciences. I have as well been befriended by several of the blacklistees and their offspring. Unfortunately, many of them have died; as of this writing, to the best of my knowledge, only two of the blacklisted Hollywood people, Marsha Hunt and Norma Barzman, are still alive.

Given the axial changes in the entertainment/media industries (huge enterprises adroitly staying several steps ahead of regulation and control), the admonition to be "woke," and the "cancel culture," the time seemed propitious for a book that offered some new thoughts on the motion picture blacklist: its origins, its extent, its duration, its impact, and its future prospects. Also, given the large number of books published and films made on the subject, it seemed time to provide an up-to-date annotated bibliography and filmography. Finally, I wanted to undertake a last summing-up of what I have learned over the years. I decided to include three previously unpublished essays and three previously published ones. In terms of the new material, chapter 2 examines the question of Jewish anti-Communism in the movie industry and its connection to national Jewish anti-Communism, shedding light on the movie executives' thought processes as they promulgated the blacklist. I have always been fascinated with Dashiell Hammett as a mystery writer and political activist. His transformation from hugely successful short-story writer and novelist to the least-likely Communist imaginable seemed worthy of discussion. Finally, an objective comparative analysis of the respective moral postures of the friendly and unfriendly House Committee on Un-American Activities witnesses has not been done. And the two books I review about the witnesses' morality failed to meld those individual stories into a satisfactory explanation.

From my roster of previously published articles, I have selected those on Ring Lardner Jr., an unfriendly witness, and the friendly witness Isobel Lennart. As a coda to them, my article on the blacklist-induced broken friendship and business relationship between Carl Foreman and Stanley Kramer seemed useful. The four of them navigated the rapids of the blacklist era in different and instructive ways. (I have made a few alterations in the Lardner article.)

In sum, the three new chapters and three previously published articles represent a change in my perspective about the blacklist. When Steven Englund and I composed *The Inquisition in Hollywood* some forty years ago, the institutional arc of the story we were telling, from the formation of the Screen Writers Guild to the blacklist, dominated our thinking. Although we inserted many personal stories along the way, the arc always took precedence. But ever since I began doing oral histories for UCLA, I have come to the conclusion that one can learn much more about the complexities and contradictions of the blacklist era via personal life stories. Generalizing categories can be useful, but they must be very carefully employed. For example, Steven and I spent weeks crafting what we thought would be our opening chapter—the prescreenwriting lives and careers of our protagonists. We finally realized that this was a waste of time, that there were too many variations on the theme. There is no screenwriter type, no informer type, no unfriendly witness type, no producer type, and no Communist Party member type. It is only through examining the lives and thoughts and motives of individuals that one can come to a genuine understanding of the blacklist era.

In chapter 1, "Looking Back," I have tried to summarize what I have learned about the origins and operation of the blacklist. In chapter 8, "Looking Ahead," I have essayed a glance at the probability of future proscriptions of the blacklist type. That chapter represents the final iteration of my long-standing belief that the history of the United States is replete with banishments of typed people from full citizenship, civil rights, and civil liberties. Although progress has been made on many fronts, the United States remains a racist, misogynist, nativist, and anti-Left country, dominated by huge media entities. And, as the Trump presidency has demonstrated, it does not take much for the pendulum of history to swing back to an intolerant, suppressive, and frankly scary phase.

Should Trump or someone like him become president of the United States in the coming years, the words of two formerly blacklisted Hollywood screenwriters, spoken on the occasion of their respective acceptance of the Writers Guild of America's Laurel Award for Screenwriting Achievement, are pertinent. Dalton Trumbo (1970) invited those in their forties or younger to occasionally "look back with curiosity on that dark time," to see it as "a time of evil"; "a situation that had passed beyond the control of mere individuals"; "a long nightmare"; and a time in which all concerned became "victims." (In 2018, two years before he died, the civil rights legend John Lewis warned that the United States was descending into another dark time [*John Lewis: Good Trouble*, Magnolia Pictures, 2020.]) Michael Wilson (1976) foresaw a day coming in the lifetime of younger Guild members "when a new crisis of belief will grip this republic." If it should, he trusted that "you younger men and women will shelter the mavericks and dissenters in your ranks and protect their right to work."[1]

Looking Back

The pendulum swing of historiography is very noticeable in writing about the blacklist. At the height of the domestic Cold War, aside from one book by Gordon Kahn, a blacklisted writer (*Hollywood on Trial,* 1948), occasional articles by the blacklistees, and the groundbreaking article by Elizabeth Poe ("The Hollywood Story," 1954), all those who wrote about the subject either denied its existence or approved of it and condemned the blacklistees.[1] Perhaps the peak of the campaign to diminish the blacklisted as artists, and by extension serious political players, occurred in Murray Kempton's *A Part of Our Time* (1955), his book of essays on the 1930s. "Their story," he wrote, "is a failure of promise.... The promise at the beginnings of most of them appears now to have been largely smoke and thunder.... [T]hey got rich fabricating empty banalities to fit Hollywood's ideal of life in America." Even John Cogley's two-volume *Report on Blacklisting* (1956), the mainstream book that exposed the mechanics of the blacklist in film and television, which was based to a large extent on Poe's reporting, is riddled with the anti-Communist bias of Cogley and his other main reporter, Paul Jacobs. The unfriendly witnesses are treated in a hostile manner and falsely accused of having administered their own blacklist in the preceding decade. Nor did the erosion of the blacklist, beginning in 1960 with Dalton Trumbo's screen credits for *Exodus* and *Spartacus,* change the tenor of the commentary. Richard Corliss, in his series of essays on thirty-five screenwriters, singled out Dalton Trumbo for some of his sharpest barbs, including him among the left-wing writers who were, in his words, "footnotes in Hollywood history." (He did, however, praise the work of two other left-wing writers, Donald Ogden Stewart and Sidney Buchman.) Walter Goodman, in his critical study of the

House Committee on Un-American Activities, called the unfriendly witnesses "craftsmen, more or less adept at setting down on paper the ideas in a producer's head. It was not arduous work," and their "careers parodied the writer's craft." These supercilious comments continued into the 1970s, with Stefan Kanfer ("they were responsible for pap, but they were also concerned with the Little Man") and Hilton Kramer ("loyal, pampered, high-priced hacks").[2]

A major swing in viewpoint occurred in 1968, with Howard Suber's doctoral dissertation fully exposing the mechanics of the blacklist. He was the first person since Poe to interview some of the people involved. He spoke with six of the Nineteen, unfriendly witnesses who were subpoenaed by the House Committee on Un-American Activities to appear at its October 1947 hearings into "Communist Infiltration of the Motion-Picture Industry" (John Howard Lawson, Lester Cole, Albert Maltz, Ring Lardner Jr., Howard Koch, and Edward Dmytryk), studio head Dore Schary, and Robert Kenny, an attorney for the Nineteen. Unfortunately, he could not find a publisher. Four years later, however, the actor Robert Vaughn succeeded in turning his Ph.D. dissertation on blacklisting into a book: *Only Victims.* He also interviewed the blacklisted people, and he performed a significant service by including the statements that ten of the members of the Nineteen who actually testified in October 1947 were not permitted to read during their testimonies before the House Committee. Then, in 1976, the documentary film *Hollywood on Trial* allowed the blacklistees to speak for themselves. They came across as serious, intelligent people and stirred the curiosity of some of its watchers to learn more about them, especially their political pasts, which had been ignored by the previous naysayers.[3]

The tide turned fully in the early 1980s, with the publication of *The Inquisition in Hollywood; Naming Names;* and *The Hollywood Writers' Wars.* All three were deeply researched; Larry Ceplair, Steven Englund, and Nancy Schwartz moved the story arc back to the 1930s, demonstrating that the blacklisted people had been dedicated and serious political activists, as well as hardworking, successful writers, directors, and actors; Victor S. Navasky interviewed dozens of friendly and unfriendly witnesses and unveiled the dense supportive network for those who cooperated with the Committee. All four authors admired and respected the blacklistees.[4] (For a full discussion of *Naming Names*, see chapter 3.)

For about fifteen years, this new left/liberal generation of historians held sway, but, starting in 1995, the pendulum again swung back to the conservative right, fueled by the administrations of Ronald Reagan and George H. W. Bush and the collapse of the Soviet Union. The latter event paved the way for the release of the Venona decryptions (of telegrams between the Soviet Union and US Communists) and the opening of the Soviet archives to historians. Documents relating to the Communist Party of the United States were collected, with commentary, in the Yale University Annals of Communism series. (Each book in the Yale series is coedited by a US historian and a Russian academic or archivist. Virtually all of the former are zealous anti-Communists.)[5] The editors of those volumes concluded, to the surprise of no one who had been paying attention, that there was a very close link between Soviet Communist leaders and the Communist Party of the United States. There was a "see, the domestic Cold War was necessary" leitmotif in all these books. In addition, a number of biographies of Ronald Reagan appeared, documenting his efforts to suppress Communism in Hollywood. These books resurrected the specter of evil Communism and its Stalinist dupes. In 1998, Kenneth Lloyd Billingsley, an acolyte of Roy Brewer, the doyen of Hollywood anti-Communists, produced a book faithfully mirroring Brewer's version of the blacklist in Hollywood.[6]

Paul Buhle and Dave Wagner countered with four books covering most facets of Hollywood radicalism.[7] But Richard Schickel, a well-versed student of the topic and a firm believer that the Hollywood Ten's "lack of candor" in their appearances before the House Committee in 1947 was as responsible for the blacklist as the House Committee itself, subjected one of those books, *Radical Hollywood*, to a negative review.[8] During the following decade, Ronald and Allis Radosh and Allan H. Ryskind wrote two rightist revisions, strongly advocating the anti-Stalinist line. In the latest book, Thomas Doherty has taken an evenhanded approach.[9]

Both sides are clear on a central issue: The vast majority of those blacklisted were or had been members of the Communist Party. They differ on whether or not this membership and the refusal of those subpoenaed by the House Committee to affirm Party membership should have led to blacklisting. It is a huge conceptual leap from what the Hollywood Communists did—attend meetings (Party branch, front groups, guild, and union), contribute their names and money to what they called "progressive causes" (antifascism, union organizing, election of "progressive" candidates)—and what they were accused of doing: subverting the political, social, economic, and cultural structures of the United States.

Most of the sympathetic authors do not bother to answer the main charge of the antipathetic authors: Communists (Stalinists in the parlance of the anti-Communists), especially those in media and education, were complicit in the evils of Stalin's regime, and, as such, must be assigned blame for its crimes. (It should be pointed out that the terms "Stalinist" and "Stalinism" have become, like "fascism," forms of abuse and polemic with little substantive content, used so loosely that they have no validity as tools of analysis or explanation.) Steven Englund and I did point out the ideological blinders of the Hollywood Communists, noted their support for a regime that killed and imprisoned tens of millions of people, and showed how they obediently followed every change in the Party line, no matter how abrupt and contradictory it was. We criticized the Hollywood Communists for their failure to look deeply into Soviet Communism and for propounding facile explanations for the twists and turns of the Party line emanating from Moscow. But those conclusions did not satisfy anti-Communists, who seem unable to distinguish myopia or Party discipline from criminality. Contra their contentions, there is not a shred of evidence to link any Hollywood Communist to espionage or sabotage. Nor did they, because they could not, pour an unrestrained flood of subversive messages into the movies they worked on, dominate any of the studio guilds and unions, or engage in blacklisting conservatives in the movie industry. The Communists in Hollywood only succeeded when they acted like, and in unity with, liberals (1935–1939) or when they assumed a patriotic stance (1941–1945). As soon as they abandoned those positions, they became isolated, politically ineffective, and the objects of obloquy and prosecution. But that is not enough for anti-Communists, who reject any book that is at all sympathetic to the unfriendly witnesses, that does not excoriate the blacklisted people for their refusal to "apologize" for their political past.

So, here we stand, on the blacklist's seventy-fifth anniversary, on the same contested ground of interpretation. Clearly, the fact-gathering approach of leftists and liberals has accrued more points than the polemical, anecdotal approach of the conservative and reactionary Right. From the former's books and articles we have learned a few undeniable facts: The vast majority of those blacklisted were or had been members of the Communist Party (though, it is interesting to note, the Party did nothing to support the Hollywood Ten or future blacklistees); an unknown number of them stayed loyal to the Party through thick and thin (notably John Howard Lawson and Lester Cole); very few fit the definition of the "Stalinist" epithet constantly hurled at them by anti-Communists; none have been accused of spying for the Soviet Union; none have been discovered planning a revolutionary overthrow of the US government; all attempted, in one way or another and with varying degrees of success, to add "realistic" or "progressive" elements to the films they worked on; all supported a progressive or liberal reform agenda (civil rights, civil liberties, protection for immigrants, rights for women [though most of the males were patriarchal]); engaged in labor union organizing, opposition to fascism and anti-Semitism, and support for world peace (with the exception of their fervent support for World War II). Two big questions remain unanswered, probably because they are unanswerable: Did the blacklist in particular, and the anti-Communist crusade in general, do more harm to the United States than Communists, left alone, would have done? Would the political and film culture of the United States have been healthier if not for the blacklist, in particular, and anti-Communism, in general?

What, then, was the blacklist, how did it function, and what effect did it have on the United States? A blacklist is one of several mechanisms used by employers and governments to proscribe and silence undesirable individuals and groups. It has a long and unsavory history that can be traced back to the early seventeenth century, when the term was coined by Philip Massinger, an English playwright. It was first used politically during the English Civil War, to refer to the Royalists whose estates were being expropriated by the Commonwealth. Then, the newly restored king Charles II applied the term to those who were to be punished as regicides (involved in the execution of his father, Charles I). It came into use as a political weapon in the late eighteenth century, as a device to deny employment to "troublemakers," those who challenged the authority of their employers or who tried to organize the workforce into a trade union. (It was occasionally used by workers to warn other workers of undesirable employers.) During the nineteenth century in the United States and United Kingdom, it was used extensively as a union-busting tool. Though it was ostensibly outlawed as an unfair labor practice by the National Labor Relations Act (1935), the language of the statute is vague: "It shall be an unfair labor practice for the employer to discriminate in regard to hire or tenure of employment or any term or condition of employment to encourage or discourage membership in a trade union."[10] This law did not, for example, end the most pernicious and longest-lasting blacklists: Organized baseball banned African Americans from 1889 to 1947; the National Football League banned them from 1934 to 1945; and the National Basketball Association did not sign Blacks between 1946 and 1949.[11]

What was unusual about the motion picture blacklist, 1947–1960, was that it was not a response to union organizing (albeit a blacklist had been used against some of the organizers of the Screen Writers Guild during the 1930s) but to a government-generated "Red Scare." The domestic Cold War was the third such "Red Scare" of the twentieth century (the first occurred in the aftermath of World War I and the second in response to the Nonaggression Treaty signed by Nazi Germany and Soviet Russia, 1939–1941). These Red Scares were, themselves, episodes in a history of government assaults on freedom of speech, assembly, and due process, recurring approximately every thirty years in US history. (There is also a recurring cycle of ethnic and religious prejudice, in the form of nativism, that stretches from the late 1790s to the present, and the two cycles regularly coexist.)[12] This sad cycle of political suppression began with the Sedition Act of 1798, making it unlawful to "write, print, utter, or publish . . . any false, scandalous and malicious writing" against the government of the United States, either house of Congress, or the president. Twenty-five people, mainly editors of newspapers hostile to the John Adams administration, were arrested, and ten were convicted.

In 1835, Postmaster General Amos Kendall ignored federal postal law guaranteeing the security of the mail and gave permission to southern postmasters to refuse delivery of abolitionist materials. And when a mob in Charleston, South Carolina, broke into the main post office and seized and burned bags of mail containing abolitionist literature, the Andrew Jackson administration did nothing. In fact, in December of that year, Jackson proposed a new federal statute to prohibit the circulation via the mail in the southern states of any incendiary publication intended to instigate a slave insurrection. Senator John C. Calhoun (D-SC) proposed a bill to close the mails to any publication made criminal by a southern state. When the *New York Tribune* published a letter from Harriet Jacobs, a fugitive slave, southerners tried to destroy all copies of that issue. In addition, several abolitionist newspaper offices in the North were ransacked, and one editor was murdered.

Throughout the Civil War (1861–1865), newspaper reporters and editors were arrested without due process for opposing the draft, discouraging enlistments in the Union army, or even criticizing the income tax. In 1873, An Act for the Suppression of Trade in, and Circulation of, Obscene Literature and Articles of Immoral Use (aka the Comstock Act) made it illegal to send "obscene, lewd or lascivious," "immoral," or "indecent" publications through the mail. The law also made it a misdemeanor for anyone to sell, give away, or possess an obscene book, pamphlet, picture, drawing, or advertisement. Two dozen states followed suit, enacting "little" Comstock laws. Twenty-two years later, the US government sought an injunction to break the strike of the American Railway Union against the Pullman Palace Car Company. Communication from union headquarters to its members was enjoined as well. When Eugene V. Debs, the union's president, made such a communication, he was arrested, charged with contempt of court, and convicted. (The Supreme Court of the United States unanimously upheld his conviction, *In re Debs*, 1895.)

In the years leading up to World War I, labor unions, particularly the Industrial Workers of the World, had their speech, press, and assembly rights constantly violated by local, state, and federal governments. The 1903 Anarchist Exclusion Act barred people with those views from entering the United States. When a case challenging the act reached the Supreme Court, the justices ruled that Congress has unlimited power to exclude anarchists. And the 1908 Postal Exclusion Act added antigovernment writing to "indecent" postal matter banned by the Comstock Act. At the outset of US entry into World War I, Congress passed the Espionage Act of 1917, granting the postmaster general the authority to ban from the mail any material "advocating or urging treason, insurrection, or forcible resistance to any law of the United States."[13] When Debs criticized the war and the draft, he was charged with violating this act and sentenced to prison. The US Supreme Court upheld his conviction in *Debs v. United States* (1919).

In 1918, Congress enacted an amendment to the Espionage Act, the Sedition Act, which prohibited "Uttering, printing, writing, or publishing any disloyal, profane, scurrilous, or abusive language intended to cause contempt, scorn . . . as regards the form of government of the United States or Constitution, or the flag or the uniform of the Army or Navy . . . urging any curtailment of the war with intent to hinder its prosecution; advocating, teaching, defending, or acts supporting or favoring the cause of any country at war with the United States, or opposing the cause of the United States."[14] One year later, state legislatures began passing criminal syndicalist laws, which, in the words of the California statute, criminalized "any doctrine or precept advocating . . . the commission of crime, sabotage . . . or unlawful acts of force and violence . . . as a means of accomplishing a change in industrial ownership or control, or effecting any political change."[15] Those who knowingly associated themselves with such a group were criminally liable. By the mid-1920s more than half of the states had passed such laws.

In 1940, Congress passed the country's first peacetime sedition law, the Alien Registration Act of 1940 (usually referred to as the Smith Act because Title I of the law was named after its sponsor, Democratic Rep. Howard W. Smith of Virginia). The law prohibited advocating or teaching the "propriety of overthrowing or destroying any government in the United States by force or violence" and the printing or publishing of any material advocating or teaching the violent overthrow of the country.[16] This law, combined with a host of state and local laws, the Attorney General's List, loyalty oaths, blacklists, and boycotts, effectively limited free speech during the worst of the domestic Cold War period, 1946–1961. Producers and sponsors tightly controlled the content of movies and television shows, and writers and directors practiced self-restriction and self-censorship. The creative artists feared that suggesting the wrong topic or fabricating the wrong scene or dialogue could lead to loss of employment. In fact, it is arguable that these self-limitations exceeded those imposed by the networks and sponsors.

During the Richard M. Nixon administration (1969–1974) reporters' telephone lines were repeatedly tapped, and the Internal Revenue Service was directed to investigate tax returns filed by Seymour Hersh and other journalists whom the White House disliked. Several provisions of the Patriot Act (2001) impacted First Amendment freedoms in a fundamental way. Section 215 allowed government officials to read business records, library records, healthcare records, logs of Internet service providers, and other documents and papers without the traditional protections that individuals have. The act also added "expert assistance or advice" to the definition of providing "material support or resources" to terrorist organizations. Of course, the label of "terrorist organization" can be haphazardly applied, as was the label "subversive organization" during the Cold War. Finally, the Department of Justice in the Donald J. Trump administration tried to obtain telephone and email records of hostile newspaper reporters.

The motion picture blacklist was the first institutionalized, politically based proscriptive list. It was also the most highly publicized list that emerged during the domestic Cold War. But the Hollywood blacklistees were a small percentage of those blacklisted during that era: thousands of professors and teachers, government employees, and trade unionists were proscribed during that period. In 1952, for example, twenty-eight California private and public colleges agreed to collaborate with the California Senate Fact-Finding Committee on Un-American Activities, to install on each campus an official representative of the committee. In its first year of operation, this enterprise dismissed or forced the resignation of more than one hundred employees, and two hundred new appointments were blocked.[17] The motion picture industry, though, was unique in having a recognized complementary graylist that included people who had not been identified as Communists, but who had been members or supporters of causes deemed "subversive" (antifascist, pro-Republican Spain, antiracist, support for progressive political candidates) by anti-Communists. The names of the organizations could be found in the Attorney General's List of Subversive Organizations (mandated by President Harry S. Truman in 1947), and the names of entertainment industry people who had joined one of those groups or signed petitions on their behalf could be found in *Red Channels*, a list of 151 names compiled by former FBI agents (see below).

In what follows, I use "producers" to refer to the Hollywood studio bosses and New York executives of the major moviemaking companies, all of whom belonged to the Association of Motion Picture Producers and the Motion Picture Association of America. The former was an industry group representing only the studios that actually produced films (United Artists, a major distributor, was not a member); it collectively bargained with the studio unions and guilds. The latter engaged in public relations and self-regulation. It administered the motion picture codes.

Blacklisting began in Hollywood, in the 1920s, in two forms. In the first, the producers, in the aftermath of a series of public scandals (involving three murder cases), fired 117 employees with unsavory personal lives.[18] In the second, the International Alliance of Theatrical Stage Employees (IATSE) targeted the leaders of the unions challenging it during the brutal jurisdictional contests of the 1920s and 1930s. Some studio bosses later used a blacklist to promote their company union, the Screen Playwrights, and thereby undermine the rival Screen Writers Guild. The infamous motion picture blacklist began in November 1947, when the movie executives fired five of the Hollywood Ten who were under contract and pledged not to rehire them or the other five until they had purged themselves of their Communist taint. This blacklist grew from ten to nearly three hundred in the early 1950s. People found themselves on that list if they had been publicly alleged to be a Communist Party member, one named, that is, by an informing witness, who had been coached to name as many names as he/she could. (Even though the Committee had the names of Hollywood Communists, those names had to be publicly exposed by witnesses to give the producers the cachet they needed to blacklist.) Then, if they did not appear, or did appear but invoked the Fifth Amendment, they would be fired or not be hired in the future.

There was no "list" per se. The studio bosses derived their information about who not to hire from the indexes of the transcripts of the hearings of the House Committee on Un-American Activities, and a list of more than three hundred names collected by the American Legion and distributed to the major studios. To get one's name off the blacklist, one had to appear before the House Committee, apologize for joining the Party, laud the Committee, and name names (see below for what was required to get off the graylist).

We should also be clear on the identity of the blacklisters. The Federal Bureau of Investigation, the House Committee on Un-American Activities, the Senate Permanent Subcommittee on Investigations (Joseph McCarthy's [R-WI] subcommittee), and the Senate Internal Security Subcommittee lacked the power to blacklist. They could only expose and intimidate. The motion picture blacklist was the work of the producers; the television blacklist was the work of the networks and advertisers. They completely controlled hiring and firing decisions. In order to avoid censorship by the government and boycotts by such organizations as the American Legion and Catholic Church, the movie executives created a de facto mode of censorship, which severely weakened dissent and political expression in the United States. Despite nearly a dozen legal suits brought by blacklistees charging a conspiracy not to hire, no court ever recognized the existence of a blacklist. When a few blacklistees secured a favorable decision, it was for proving breach of contract. The movie producers scrupulously adhered to the blacklist. If, as it turned out in several famous cases, a blacklisted writer had written a script for a major studio, it was only because great care had been taken to hide that fact. The blacklist only ended when the producers became convinced that open hiring of blacklisted people did not negatively impact box-office receipts. No production company ever admitted to having utilized a blacklist. However, in 1997, the four major talent guilds —Writers Guild of America, Screen Actors Guild, Directors Guild of America, and American Federation of Television and Radio Artists— publicly apologized for their role in the blacklist mechanism.[19]

Anti-Communists have, since the 1940s, regularly claimed that the Communists, prior to the blacklist, had themselves engaged in blacklisting. They base their case on allegations made by a few Hollywood anti-Communists, like the actors Adolphe Menjou and Ronald Reagan. However, no Communist, save Sidney Buchman, reached an executive position in the studios, and Buchman worked for Harry Cohn, who held all the reins of hiring and firing. In sum, the Communists in Hollywood, even at the peak of their enrollment in the Party, had no leverage over employment decisions, film projects, or film content. Certainly, they could asperse anti-Communists and try to promote "progressive" films, but that was the extent of their influence.

Finally, we should also not fall into the trap of conflating the blacklist and McCarthyism. During the course of the last several decades, historians have promiscuously used the "McCarthyism" label, applying it to decades and even to the entire twentieth century. What began as a label on a tar barrel in a Herblock political cartoon was stretched, by Ted Morgan, to cover the history of the United States from the Russian Revolution to 2004.[20] Those writers who have elasticized this label do not seem to know that techniques they ascribe to McCarthy—guilt by association, irresponsible accusations, exaggeration of national security threats, browbeating and badgering of committee witnesses—had been wielded and honed by the House Committee on Un-American Activities years before McCarthy made his famous speech of February 1950, "revealing" that hundreds of Communists were employed by the United States Department of State. And compared to the Committee's thirty-year existence, McCarthy enjoyed a relatively short time in the spotlight (1950–1954). Further, McCarthy's focus was much narrower than that of the House Committee. He concentrated on the Departments of State and Defense, whereas the House Committee ranged far and wide, over labor organizations, educators, media, and professionals. And even in allegations of government infiltration by Communists, the former chair of the

House Special Committee on Un-American Activities, Martin Dies Jr. (D-TX), had preceded McCarthy, telling the House of Representatives, in 1943: "I intend to read [into the *Congressional Record*] the names and positions and records of many of the bureaucrats who have wormed their way into [the Roosevelt administration]."[21] In sum, the period 1945–1960 should be labeled "The Blacklist Era" or "The Un-American Era," not the "McCarthy Era."

It will also be useful to list and discuss the charges made against the Ten (and the subsequent blacklistees) by anti-Communists. They charge the unfriendly and Fifth Amendment witnesses with a lack of "candor," meaning that they, by not answering the House Committee's questions about their political and guild affiliations, opened the door to "McCarthyism." That is, had those witnesses fully disclosed their political affiliations, they would have cut the ground from under conspiracy theorists. The anti-Communists, by demeaning the unfriendly witnesses' refusal to answer those types of questions, think they have demonstrated that the witnesses were not defenders of the First Amendment; they were simply trying to protect themselves by hiding their membership in a subversive organization; and they were complicit in the depth and duration of the domestic Cold War. The Ten did commit a tactical blunder by not specifically stating that they were standing behind the First Amendment, but anyone who cares to read their speeches, letters, legal briefs, and memoirs can have no doubt about the centrality of the First Amendment to their resistance. And it is stretching credulity to think that the domestic Cold War juggernaut or the Communist-conspiracy ideology could have been even slightly sidetracked by the "candor" of ten (or, subsequently, seventy-six) Hollywood movie-studio employees.

Almost on a par in falsity with the above charge is the anti-Communists' claim that the witnesses were "unrepentant Commies." "Unrepentant" is the key term. By which they mean that the unapologetic witnesses did not get down on their hands and knees before the FBI and the House Committee and forsake their entire political past, confess they had been duped, and then inform on their friends and colleagues, none of whom represented a danger to the national security of the United States. Nor did they do so in the succeeding years. As noted above, "repentance" would not have changed the course of the domestic Cold War. It would simply have put a seal of approval on Cold War prosecutions.

The anti-Communists most egregiously exaggerate when they accuse the Hollywood Communists of being "hard-core, fervent Stalinists" and "Hitler apologists" or allies. As to the first, the preponderant majority of Hollywood Communists were not hard-core ("stubbornly resistant or inveterate") anything, nor were they fervent ("showing great emotion or warmth; ardent") about Soviet Russia. They can, to be sure, be accused of being uncritical, of not probing more deeply into the Soviet regime. But it is ludicrous to maintain that their secrecy about their Party membership helped pave the way for Stalin's internal purges, deportations, and incarcerations or the Soviet incursion into, and occupation of, Eastern Europe.

As for the second charge, my dictionary defines an apologist as one who argues in defense or justification of another person or cause and an ally as one who is formally connected to another. Not once did the blacklistees defend, justify, or enable the words and deeds of Hitler and the Nazi Party. Many of the blacklistees had criticized the United States, Great Britain, and France for not supporting the democracies being destroyed by Germany, Italy, and Japan. That is, they criticized the validity of the Western governments' antifascism. They believed that if those countries had been more actively opposed to Germany and Italy when it mattered, 1935–1939, there might not have been a war. Their support of the German-Soviet Nonaggression Treaty of 1939, though it did remove them from the antifascist struggle, was motivated solely by their obedience to, and belief in, the Party line, which stated that Communists must support the policies of the world's only proletarian state and that the war between Germany and the United Kingdom and France was an "imperialist" struggle.

But the right-wing mythologizers are not interested in facts and definitions; they abhor complexity and nuance. The attitudes or motives of Communists are unwelcome intruders in the simplistic and reductionist world of anti-Communism, in which anyone who dared to oppose the policies and acts of the domestic Cold War was to be demonized. Indeed, the words "fervent" and "slavish" better describe their defense of the Cold War national security state and the members of the congressional investigating committees. It is, rather, the anti-Communists who should apologize for J. Edgar Hoover, Martin Dies, Richard Nixon, and Joseph McCarthy. And if assignment of blame is indeed possible, it is the anti-Communists who must be assigned responsibility for the perpetuation of investigations and proscriptions and the ruined lives of the thousands of people caught up in the jaws of the Cold War juggernaut they assembled and operated. This behemoth emboldened a rogues' gallery of demagogues to inflate, often for their own agendas, the threat posed to national security by domestic Communists.

The motion picture blacklist era began on May 9, 1947, the day when two members of the House Committee on Un-American Activities convened executive sessions at the Biltmore Hotel in Los Angeles. They interviewed fourteen friendly witnesses, most of whom were members of the anti-Communist Motion Picture Alliance for the Preservation of American Ideals, and studio head Jack Warner; the witnesses gave the congressmen the names of suspected Communists employed by the studios. Though Eric Johnston, the president of the producers' associations, had pledged the full cooperation of the industry to this investigation, Committee chairman J. Parnell Thomas (R-NJ) publicly expressed his dissatisfaction with the movie executives. In response, Johnston convened a meeting of the producers on June 2 and advised them to call for an open investigation by the House Committee and not to employ "proven Communists" in jobs that had influence over film content. The producers rejected his second demand because it "would be a potential conspiracy" not to hire, and the producers lacked a mechanism for proving whether someone was a Communist.[22]

In July, Thomas sent two of his investigators to Hollywood to intimidate the producers into acting more cooperatively. When that did not work, Thomas authorized the serving of subpoenas. On September 22, 1947, the *Hollywood Reporter* divulged the names of forty-two motion picture personnel who had received subpoenas from the House Committee.

Nineteen of those listed were labeled "unfriendly" (unlikely to cooperate) by a few publications. Eighteen of those subpoenaed and their lawyers met regularly for the next month to plan their strategy. (The nineteenth, Bertolt Brecht, who had been labeled an "enemy alien" by the US government and therefore needed to take a different position, did not participate in those meetings.) The other eighteen decided to challenge the right of the Committee to subpoena them or ask them questions about their guild and political affiliations. They also decided that each would write a statement criticizing the Committee, to be read when they were called to the stand. Finally, they made what turned out to be a disastrous decision: they would not outright refuse to answer any of the questions, but they would use the questions to attack the Committee, that is, they would answer those questions "in their own way." (They were advised to do so by one of their attorneys, who told them that their lack of cooperation would result in a contempt citation, trial, and conviction. They would fare better in the courts of appeal, he told them, if they had not outright refused to answer questions about their Communist Party membership.) This decision obfuscated their core position—the Committee was violating their First Amendment rights—and it provoked the kind of behavior from some of the witnesses that gave ammunition to those movie executives who wanted to make a show of cooperation.

The solid wall of opposition that the unfriendly witnesses had been told to expect from industry leaders crumbled immediately when leadoff witness Jack Warner testified on October 24, the first day of the hearings. He crawled before his questioners, telling them, "It is a privilege to appear again before the Committee to help as much as I can in facilitating its work." He claimed that he had been aware for more than a decade of Communists working in the industry, and that he had fired many of them. He then reeled off a list of names of those he had heard or read about who were Communists. Of the fourteen he named, three were not Party members. He did, however, strongly defend his studio's pro-Soviet film *Mission to Moscow* (1942) as an effort to aid the war by promoting the US-Soviet alliance.[23] Louis B. Mayer, who testified a few days later, insisted that the producers could handle the Communist problem, and he defended his studio's pro-Soviet film *Song of Russia* as a sign of friendship for an ally. The last studio boss to testify, Walt Disney, complained about Communist efforts to organize his cartoonists and acknowledged that there was a Communist threat in Hollywood.

John Howard Lawson, the first unfriendly witness called to the stand, on October 29, exhibited the behavior that provided the producers with their rationale for instituting a blacklist. Goaded by Thomas's refusal to allow him to read his prepared statement and cutting off his attempts to answer questions "in my own way," Lawson grew angrier and more argumentative. Thomas ordered the sergeant-at-arms to remove Lawson from the witness chair. Eric Johnston, cleverly slotted by Thomas to follow Lawson to the stand, trod carefully. Johnston stated that he welcomed this investigation and hoped that it would expose Communists in the industry. Though only two of the other ten unfriendly witnesses, Dalton Trumbo and Lester Cole, expressed anger, and only Trumbo and Lardner were ordered to leave the stand, the die had been cast. (Brecht, the eleventh, and last, unfriendly witness called to the stand, answered the Committee's questions. He did so because he was eager to return to Germany, and he feared that any show of resistance might lead to him being detained. He left the country the day after his appearance.)

The leaders of the industry at first masked their concern when the Ten were cited for contempt of Congress. Samuel Goldwyn announced, "I believe that the entire hearing is a flop; I think the whole thing is a disgraceful performance." Paul V. McNutt, an industry counsel, said: "The truth is, there are no pictures of ours which carry Communist propaganda and we do not care how many so-called experts the Committee employs to try to find out. The search will be fruitless." Eric Johnston told the unfriendly witnesses, "As long as I live, I will never be a party to anything as un-American as a blacklist." But some producers, like M-G-M's Eddie Mannix, had decided that the Ten had to go, not because they might be Communists but because they "had become of great disservice to the industry."[24]

One month after the hearings ended, while the members of the House of Representatives were voting to cite the Ten for contempt of Congress, the movie company executives and studio bosses met at the Waldorf-Astoria Hotel to decide how to deal with them. Two of the major studios, RKO and Fox, had already decided to fire the three witnesses under contract to them: Edward Dmytryk, Adrian Scott, and Ring Lardner Jr. M-G-M was close to such a decision on Dalton Trumbo and Lester Cole. The big question confronting the executives was the stance they should take about the overall question of Communism in the industry. No transcript of the meeting has come to light, but the anecdotal evidence indicates that the majority of those present did not want to inaugurate a blacklist. However, Johnston and the two special counsels, Paul V. McNutt and James Byrnes, insisted that the only realistic course of action was to publicly announce the firing of the five under contract and to state that none of the Ten would be employed until they had purged themselves of their Communist taint. Johnston cited as evidence the negative response of newspaper editorials to Hollywood and the threats of boycotts. Only Samuel Goldwyn, Dore Schary, and Walter Wanger objected to firing those under contract. The executives finally agreed that they would draw the line at the Ten and institute a policy of self-regulation. The so-called Waldorf Declaration announced that the Ten, by "their actions have been a disservice to their employers and have impaired their usefulness to the industry." Therefore, "We will forthwith discharge or suspend without compensation those in our employ and we will not re-employ any of the ten until such time as he is acquitted [of contempt] or has purged himself of contempt and declares under oath that he is not a Communist." Furthermore, "We will not knowingly employ a Communist or a member of any party or group which advocates the overthrow of the Government of the United States by force of by illegal or unconstitutional methods." Finally, the executives promised to "invite the Hollywood talent guilds to work with us to eliminate any subversives, to protect the innocent, and to safeguard free speech and a free screen wherever threatened."[25] The talent guilds agreed to cooperate, and a Motion Picture Industry Council (MPIC), consisting of representatives of the producers, guilds, and trade unions, was created to bring the "Communist problem" to the attention of all studios, publicize the efforts of the industry to purge itself of subversives, "clear" repentant Communists for reemployment, and criticize House Committee witnesses who refused to cooperate with the Committee. Committees were appointed to inform the talent guilds of these decisions. Only the committee sent to the writers' guild was received with open hostility by some of the members.

There matters stood for three years. Two of the Ten, John Howard Lawson and Dalton Trumbo, were tried for contempt of Congress. (The other eight, to save the expense of multiple trials, agreed to accept whatever verdict was rendered.) When they were convicted, they appealed and launched a national campaign to rally support to their cause. Clearly waiting to see the outcome of the appeal process, the House Committee did not resume its hearings. On April 10, 1950, the Supreme Court of the United States refused to grant certiorari, and the Ten began turning themselves in to federal authorities to begin serving their one-year sentences. (Herbert Biberman and Edward Dmytryk were sentenced to six-month terms.) On May 4, the Motion Picture Alliance predicted that within a year the House Committee would resume its investigation of the industry, and they warned the producers that this time they must fully cooperate.[26] When the Committee formally announced it was reopening the hearings, in March 1951, the producers promised their full cooperation and stated that those witnesses who did not deny their Communist affiliation would find it difficult to get work in the studios. The Motion Picture Industry Council promised to commend and encourage all witnesses who "openly admit their membership or association to the Communist Party or any Communist-controlled organization," while deploring those witnesses "who stand on constitutional privileges . . . or who refuse to recognize the authority of Congress."[27] One other thing had changed, to the detriment of those who chose not to cooperate: they lacked a support network. There was no Committee for the First Amendment (and no organized support from liberals); the democratic unions had been decimated by the failure of the Conference of Studio Unions and the Taft-Hartley Act; and the Communist Party in Hollywood had been reduced severely in number.

The Committee also modified its approach, focusing on Communists rather than Communism in the industry. Subpoenaed witnesses also learned a key lesson from the October 1947 hearings. They had only two paths open to them if they wanted to avoid a prison sentence: invoke the Fifth Amendment and be fired, or cooperate fully with the Committee, admit to membership in the Communist Party, apologize for this membership, provide the names of other members, and praise the Committee. Larry Parks, the leadoff witness, who had not been adequately coached, refused at first to give names; by the time he did so, he had effectively ended his career. The friendly witnesses who followed rattled off hundreds of names. (One witness, Martin Berkeley, provided more than 150.) When Edward Dmytryk decided to follow the formula of the Waldorf Declaration and recant, he met with members of the MPIC, who prescribed the path to his return to work: coauthoring a lengthy apology in the *Saturday Evening Post*, testifying anew before the House Committee, naming names. The MPIC issued a statement explaining its role:

> We are just a few of the many loyal Americans in Hollywood who have helped bring about the complete frustration and failure of the Communist Party in the motion picture capital. On February 2, 1951, we met with Edward Dmytryk at his request. Dmytryk told us he wished to rehabilitate himself and he asked our advice and help. We told him that we were not interested in him personally or whether he ever got a job again. We made sure in our own minds that it was not principally economic pressure which had led Dmytryk to want to come clean, although of course it had something to do with it. We made sure that Dmytryk was really trying to escape the Communist trap.[28]

But the vast majority of witnesses took the first option and joined the blacklist.

The MPIC also had to contend with a different type of list, made necessary by the publication, in 1950, of *Red Channels: The Report of Communist Influence in Radio and Television*. This book, a compilation of 151 names (mainly actors and actresses) and the "subversive" organizations to which they lent their names, was published by three former FBI agents, who also published *Counterattack*, a magazine purporting to expose Communist influence on movies. Shortly after it appeared, Ronald Reagan, president of the Screen Actors Guild, received permission from its board of directors to enlist the MPIC to protect the actors and actresses named in *Red Channels*. The MPIC plan allowed employees under suspicion of subversive activities to write a statement of facts to clarify their position against Communism and explain their relations to any organization to which they belonged that had been linked to Communism. Members of the MPIC, notably Reagan and Roy Brewer, evaluated the letters and worked with letter writers to improve their credibility. The writers were told that their "voluntary" statement should include: an oath of allegiance to the United States, a promise to support it faithfully and honestly against all its enemies, support for US involvement in the Korean War, repudiation of Stalinism, and a pledge to support Americanist activities or organizations. The MPIC, after carefully scrutinizing the letter and, sometimes sending it back to be reworked, in some cases several times, would then direct the letter to the producer or studio of the writer's choice. The decision to hire was left with the studio.[29] (Some letter writers, like the composer Johnny Green, had to rewrite his letter two times to maintain his job at M-G-M;[30] others, like the actor Alexander Knox, wrote lengthy letters, to no avail.)

In addition to the blacklist, the movie executives produced nearly fifty anti-Communist movies. They did so not out of patriotic duty or ideological convictions or short-term economic benefit (none of the films did well at the box office) but out of fear for the long-term economic consequences of not marching in step with the domestic Cold War. During the March 1947 hearings of the House Committee, regarding bills to curb or outlaw the Communist Party, at which J. Edgar Hoover and Eric Johnston testified, Richard Nixon (R-CA) and J. Parnell Thomas had commented on the paucity of anti-Communist films being made in Hollywood. Twentieth Century-Fox was the first studio to get the message. It announced in April that it would be producing *The Iron Curtain*, based on a recently exposed atomic spy ring in Canada. But it was not until five months after the October 1947 hearings ended that *Variety* announced, in March 1948, that anti-Communist films would become "the hottest" theme to hit the screens in the coming year.[31] Of note, RKO, the studio owned by Howard Hughes, the most virulent anti-Communist mogul, produced only one notable anti-Communist movie, *I Married a Communist/The Woman on Pier 13*.[32] Of the four dozen produced, *My Son John* (Paramount, 1952, written by John Lee Mahin, an ultraconservative, and directed by Leo McCarey, a friendly witness) and *Big Jim McLain* (Warner Bros., 1952, produced by and starring John Wayne) are the two that usually garner the most attention.

The studio heads also stopped making "social problem" films. Dorothy B. Jones estimated that those films constituted 28 percent of movies made in the last half of 1947. After the Waldorf Declaration, however, one script reader told Lillian Ross: "I now read scripts through the eyes of the D.A.R. [Daughters of the American Revolution], whereas formerly I read them through the eyes of my boss. . . . I am loused up. I'm scared to death, and nobody can tell me it isn't because I'm afraid of being investigated." In August 1948, *Variety* reported that "studios are continuing to drop plans for 'message' pictures like hot coals."[33]

The executives of the major studios fully adhered to the blacklist, even in the face of blacklisted writers, behind pseudonyms, winning Academy Awards for their uncredited scripts: *The Brave One* (King Brothers, 1956), *The Bridge on the River Kwai* (Columbia 1957), and *The Defiant Ones* (United Artists, 1958). A major crack appeared in 1960, when Otto Preminger and Universal Pictures announced that Dalton Trumbo would receive screen credit for *Exodus* and *Spartacus,* respectively. One by one, on their own merit, many of the blacklistees returned to work. A significant number, however, found it difficult to regain their footing in the industry. The producers' associations never stated that the blacklist had ended, because they had consistently maintained that there had never been a blacklist in the first place. The producers' position was voiced in a 1980 interview by Ronald Reagan, the Republican candidate for president, and one of the signatories of the above MPIC announcement. He told Robert Scheer that the industry had responded to Communist domination of several unions and the efforts of Communists to take over the industry: "And all of the re-writing of history today, and the stories that we have seen, and screenplays and television plays, and so forth, about the persecution for political belief that took place in Hollywood, believe me, the persecutors were the Communists who had gotten into positions where they could destroy careers, and did destroy them.

There was no blacklist in Hollywood. The blacklist in Hollywood, if there was one, was provided by the Communists."[34]

In many ways, the television blacklist replicated the motion picture one. But here too there was a thriving black market (*You Are There, The Adventures of Robin Hood,* among others) and, in terms of content, there were significant outliers: *See It Now,* the Army-McCarthy hearings, and the great playhouses (Kraft, Philco, Goodyear, and Studio One). In fact, the best movie about the blacklist, *The Front* (Columbia Pictures, 1976), focused on the television black market.

What had the motion picture blacklist accomplished, aside from barring approximately three hundred people from their chosen vocation, hastening the exit of hundreds of people from the Hollywood Communist Party, altering the content of movies, and creating an informer subculture in Hollywood? There is no evidence that it strengthened the country's national security or improved the quality of moviemaking. It was probably a very small factor in the decline of the studio system, which had been much more strongly impacted by the rise of television and the antitrust decree ordering the companies to divest themselves of their exhibition venues. It did not weaken the will of the blacklisted to resist. Dalton Trumbo waged a twelve-year, ultimately successful, war in print and behind the scenes. Nearly a dozen legal suits were filed. Three of the blacklisted, Paul Jarrico, Herbert Biberman, and Michael Wilson, created the pro-labor, pro-Chicano, pro-feminist movie *Salt of the Earth* and distributed it in the face of a vast campaign by anti-Communists to block it. And a small group founded countercultural periodicals, *Hollywood Review* and *California Quarterly.*

Bloody but unbowed, the blacklistees would in their later years inspire dozens of historians and documentary filmmakers to revise the history of the domestic Cold War and offer a counter to the anti-Communist version that had dominated for over two decades.

2

Jewish Anti-Communism in the United States and Hollywood

Anti-Communism in the United States was not a monolithic entity. In my book on the subject, I divided it into two large categories.[1] Official (or government) anti-Communism was the work of federal, state, and local governments. Unofficial (nongovernment) anti-Communism consisted of several subcategories, including liberal, conservative, Socialist, labor, academic, and religious. Jewish anti-Communism was a distinctive subcategory of religious anti-Communism, and it, like the other categories and subcategories, displayed marked diversity. In general, Jewish anti-Communists publicly declaimed a deep disdain for Communism as a theory and practice but harbored a hidden or, sometimes, not-so-hidden agenda. This hidden agenda focused on dissolving the public image linking Jewishness and Communism,[2] protecting and advancing thereby the interests of Jewish communities, both in the United States and abroad, while not calling attention to their Jewishness. The hidden agenda of the motion picture industry leaders, most of whom were Jewish, was to protect their product against outside censorship and to avoid boycotts of their movies, while not calling attention to themselves as Jews. The Jewish organizations spoke for a large community; the motion picture executives, for an oligopoly. The Jewish organizations refused to associate with Communists, whereas the movie executives knowingly employed hundreds of them. The Jewish organizations made at least nominal attempts to balance their anti-Communism with respect for civil liberties, whereas the motion picture executives made no effort of any kind to respect the

24

civil liberties of those accused of being Communists. In effect, the Jewish organizations were true-believing anti-Communists; the motion picture executives were de facto anti-Communists. The former were motivated by ideals of a sort; the latter's motives were purely mercenary.

A Brief History of the Anti-Communism of the Jewish Organizations, 1917–1950

Organized Jewish defense groups began to respond to the association of Jews and Communism in 1918. What was then labeled "Judeo-Bolshevism"[3] had a long history of antecedents: Judeo-witchcraft, Judeo-pollution, Judeo-antichristism, Judeo-lèse-majesté; Judeo-capitalism. In David Nirenberg's words: "it is difficult to think of a financial innovation, practice, or crisis which was not discussed in terms of Judaism in the nineteenth and the early-twentieth century."[4] As a result, many Jews were justifiably hypersensitive to overt and coded racial slurs and threats.

As of 1918, there were three main Jewish defense groups in existence: the American Jewish Committee (AJC), the Anti-Defamation League of B'nai Brith (ADL), and the American Jewish Congress. The main concern of the American Jewish Committee, founded in 1906 by wealthy German Jews in the wake of a series of pogroms in czarist Russia, was, via informal methods, to battle against anti-Semitism, but, after 1917, it was also concerned with disavowing any connection between Jews and the Bolshevik-led revolution in Russia. In September 1918, its Executive Committee issued a statement intended "to clarify public opinion with regard to the relationship of the Jews to that species of radicalism which has come to be called Bolshevism."[5] Its main foreign effort in 1918 and 1919 was to publicize the pogroms in Poland and Ukraine, including a mass demonstration and rally in New York, on May 21, 1919. In addition, Louis Marshall, the president of the AJC, traveled to Versailles to lobby the peace conferees on the situation of Jews in Poland. It also quietly joined with another Jewish organization, the American Jewish Joint Distribution Committee (founded in 1914, to provide aid to Jewish communities affected by the war), to secure permission from the

Department of State to work with the Soviet Jewish Public Committee, to aid Jews in the Ukraine.

When, during the course of a nine-month US Senate investigation of the impact of Bolshevism in the United States, a witness stated that Bolshevik Russia received financial and moral support from East Side Jews, Marshall publicly stated, "Everything that real Bolshevism stands for is to the Jew detestable."[6] But he and the other AJC leaders chose to ignore the conclusion of the Senate investigating subcommittee associating Jews with "the doctrine of force, violence, assassination, confiscation, and revolution."[7]

The ADL, founded in 1911, used an educational approach to combat domestic anti-Semitism, whereas the American Jewish Congress, founded in 1918 by middle-class Eastern European Jews, took a pro-Zionist position, using boycotts and demonstrations as part of its strategic response to anti-Semitism. The AJC feared that such overt tactics implied that Jews prioritized their Jewishness over their Americanness.[8] As well, it feared that overt attacks on Bolshevism might provoke anti-Semitic repercussions in Soviet Russia.

During the 1920s, these three agencies, in their different ways, consistently attempted to dissociate Jewishness from Communism and demonstrate the anti-Communist credentials of American Jews.[9] And in that decade, the ranks of Jewish anti-Communism grew progressively larger as many Jewish Socialists, angered by the splits in the Socialist Party provoked by Communists, joined the chorus. Jewish Trotskyists followed, as did many Jewish liberals, alienated by Communist tactics. Saul Bellow's friend Sydney Harris recalled: "In those days [1930s] the Stalinists were a terribly brutal lot. They were like thugs."[10] That thug-like behavior was demonstrated in February 1934, when several thousand Communists invaded a Socialist Party rally in Madison Square Garden, "shouted down the speakers, threw folding chairs from the balcony, and started fights all over the floor."[11]

The ranks of Jewish Communists also swelled during those years, and several polls indicated that during the 1930s there was a predilection among people in the United States to associate Jews with radicalism. A series of polls taken by the Opinion Research Corporation between March

1938 and September 1939 reported that from 25 to 32 percent of those asked believed that Jews tended to be more radical than other people. A 1940 poll placed Jews second only to Russians as a nationality or religious group with a propensity for being radical or Communistic.[12] Archibald E. Stevenson, a member of the National Civic Federation, warned James N. Rosenberg, a Jewish activist, that Jewish organizations should not minimize the seriousness of the so-called link and "should counteract the effect of this anti-Jewish campaign."[13] In response, the American Jewish Congress's founder and leader, Rabbi Stephen Wise, said in May 1933, "We cannot afford to side with Communists or give sympathy and support to them."[14] The following year, the AJC, B'nai Brith, and the newly formed Jewish Labor Committee issued "A Public Statement on Communism and Jews." It denied any link between Jews and Communism. The American Jewish Congress refused to join as cosponsor.[15]

The Jewish Labor Committee (JLC), formed by the United Hebrew Trades, International Ladies Garment Workers Union, and Amalgamated Clothing Workers of America, among others, and strongly backed by the American Federation of Labor, took a more robust anti-Communist line than the older organizations. Its goal was to "give aid to Jewish and Jewish labor institutions overseas; provide succor to victims of oppression and persecution and to combat antisemitism and racial and religious intolerance abroad and in the United States."[16] Its first major activity was to organize a boycott of Nazi goods, but it refused to ally with any Communist-led groups, and, in 1938, it resolved to ally "only with those Jewish and non-Jewish bodies which adhered to the viewpoint of broad state liberty and democracy of all countries." During the 1940s, the JLC, increasingly concerned about the lot of Soviet Jews, became even more strongly anti-Communist.[17]

At about the same time, a group of college students organized Avukah, a Zionist group to fight against anti-Semitism, fascism, and reaction. According to an article in the *Harvard Crimson*, it had chapters at every important college or university.[18] Nathan Glazer, a student at City College of New York who edited *Avukah Student Action* in the early 1940s, recalled, "We were generally allied on campus issues with the anti-Stalinist Left— the socialists and the Trotskyites."[19]

The AJC, however, still moved carefully. In 1935, under strong pressure to issue an anti-Communist statement, the executive committee cited several reasons not to do so: It would add weight to anti-Semitism, cause the loss of liberal sympathy, and harm Jews in the Soviet Union.[20] The ADL, for its part, allied itself with Martin Dies Jr. (D-TX), the anti-Communist chairman of the House Special Committee on Un-American Activities, even though there were concerns that he might be anti-Semitic. According to Dies: "In the beginning our Committee obtained much valuable information from Jews and Jewish organizations, including the Anti-Defamation League. However, over a period of time, I noted that the Anti-Defamation League . . . became arrogant, overbearing and uncooperative in some of its activities."[21]

From 1941 to 1945, during the time of the wartime alliance between the United States and the Soviet Union, anti-Communism of all types moderated. It resumed at the end of the war, and Paul Jacobs recalled that the growing tensions between the United States and the Soviet Union "were inevitably reflected" inside the AJC and many other Jewish organizations.[22] Executives and staff members, despite public opinion polls to the contrary, believed that the temporarily silenced anti-Semitic agitators of the 1930s were reemerging in a new and threatening guise, using anti-Communism as a cover.[23]

Their fears escalated when the Communist Party strongly increased its effort to recruit Jews and began to wield opposition to anti-Semitism as a means to discredit the democratic countries. On November 29, 1946, the Party convened a national conference on the Jewish question. Its resolution proclaimed: "Our major task is to combat the reactionaries among the Jewish masses, to build among them the labor-progressive-democratic coalition for the major struggle against anti-Semitism and for equal rights; and to organize and expand the influence of our party."[24] The Communist press published a series of stories on the subject of anti-Semitism and launched public demonstrations, including efforts to boycott the film *Oliver Twist* (Cineguild, 1948), in protest of the Fagin character, a stereotypical anti-Semitic image. When, however, Golda Meir, Israel's first minister plenipotentiary to the Soviet Union, raised the issue of the emigration of Soviet Jews to Israel, and Stalin became convinced that Israel was pro-Western and that Soviet Jews were secretly working against the USSR, bilateral relations between the Soviet Union and Israel began to deteriorate, leading to a change in the Communist Party line. Attacks commenced on Israel, Jewish culture, and Zionism. In response, Jewish groups and publications denounced anti-Semitism in the Soviet Union. Communists in the United States hotly contested that accusation, and the Party established a new front group: the Joint Committee to Combat Anti-Semitism.[25] In sum, no matter the Party line, Communists stressed anti-Semitism to a degree unpalatable to the Jewish organizations.

In the AJC executive committee, a sharp, inconclusive debate raged over whether to attack Communism publicly or to more quietly combat the attempts by reactionaries to identify Jews with Communism. Finally, the committee decided it should educate Jews on the incompatibility of Communism and liberalism and publicize Soviet anti-Semitism.[26] Elliot Cohen, the editor of the AJC's new magazine, *Commentary*, founded in 1945, made no mention of anti-Semitism, anti-Communism, or antifascism in his inaugural editorial; instead he spoke vaguely of searching "for the light on the basic issues of peace and freedom and human destiny which challenge all mankind."[27] According to Nathan Glazer, the magazine's editors were not outspokenly anti-Communist: "I seem to recall a hesitation in making a full-blown attack on Communism. Perhaps we were inhibited by the idea that, as a Jewish magazine, a criticism of Communism legitimately fell within our purview only when it affected Jews."[28] However, in January 1948, Cohen composed an essay titled "The Problem Dissociating Jews and Communists in the Public Mind," which was not published.[29] By my count, the magazine printed ten anti-Communist articles between 1945 and 1950. Three mildly criticized Henry Wallace and his third-party effort and warned of the Communist threat to liberalism; three exposed anti-Semitism in the Soviet Union; two examined Communist threats in Europe; and one discussed the mentality and morals of a Communist. The tenth, and most strongly worded (and by far the longest) article sharply criticized the Communists' role in the riots that broke out at Paul Robeson's concerts at Peekskill in 1949. (Robeson, an African American singer and actor, had strong ties to the Communist movement, and the concert was a fundraiser for the Communist-run Civil Rights

Congress.) The authors downplayed the role of anti-Semitism among the protesters and accused Communists of using the concert "to increase civil strife to inflame the racial and religious passions and antagonisms that are already this country's shame, and in fact to play the same role in weakening this country before a foreign enemy that Nazi agents and their domestic supporters played during World War II."[30] AJC executive S. Andhil Fineberg criticized the ACLU for publicizing the anti-Semitic aspects of the Peekskill riots, while the American Jewish Congress publicly criticized the protesters.[31]

The ADL, in its 1947 report on anti-Semitism in the United States, stated that though there had been less organized anti-Semitic activity than at any time since 1933, there was "a very real increase in unorganized anti-Semitism." The report blamed the House Committee on Un-American Activities' investigation of Communism in Hollywood, because it provided overtly anti-Semitic newspapers "great opportunity to spew forth antisemitic venom. The false notion that the motion picture companies are controlled by Jews was stated and restated."[32] The AJC leaders, for their part, cultivated the staffs of the congressional investigating committees, advising them how to question Jewish Communist witnesses and, in coordination with the National Council of Churches for Christ and the National Catholic Welfare Conference, trying to set guidelines on investigations of Communism in religious organizations.

Jewish Anti-Communism in the Movie Industry

The Jewish movie executives—mainly immigrants or sons of immigrants from Eastern Europe (Adolph Zukor, Carl Laemmle, Louis B. Mayer, Marcus Loew, Schenck brothers, William Fox, Warner brothers, Samuel Goldwyn, Barney Balaban, B. P. Schulberg, Harry Cohn, Schneider brothers)—who dominated the motion picture industry in Hollywood from its origins were not conspicuously active in the national Jewish organizations. They preferred to keep their Jewishness unobserved. But they were unsuccessful. The wealth they amassed did not gain them entry into high society. They were excluded from the best country clubs and private schools, and they were regularly attacked by a variety of groups as money grubbers, sexual immoralists, and "dirty Jews." They did not renounce their Judaism—they were prominent members of their synagogues, they quietly supported Jewish causes, and they hired and promoted many Jews for executive positions—but they did try to keep it hidden, to pretend they were fully assimilated Americans. The films they produced avoided Jewish themes, and they did not hire many Jewish character actors. The Warner brothers' *The Life of Emile Zola* (1937), about anti-Semitism in fin de siècle France, did not use the word "Jew."

Most of them were politically conservative. The Warner brothers and Walter Wanger supported a liberal agenda, backing, financially and in their movies, Franklin D. Roosevelt and his New Deal, and they supported antifascist organizations. And yet, when Wanger visited Italy in 1937, he met with Mussolini, offered him advice on filmmaking, and referred to him as "a marvelous man."[33] In 1934, M-G-M and Columbia executives led the effort to defeat Upton Sinclair in his campaign to become governor of California. Sinclair, a Socialist, had won the Democratic primary, promising to end poverty in California. Three weeks before the election, the studio bosses arranged for anti-Sinclair speakers to address their employees, and some bosses demanded that their employees contribute to the campaign of the Republican nominee, Frank Merriam. Irving Thalberg, the Jewish head of production at M-G-M, produced a series of short-subject films designed to undermine Sinclair's appeal.[34] (Thalberg also promoted the formation of the Screen Playwrights, a group of older, more conservative screenwriters, to oppose and destroy the newly created and, in his mind, radical, Screen Writers Guild.)

Harry Cohn (Columbia) and Louis B. Mayer (M-G-M) admired Benito Mussolini and attempted, in various ways, to collaborate with his regime. Columbia made a favorable documentary about him, and William Randolph Hearst's newspapers promoted it and other films that portrayed the Italian dictator in a favorable light. (Hearst owned Cosmopolitan Films.) Mussolini's son Vittorio was warmly received by Mayer, Hearst, Walt Disney, Will Hays, and Wilfred Sheehan (Twentieth Century-Fox) when he came to Hollywood in 1936 to discuss possible production deals.[35]

Though the industry knowingly employed hundreds of people who were members of the Communist Party, prior to 1944 there was no organized effort to purge them from the industry. In fact, during the first Red Scare (1918–1921), only six movies with antiradical content were made, and even fewer were made in response to the request of Secretary of the Interior Franklin K. Lane that moviemakers should help "combat social unrest" by producing more movies extolling the United States. But a few months after the Red Scare ended, a title card in D. W. Griffith's *Orphans of the Storm* urged the audience to exercise great care not to exchange the good government of the United States for "Bolshevism and license."[36]

In 1922, when movie executives decided to placate right-wing censors by establishing the Motion Picture Producers and Distributors of America (MPPDA) and selecting a conservative Republican, former postmaster general Will Hays, as its head, political censorship did not loom large. Hays spoke in general terms about the new organization, announcing that it would uphold high moral standards in films, and the 1927 and 1930 codes did not include any taboos on politics or political movements. Continuing pressure for a stricter code led to the creation, in 1934, of a new enforcement mechanism, the Production Code Administration (PCA), headed by the ultra-Catholic Joseph Breen. All scripts had to be submitted to the PCA before shooting could commence, all negatives had to be approved before being printed, and no movie could be released with a PCA seal of approval until all changes demanded by the PCA had been made. Though this new office did not specifically warn against political commentary in films, all scripts with contemporary domestic content or those alluding to foreign affairs became subjected to the conservative principles of Hays and Breen. Breen responded to M-G-M's adaptation of Sinclair Lewis's novel *It Can't Happen Here* (about a fascist takeover of the United States) with a nine-page, single-spaced letter enumerating fifty-nine necessary changes. M-G-M canceled the project. Breen also forced United Artists to obfuscate most of the pro–Spanish Loyalist content of *Blockade*.[37]

Despite the urgings of two of the leaders of anti-Communist Jewish organizations in Los Angeles, Max Mont of the Los Angeles branch of the Jewish Labor Committee and Joseph Roos of the Los Angeles Jewish Community Committee, the studio bosses did not adopt an anti-Communist posture. They believed, foolishly as it turned out, that if they trod carefully the enemies of the industry would not publicly associate Communism and Judaism.[38] In 1935, Harry Warner warned the aspiring screenwriter Maurice Rapf (son of M-G-M executive Harry Rapf), newly returned from a visit to the Soviet Union and deeply radicalized by it: "I don't want to talk to no goddam Communist. Don't forget you're a Jew. Jewish Communists are going to bring down the wrath of the world on the rest of the Jews."[39] A few years later, Warner told his studio employees, "This industry has no sympathy with Communism, Fascism, Nazism or any other 'ism' than Americanism."[40] And he told the Ancient Order of Hibernians: "I am not accepting your hospitality as a *Jewish*-American. I am here as an American."[41] Art Arthur, a producer at Twentieth Century-Fox, urged the AJC to take seriously the allegations linking Jews to Communism, to reply to them and to make each reply "a springboard for a true report of what Jews mean to America." The AJC did nothing.[42]

Much more than they feared Communism, the movie executives feared anything that called attention to their Jewishness. They were, for example, hostile to the Hollywood Anti-Nazi League; they wanted it renamed the Hollywood Anti-Nazi, Anti-Communist League.[43] Alone among the studio bosses, Harry and Jack Warner supported the Jewish People's Committee for United Action against Fascism and Anti-Semitism, the Hollywood Anti-Nazi League, and the American Committee for Anti-Nazi Literature. And yet, as Jewish screenwriter Ben Hecht illustrated in his wonderful anecdote about David O. Selznick, the producers' efforts to mask their Jewishness was in vain. Selznick had refused to cosponsor a mass meeting to raise funds for a Jewish army, because, he told Hecht: "It's a Jewish political cause and I'm not interested in Jewish political problems. I'm an American and not a Jew." Hecht responded: "If I can prove you are a Jew, will you agree to co-sponsor the meeting?" "How will you do that?" asked Selznick. "I'll call up any three people you name and ask them what would you call David O. Selznick, an American or a Jew?" All three replied, "Jew."[44]

The movie executives also believed that they could not produce certain types of movies (anti-anti-Semitic or antifascist), because critics regularly misconstrued their purpose. Harry Warner said, "We've got to

33

be aware we are Jews . . . and that we will be looked upon by the community, not just Hollywood, of saying certain things *because* of being Jewish."[45] Hecht sharply criticized the studio bosses for their retreat from their Jewishness: They are "fretful toward keeping any Semitic color from their product," and, "though they have the hearts of lions, they will not fight as Jews. As anything else, yes. For any other cause, yes. For ideals they never heard of and that mean nothing to them—yes. As Jews—no."[46] And Jewish screenwriter Michael Blankfort wrote: "They were accidental Jews, terribly frightened Jews, who rejected their background to become super-Americans. They were interested in power and profit."[47]

And when the producers did green-light an antifascist or anti-Nazi movie, Jewish groups brought pressure on the studios to cancel it. For example, when it became known that M-G-M was adapting Sinclair Lewis's novel *It Can't Happen Here,* the chairman of the film committee of the Central Conference of American Rabbis urged the company's bosses and Will Hays not to make it: "The only wise method to pursue in these days of virulent anti-Semitism is to have no picture in which the Jewish problem is ventilated." Ironically, pro-German groups also pressured M-G-M to drop the project.[48]

But the bosses did want to do something about the growing strength of pro-Nazi groups in Los Angeles, but as private, not public, Jews. To that end, they met at the Hillcrest Country Club in March 1934 and agreed to support the fact-finding work of the newly formed Los Angeles Jewish Community Council (renamed, in 1945, Community Relations Council of the Jewish Federation Council), and to launch an undercover spy organization tasked with rooting out un-American groups in the Los Angeles area. This support group, the Studio Committee, was chaired by attorney Mendel Silberberg. Leon Lewis of the ADL, who had overseen the meeting, was later asked by Joseph Breen to head a newly established ADL advisory committee that would work with the producers to monitor anti-Semitic images meant for the screen and put pressure on the studios to abide by this committee's decisions. One project, *The Mad Dog of Europe,* was considered so extremely anti-German that the committee succeeded in getting RKO to drop it and to convince M-G-M not to pick it up. The film's producer, Al Rosen, excoriated the industry leaders for caving into German pressure, stating: "Most of these large producers are Jewish firms, and they call themselves Jews." The committee also opposed what its members saw as the stereotypical portrayal of Jews in *The House of Rothschild* (Twentieth Century-Fox, 1934), but to no avail.[49]

When Warner Bros. began making anti-Nazi and pro-British movies, an overt anti-Semitism became evident. A scurrilous broadside, with a cartoonish figure of a man with a long, hooked nose, read: "How 'A Star Is Born'/Ask the Hollywood Jew Who Owns One/ . . . Boycott Every Motion Picture Starring Any Member of the Pro-Communist Hollywood Anti-Nazi League/Destroy Jew Monopoly of the Motion Picture Industry."[50] Breen warned the studio heads that they were opening themselves to the charge that "Jews as a class" were trying to capture the screen of the United States for Communistic propaganda purposes, and, he added, most agitators in Hollywood were Jews.[51] Joseph Kennedy, a former studio owner and the US ambassador to the United Kingdom, stated: "Jews are on the spot, and they should stop making anti-Nazi pictures or using the film medium to promote or show sympathy to the cause of the democracies versus the dictators. Anti-Semitism was growing in Britain and the Jews were being blamed for the war."[52] And Congressman John Rankin (D-MS) charged that "Wall Street bankers and international Jews are dragging the country into war."[53] The curious logic of these and other critics of Hollywood went something like this: Hitler had come to power because of his anti-Communism. Therefore, those who criticized Hitler were, ipso facto, Communists.

In the years leading up to World War II, the industry faced threats from two congressional investigating committees, replete with coded anti-Judaic rhetoric. In August 1938, Martin Dies Jr., chairman of the House Special Committee on Un-American Activities, who had not shown any previous interest in the movie industry, announced that he was going to Hollywood to investigate charges that the Hollywood Anti-Nazi League was a Communist-dominated organization. Dies said he would afford the League's members, whom he labeled "dupes," "the opportunity to reply to charges that they were participating in communistic activities." He also pointed out that most of the movie bosses were

Jews, and, therefore, much more susceptible to Communist influence than any other group.[54]

Prior to this announcement, Dies had made no comments in the *Congressional Record* pertaining to Communism in Hollywood, and none of the witnesses testifying before his committee had alluded to Hollywood. His first hint that this might be a headline-grabbing investigation came when Edward E. Sullivan, a committee investigator sent to the West Coast to dig up incriminating evidence against labor leader Harry Bridges, reported that he, Sullivan, had uncovered "evidence of subversive activities in Hollywood" and that "all phases of radical and Communistic activities are rampant among the studios." At a set of hearings in August 1938, Sullivan reported on his findings, and J. B. Matthews, a newly minted anti-Communist professional witness, alleged that "almost everybody in Hollywood except Mickey Mouse and Snow White" had been members of the Party. Walter Steele, editor of *National Republic* magazine and chairman of the American Coalition Committee on National Security (an umbrella organization for 114 patriotic groups), submitted for the record a voluminous report asserting that many studio employees were "strongly sympathetic to communism" and were attempting to sneak subversive messages into films.[55]

The Anti-Nazi League responded with a barrage of telegrams to the president and Congress, a mass rally, and a national radio broadcast. The producers' associations and the guilds announced their hostility to the investigation. And Dies, finding no significant group or organization willing to cooperate with him, postponed, then canceled, the planned hearings. On his way out, though, he called the industry a "hotbed of Communists and radicals."[56] In the book Dies authored a year later, *The Trojan Horse in America*, he made no charges about the movie industry harboring Communists.[57] Invited to Warner Bros. Studio to watch its first outspoken anti-Nazi movie, *Confessions of a Nazi Spy* (1939), Dies admonished Harry Warner for ignoring or soft-pedaling Communism and portraying Nazism as the greater menace.[58] Despite his remarks, anti-Nazi movies of all types and quality flowed out from the smallest to the largest studios.

In early 1940, Dies announced that his committee planned to resume its investigation of "alleged subversive activities" in Hollywood. He was moved to do so in response to his committee's investigation of various fascist and left-wing groups and information from a colleague with close ties to the International Alliance of Theatrical Stage Employees (IATSE), which used red-baiting to defeat the efforts of rival unions. This man told the committee's investigator that Communists were fomenting an internal struggle in the Hollywood unions. He was, Dies said, "determined to expose Hollywood thoroughly." IATSE executives welcomed the probe, and studio executives did not publicly protest, claiming, "We're Clean." In two articles for *Liberty* magazine, "The Reds in Hollywood" and "Is Communism Invading the Movies?," Dies stated that Hollywood "has been completely duped by Communists." Right-wing gossip columnist Hedda Hopper exulted that Dies was going to "bring the names of the guilty into the open." Sitting as a one-person committee in his home in Beaumont, Texas, Dies questioned John L. Leech, a former Communist turned informer. Leech provided the congressman with the names of forty-three people who were, he alleged, "members of, contributors to, or interested in the Communist Party." A significant number of those named were liberals. Dies then traveled to Los Angeles and San Francisco, offering "clearance" to any of the forty-three who agreed to testify before him in executive session. Nearly a dozen liberals appeared, and, at the end of August, Dies announced that he had "cleared" forty-two (the forty-third, Lionel Stander, was immediately fired from the movie he was working on). Y. Frank Freeman, president of the Association of Motion Picture Producers, said that his organization welcomed "a complete and impartial investigation," and if such an investigation revealed anyone who might, "by their actions and conduct," bring discredit upon the industry, the industry will not protect them.[59]

Some studio executives instituted measures to demonstrate that they were aware of subversive elements in the industry and that they were taking steps to deal with them. Edward Dmytryk claimed that the head of publicity at RKO had been authorized to collect information of "dangerous left-wingers" and convey it to the archconservative director Cecil B. DeMille.[60] Harry M. Warner gathered his studio's employees together on June 5, 1940, to announce, "We don't want anybody employed by our company who belongs to any bunds: Communistic, Fascistic or any other un-American organization." He urged his audience to turn over any "disunifier" to the FBI. One month later, his company released *Murder in the Air,* starring Ronald Reagan as an FBI agent investigating a foreign spy ring. The film included a scene from a "Rice Committee" hearing. Unsatisfied with Hollywood's response to Dies's charges, Eugene Lyons, in his book *The Red Decade,* included a chapter on Communists in Hollywood.[61]

On August 1, 1941, the industry was rocked by two events: The Senate approved S. Res. 152, authorizing "a thorough and complete investigation of any propaganda disseminated by motion pictures and radio or any other activity of the motion picture industry in the direction of the participation by the United States in the present European war."[62] That night, the resolution's cosponsor, Gerald Nye (D-ND), addressed a meeting of the America First Committee (AFC) in St. Louis.[63] Though the AFC had made strong efforts to weed out anti-Semites in the organization, anti-Semites were attracted to it, and, at many meetings, were very vocal. Though Nye was not an anti-Semite, he used anti-Judaic language. At one point he accused the studio heads of "operating as a war propaganda machine as if they were being operated from a central agency," coded language for the existence of an international conspiracy as outlined in the *Protocols of the Elders of Zion.* He then named the culprits, listing eighteen Jewish names. Finally, again using coded language, he accused them of having, a few years ago, "filled their pictures with so much immorality and filth that the great Christian churches had to rise up in protest and organize the Legion of Decency to stop it."[64] According to a report in *In Fact,* Nye's list of names was "accompanied by howls of 'The Jews, The Jews.'"[65]

This time, the movie executives responded vigorously in their defense. According to *Weekly Variety,* the executives were "thoroughly aroused" by "the intolerant implications by Senator Nye of racial motivations," and they appointed a steering committee to oversee their defense. They hired as their lead attorney Wendell Willkie, who had been the unsuccessful Republican candidate for the presidency in 1940, and he regularly implied that the investigation was motivated by anti-Semites. The Jewish War Veterans supported the movie executives, and John J.

Stanley, the secretary-treasurer of the American Federation of Labor, stated, in a letter to Vice President Henry Wallace, that the investigation was anti-Semitic.[66]

Nye was the leadoff witness on September 9. He denied that he disliked Jews, and he accused his critics of using charges of anti-Semitism to cover the interventionism of the movie studios. "If antisemitism exists in America," he added, "the Jews have themselves to blame."[67] The first session of the hearings did not go well for the investigation subcommittee. The accusations of Nye and other senators were effectively refuted by a member of the subcommittee, Ernest W. McFarland (D-AZ), and the press was hostile. Dorothy Thompson called the hearings an "American Dreyfus case."[68] The hearings were adjourned on September 11. That night, however, Charles A. Lindbergh, the most prominent member of America First, delivered a speech, stating that "Jewish ownership and influence in our motion pictures, our press, our radio, and our government" was the greatest danger facing the United States, and that Jews were among the three groups inciting the United States to war. He went on to say that Jewish opposition to the Nazis was understandable, but their prowar policy endangered them: "Tolerance is a virtue that depends upon peace and strength. History shows that it cannot survive war and devastations."[69] This speech drew powerful criticism across the country, but the America First National Committee responded by deploring the interventionists' "injection of the race issue into the discussion of war and peace."[70] On the day the hearings resumed, September 22, an article in *New Republic* called the hearings a "kangaroo court," the purpose of which is "to incite racial hatred . . . and to threaten Hollywood producers that unless they abandon the anti-fascist struggle and support the America First Committee, an anti-Semitic campaign will be organized on a large scale in America."[71] During the second session, Nicholas Schenck, Harry Warner, Barney Balaban, and Darryl F. Zanuck strongly defended the industry against the charges levied against it. Harry Warner said: "You may correctly charge me with being an anti-Nazi. But no one can charge me with being un-American."[72] After the hearings ended, Nye added fuel to the flames of his St. Louis speech by saying that had he continued naming members of the motion picture industry responsible for prowar propaganda, "the proportion of Jewish names would, if anything, have increased."[73]

Both anti-Semitism and anti-Communism in Hollywood abated during the war, with one glaring exception: In 1941, when the Screen Cartoonists Guild struck Walt Disney Studio to gain recognition as a bargaining agent, Disney blamed the strike on Communists. The cartoonists were successful, and Disney, in 1944, became a founding member of the anti-Communist Motion Picture Alliance for the Preservation of American Ideals. Many of the other studios made, among their dozens of prowar movies, ten favorable to the Soviet Union. Three of them would become the targets of anti-Communists, and the writers of all three would be subpoenaed by the House Committee: Lillian Hellman (*North Star*), Howard Koch (*Mission to Moscow*), and Paul Jarrico and Richard Collins (*Song of Russia*). Three of the writers were Jewish.

Toward the end of the war, anti-Communism in Hollywood leaped back into prominence, with the formation of the Motion Picture Alliance for the Preservation of American Ideals and a flood of anti-Communist editorials and stories in the *Hollywood Reporter*. At the same time, the studio bosses' fear of anti-Semitism waned. Three studios, greenlighted anti-anti-Semitic projects: *Crossfire* (RKO), *Gentleman's Agreement* (Twentieth Century-Fox), and *Earth and High Heaven* (Samuel Goldwyn). The last was canceled, but the first two received six Academy Award nominations each, *Gentleman's Agreement* winning three, including best picture.

But trouble loomed. Congressman John Rankin, the most zealous anti-Communist and anti-Semite in the House of Representatives, successfully moved that the Committee on Un-American Activities be made a permanent committee, and he then pushed the Committee to investigate "Communist Infiltration of the Motion-Picture Industry." At the hearings, which opened in October 1947, two of the Jewish studio bosses, Jack Warner and Louis B. Mayer, avowed their strong opposition to Communism and swore that they never allowed any subversive content into their studios' movies. (Warner became the first Hollywood witness to name, in an open session, employees he thought were Communists. He became, that is, the first informer.) Both men assured the Committee that they had the situation under control. Though ten of the Unfriendly Nineteen witnesses were Jewish and six of them were called to the witness stand, their religious affiliation was not mentioned by any of the Committee members. (It should also be noted that none of the Jewish organizations called attention to this disproportionate makeup of the Nineteen, but, according to an ADL report, before, during, and after the hearings, leaders of anti-Semitic groups in Southern California carried on an aggressive campaign, using "Zionism" and "Communism" interchangeably.)[74] But one of the unfriendly witnesses, Samuel Ornitz, directly addressed the issue of anti-Semitism in his written statement, which he was not allowed to read. Ornitz wrote, voicing the hidden fears of the Jewish organizations and Jewish studio executives:

> I wish to address this committee as a Jew, because one of its leading members is an outstanding anti-Semite in the Congress and revels in that fact. I refer to John E. Rankin. . . . In speaking out as a Jew, I speak in a deeper sense as an American, as the one who has to take the first blow for my fellow Americans. For when constitutional guarantees are overridden, the Jew is the first one to suffer . . . but only the first one. As soon as the Jew is crushed, the others get it. . . . I ask, as a Jew, based on the record, is bigotry this Committee's yardstick of Americanism and subversion?

He would not, he concluded, falter before the Committee's threat of contempt of Congress, "which word sounds like the short way of saying concentration camp." He did not, however, mention anti-Semitism in his very short oral testimony.[75]

The industry had received no support from national Jewish organizations. When Sidney Harmon, an executive at Twentieth Century-Fox, urged the AJC executive director John Slawson to challenge the House Committee, by accusing it of deliberately spreading anti-Semitism, Slawson replied that Committee investigations affected all citizens regardless of their religious or ethnic affiliations.[76] However, a group of Southern California rabbis and the Southland Jewish Organization filed a petition asking the Supreme Court to reconsider its refusal to review the contempt-of-court decisions of two members of the Hollywood Ten. The Southland Jewish Organization identified itself as a group formed to safeguard the rights of Jews and other minority groups everywhere.[77] And the American Jewish Congress supported the amicus curiae brief filed on behalf of the Hollywood Ten.

Once the hearings ended, the mostly Jewish movie executives put into effect and maintained for fifteen years a blacklist of unrepentant Communists. They did not do so because the blacklistees were Communists, but because they had refused to cooperate with the Committee by answering its questions. The executives did not want to surrender to the Committee, but they surrendered to their belief that public antipathy toward Communist actors, writers, and directors would lead to boycotts of their films by the American Legion and Knights of Columbus. Among those present at the Waldorf Conference of November 1947, which initiated the blacklist, only Samuel Goldwyn, Walter Wanger, and Dore Schary voiced opposition to a blacklist. The most insistent voices were those of gentiles: the advisors Paul V. McNutt and James Byrnes and MPAA president Eric Johnston, who threatened to resign if a blacklist was not accepted. During the next decade, however, the executives welcomed back every former Communist who had, in one form of another, publicly sworn that he or she was no longer a member of the Communist Party, claimed that he or she had been duped into joining, repudiated Communism, praised the Committee on Un-American Activities, and provided names. There is no evidence that fear of anti-Semitism influenced the decision by the movie bosses to blacklist the Hollywood Ten, but it would beggar belief to think that the executives had forgotten the outcries linking Jews and Communism and Jews and movie bosses, which had occurred only eight years previously.

A strong link between producer anti-Communism and Jewish anti-Communism was provided by the attorney Mendel Silberberg, the chairman of the Community Relations Committee of the Jewish Federation Council of Los Angeles. Silberberg also represented several of the studios and participated in the 1947 Waldorf meeting that inaugurated the motion picture blacklist. The executive director of the Community Relations Committee, Joseph Roos, worked closely with William Wheeler,[78] the Hollywood investigator for the Committee on Un-American Activities, and Martin Gang, the Jewish lawyer who represented former Communists anxious to clear themselves.[79] They, in turn, worked closely with a lay analyst and former Communist named Phil Cohen, who had become an unofficial adviser to those Communists who were considering becoming informers.[80]

Gang had a good reputation in the liberal or progressive community. He had been a member of the Independent Citizens Committee of the Arts, Sciences and Professions—originally established to aid the 1944 presidential campaign of Franklin D. Roosevelt; he had worked with some of the Nineteen; and he helped Dalton Trumbo with his suit against M-G-M for breach of contract. Gang entered the clearance process when he was approached by one of his clients, actor Sterling Hayden, who would be the first voluntary namer. After Hayden's appearance, Gang became known as a conduit to continued employment. He would investigate the circumstances that had led to his prospective client's predicament and, once convinced that his client wholeheartedly desired to clear himself/herself, would call Wheeler, who would come to Gang's office, listen to the client's recantation, and, if satisfied, arrange for a Committee appearance. If the client had not been named but exposed in a public list, such as *Red Channels*, Gang required the client to make a full list of all his/her political activities, associations, writings, articles, speeches, meetings, lectures, contributions, subscriptions, and all potentially suspicious movements. When Gang was satisfied, he would circulate the list via the offices of Roy Brewer, actors Ward Bond or John Wayne, or other notables of the Motion Picture Alliance for the Preservation of American Ideals. Gang saw himself as a "frustrated crusader," one who had tried "to keep a lot of innocent people from being hurt unnecessarily." He felt obliged, as a lawyer, to serve his clients' best interests, and, in the case of the subpoenaed or already-named Hollywood employees, their best interests were served by avoiding the blacklist and prison. So he developed a series of formats to clear them. "I didn't tell them what to do," he later said; "I only told them what the choices were."[81]

Phil Cohen had been a Party member in the 1930s. And yet, in spite of his apostasy (leaving the Party) and the Party's deep distrust of psychoanalysis, Cohen became the go-to psychotherapist for the Hollywood Left. The exact relation between the visits to Cohen for psychotherapy and the decision to cooperate is not clear. What is clear is that some of the namers were already seeing Cohen for personal reasons and that at least a dozen of his patients ended up cooperating; others did not. Cohen denied trying to convince any patient into any particular course of action. Rather, he simply attempted to assist his patients to gain insights into their problems and muster the strength to deal with them. Wheeler, however, states that Cohen was very helpful, that he did try to convince his patients to leave the Party and to testify.[82]

In the summer of 1950, as the Ten were headed for prison, Julius and Ethel Rosenberg and Morton Sobell were arrested and charged with transmitting atomic secrets to the Soviet Union. They were tried and convicted in March 1951, as the House Committee on Un-American Activities reopened its hearings into Communist infiltration of the motion picture industry. The Rosenbergs were sentenced to death; Morton Sobell received a thirty-year prison sentence.

Surprisingly, almost every section of the anti-Communist chorus observed an uncharacteristic silence during the trial. The one notable exception was the organized Jewish community. According to Deborah Dash Moore, the Rosenberg case "brought the vast majority of American Jewry, who previously had not supported Communism nor opposed it solidly, into the anti-Communist camp. The case helped to make opposition to Communism a criterion of Jewish communal membership." Anti-Communist Jewish intellectuals became the "most withering in their attacks on the defense committee, the most vehement in their insistence that the Rosenbergs be executed." Victor S. Navasky, however, claims that the case "split the Jewish community."[83] In fact, the community split between a very large anti-Rosenberg majority and a small pro-Rosenberg minority. The latter composed the bulk of the national support group for the Rosenbergs and Sobell.

The leaders of mainstream Jewish organizations were at first concerned about the Jewishness of the arrested atomic spies. A memo written to the executive director of the American Jewish Committee on July 31, 1950, following the arrests of Harry Gold (May), David Greenglass (June), and Julius Rosenberg (July), was titled "Public Relations Effects of Activities of Jewish Atom Spies." The memo writer regarded the present situation "as being potentially more dangerous [to Jews] than the situation which obtained during World War II. . . . The main reason for concern is the belief that the non-Jewish public may generalize from these activities and impute to the Jews as a group treasonable motives and activities."[84] Then, following the formation of the National Committee to Secure Justice for the Rosenbergs and Morton Sobell (October 1951), the AJC issued a statement announcing that "attempts are being made by a Communist-inspired group . . . to inject the false issue of anti-Semitism into the Rosenberg case."[85] Jewish organizations responded immediately to this threat. According to Arnold Forster, the head of the Anti-Defamation League, the major Jewish agencies, "almost without exception," cautioned every organized Jewish group to be wary of the attempt by Communist sympathizers "to use Jewish platforms to urge protests against the Rosenberg injustice." The goals of the ADL campaign were twofold: (1) to counter efforts of anti-Semites to make bigoted hay out of the Jewish background of the defendants; and (2) to prevent the case from being used by Communists for their own political purposes. First of all, the ADL argued, the Rosenbergs were indicted as Americans, not as Jews. Second, "opening a synagogue or other Jewish facility as a meeting place for a Communist-sponsored campaign" would confirm many in their belief that Jews were soft on Communism.[86] Forster told Victor S. Navasky that the heads of the Jewish organizations feared the establishment of a link between being a Jew and being a Communist. They perceived "an evident quotient of anti-Semitism in the domestic Cold War": "Jews in that period were automatically suspect. Our evaluation of the general mood was that people felt if you scratched a Jew, you can find a Communist."[87]

The Rosenberg-Sobell committee in the Los Angeles area published a newsletter, held house parties, and distributed leaflets.[88] Those blacklisted writers still politically active in the rapidly dwindling, Communist-controlled Southern California Committee of the Arts, Sciences, and Professions participated in pro-Rosenberg demonstrations. Michael Wilson told me that he and several other blacklistees participated in a vigil in downtown Los Angeles on the night of the couple's execution. Roy

Huggins, one of the informers, drove up in a Cadillac convertible with the top down and shouted, "They're going to fry you Commie bastards, too!"[89] Dalton Trumbo (who was not Jewish) drafted but did not complete a pamphlet for the National Committee to Secure Justice for Morton Sobell, and his daughter, Nikola, worked for that committee.

Blacklisted screenwriter John Wexley (who was Jewish) made the most significant contribution to the pro-Rosenberg cause with his massive tome *The Judgment of Julius and Ethel Rosenberg* (672 pages), the first detailed deconstruction of the prosecution's case. He was moved to do so by his reading of the trial transcript, in which he found a story "full of holes, big holes and little holes." [90] His effort to retrace the steps of the principal prosecution witnesses was extolled by the pros and dismissed by the cons. Malcolm P. Sharp called it "a thoughtful book on the subject." Oliver Pilat labeled it "propaganda" and called Wexley's treatment of evidence and issues "infinitely devious and unfair."[91]

I have seen no evidence to indicate what the Jewish movie company executives said or thought about the Rosenbergs and the other Jewish atomic spies. It is likely that the headlines about their arrests, trials, and, in the case of the Rosenbergs, executions, only solidified their determination to maintain the blacklist, produce anti-Communist movies, and keep their heads down.

To conclude, although anti-Semitism was not noticeably on the rise in the postwar United States, Jewish anti-Communists feared that it was lurking below the surface. Though many of them were liberals, and all paid lip service to due process, they were convinced that their most important task was to protect Jews from accusations of being unpatriotic and soft on Communism. The ADL expressed reservations about the Truman administration's loyalty oath program and the Mundt-Nixon-Ferguson anti-Communist bills, and the American Jewish Congress issued a pamphlet, written by Irwin Ross, titled *The Communists: Friends or Foes of Civil Liberties?*, which sought to balance fundamental civil liberties with national security but also advocated the exposure and elimination of Communists from private organizations.[92] In March 1951, the Community Relations Council of Los Angeles sponsored three roundtable conferences "On the

Problems of Communism and Preservation of Civil Liberties." Martin Gang participated in the third, "Jewish Communist Life as an Answer to Communism."[93] Nevertheless, neither the AJC nor the ADL ever came to the defense of Jewish Communists caught in the loyalty/investigation nets, nor did they defend the rights of Communists to be employed in educational and government jobs or in the movie industry. They did, however, strongly defend the few Jews who were, on the surface, wrongly accused. Examples of the latter include challenges to the nomination of Anna M. Rosenberg as assistant secretary of defense in the Truman administration and the Jewish scientists and engineers suspended during the investigation of Communist infiltration of Fort Monmouth in 1954.[94] In general, Jewish organizations refrained from attacking congressional investigation committees, opting instead to lobby them to investigate hate groups or to work with them to ease the path of Jewish witnesses. In October 1957, Rabbi Fineberg appeared before the Un-American Activities Committee, where he praised the Committee's efforts "to educate the American people on the nature of communism."[95] The one exception was the American Jewish Congress, which challenged the constitutionality of state loyalty oath programs and opposed New York's Feinberg Law, barring Communists from employment in the public schools.[96]

Though both the Jewish organizations and the movie companies purged known and unrepentant Communists from their ranks, the de facto anti-Communist Jewish studio bosses did so much more publicly and systematically than did the true-believing anti-Communist Jewish organizations. The motion picture blacklist and graylist directly harmed the lives of more than five hundred of their employees and their families. It also made those who remained employed fearful of putting social or political content into their movies. The movie bosses never once expressed qualms about this massive proscription, and, when the blacklist began to crumble in 1960 under the able direction of Dalton Trumbo, the bosses only slowly and reluctantly allowed blacklistees to sign contracts. During the height of the blacklist, only one studio boss, Harry Cohn, even diddled the process, likely arranging clearance deals for Sidney Buchman, Judy Holliday, and Carl Foreman.

Jewish anti-Communism was a minor element in the Cold War. It did far less harm than most of the others. But it did contribute to an oppressive atmosphere that severely damaged the main ideals of Judaism: justice and fair treatment. It also cast a pall over the cultural scene in the United States, where censorship and self-censorship predominated.

3

A Debate over the Politics and Morality of Cooperative and Uncooperative Witnesses Who Testified before the House Committee on Un-American Activities, 1947–1953

According to the data meticulously collected by Howard Suber, 214 Hollywood studio employees were named by cooperative witnesses to the House Committee on Un-American Activities.[1] Of the 120 who appeared (via subpoena or voluntarily) to testify, seventy-six refused to cooperate (invoking either the First or Fifth Amendment), and thirty-nine cooperated (naming names). Four of the witnesses refused to cooperate on their first appearance but returned later and cooperated. (By my count, twenty-two who did not appear, mainly because they had left the country to avoid a subpoena, would have refused to cooperate.) Since 1947, when the first ten of the unfriendly witnesses challenged the Committee, there has been an ongoing debate about their behavior as well as the Fifth Amendment positions of the many resistant witnesses who followed, 1951–1953. Since October 1947, anti-Communists have accused the unfriendly witnesses of a lack of candor, whereas left-wingers have accused the friendly witnesses of gross acts of betrayal.

The weight of scholarly opinion tipped toward those who resisted, in 1980, when Victor S. Navasky's *Naming Names* was published. Navasky had interviewed many of the friendly and unfriendly witnesses, and he made clear that he preferred the moral position of the latter. Two well-documented books published at the same time by Larry Ceplair and Steven Englund (*The Inquisition in Hollywood*) and Nancy Lynn Schwartz (*The Hollywood Writers' Wars*) took the same position as Navasky. There have been, to be sure, the occasional outliers (books by Kenneth Billingsley, Ronald Radosh and Allis Radosh, and Allan H. Ryskind), but they lacked depth of analysis and were too overtly skewed to be taken seriously. Twelve years ago, however, Alan Casty (*Communism in Hollywood: The Moral Paradoxes of Testimony, Silence, and Betrayal*) produced a scholarly, well-researched, and well-argued revisionist history. Though his sympathy is entirely with the witnesses who cooperated with the Committee, and he waves his anti-Communism like the checkered flag at the Indianapolis 500, his argument must be taken seriously.

Both authors claim to be on a moral quest, but both know precisely their destination: Navasky argues that the cooperating witnesses acted immorally, betraying their friends and colleagues; Casty indicts the uncooperative witnesses for being apologists for a criminal regime. The authors are from the same generation (Casty was born in 1929, Navasky in 1932). Navasky was a journalist, Casty a professor of English and film. Navasky is sympathetic to the Left, and Casty is antagonistic. Casty frequently critiques what he calls Navasky's hyperbole and aggrandizement; we do not know what Navasky thinks of Casty's work. Casty's book is filled with the zeal of the righteous (full disclosure: I and Steven Englund, my cowriter of *The Inquisition in Hollywood*, come under fire from Casty for some of our conclusions). Navasky's book bears the imprint of disappointment with his fellow humans; Casty disapproves only of unrepentant Communists. Navasky's book is based mainly on interviews, Casty's on documents.

Each author poses a set of questions to be answered in their respective moral quests (or, as Navasky terms it, moral detective stories). Navasky poses twelve questions, among them: "How did it come to pass that scores of otherwise decent individuals were compelled to betray a moral presumption [thou shalt not inform on one's neighbor]? What *are* the conditions under which good men do things they know to be wrong?

Are there justifications for the informers' actions that reasonable men would regard as extenuating, or are there perhaps even mandating circumstances? . . . What happens when a state puts pressure on its citizens to betray their fellows? . . . What are the consequences of betrayal and collaboration? . . . What, in other words, is to be learned from this episode of collaboration and betrayal American-style?" Casty poses six questions, but they are vaguer and not easily answered: He asks if one can locate "the moral balance point" between a witness's personal needs and desires and the desire to stand up for what the witness now believes, and does the former cancel out the latter, does it "deny it any credence?" Are there not, he continues, "many paths to betrayal. . . . What is it to testify, or not? What is one's full testimony, testament? Just what is it to behave decently?" It is clear from the tenor of these respective questions that each author already believes he knows the answers.

Navasky and Casty employ entirely different approaches to the subject. Navasky begins with an extensive examination of the informer genus, whereas Casty delineates the evils of Communism. Navasky uses the unfortunate testimony of Larry Parks to frame his thesis; Casty commences with a comparison of the responses of two Hollywood Communist artists to Party censorship of their work. He places the writer-director Robert Rossen, who defied the Party, at the center of his morality play, and he insists that Rossen, on his second appearance before the Committee, stood up for what "he believed, felt should be done." Rossen, it should be noted, denied he was an informer. (FBI director J. Edgar Hoover called the cooperative witnesses "informants"; the uncooperative witnesses called them "stool pigeons.") In any event, this juxtaposition is interesting, because Parks and Rossen had been two of the eight unfriendly witnesses of 1947 who had not been called to the stand.

Parks, a very successful actor who had just signed a huge contract with Columbia Pictures (among his twenty-six credits were the recently released *The Jolson Story* and *Jolson Sings Again*), was the leadoff witness of the 1951 hearings. Unfortunately for him, the ground rules for this new set of hearings had not been set, he had not been rehearsed, and he fell between the three possible stools. One could, as the Hollywood Ten had done in an obfuscating manner, invoke the First Amendment, be cited for contempt, and go to prison and be blacklisted. Or one could invoke the Fifth Amendment and be blacklisted. Or one could fully cooperate, answer all the Committee's questions, including the names of other members of the Party, and return to work. It turned out one could not, as Parks tried to do, answer questions about one's membership in the Party and not provide the names of other members (a tactic that came to be called "the diminished Fifth"). Parks posed the moral dilemma he faced: "Don't present me with the choice of either being in contempt of this Committee and going to jail or forcing me to really crawl through the mud to be an informer." Eventually, in an executive session, he provided names, but he did so too reluctantly, and he was blacklisted. (His wife, Betty Garrett, claimed Parks was given a list of names and merely indicated which ones were Party members. That is, he "read"; he did not "volunteer.")[2] No other witness made this mistake. The key for friendly and unfriendly witnesses alike was to state clearly and upfront one's position.

The Committee did not need the names of Communists in Hollywood. Its investigators had already compiled a long list. "The demand for names," Navasky writes, "was not a quest for evidence; it was a test of character. The naming of names had shifted from a means to an end." The hearings "were degradation ceremonies." The Committee members' "job was not to legislate or even discover subversives . . . so much as it was to stigmatize." He goes on to say that degradation ceremonies require denouncers, "and the most credible denouncer, with the most impeccable credentials, is the one who has been there himself. The ex-Communists constituted a steady supply of denouncers." As ceremonial denouncers, the naming witnesses not only purged themselves of their moral responsibility for the depredations of Communism but they also cleansed themselves of the redness that blocked their careers.

Navasky strongly believes that the named were "innocent"; they had not, he states erroneously, committed a crime. In fact, the Alien Registration Act (1940) had made it unlawful to advocate in any way, or to be part of a group that advocated or encouraged, the overthrow of any government in the United States by force or violence. In its prosecution of top leaders of the Communist Party, 1948–1951, US attorneys had successfully argued that Communists as self-admitted Marxist-Leninists were, ipso facto, such advocates and encouragers. In its 1951 decision, the Supreme Court of the United States, in *Dennis v. United States* (341 US 494), agreed with the government, ruling that active advocacy of Communist ideas created a "clear and present danger" that threatened the government. Since, in Navasky's view, being a member of the Communist Party was not a crime, he can unequivocally state that the namers violated their values and betrayed their fellow humans.

For his part, Navasky defines a cooperative witness as one "who betrays a comrade, i.e., a fellow member of a movement, a colleague, or a friend, to the authorities." He then categorizes the genus into four species: "The Espionage Informer," "The Conspiracy Informer," "The Liberal Informer," and the Hollywood informers, who were unwilling, onetime witnesses. The last varied widely: some testified reluctantly, others enthusiastically; some professed great knowledge about the Party, others claimed ignorance; some told the truth, others lied; some were combative, and others crawled; some were noisy, others were comic. But all of them, Navasky contends, accepted their role as key instruments in the show-trial purgation staged by the House Committee.

Navasky's most valuable contribution to blacklist history is his long, detailed chapter on the informer "subculture." He shows how the trio of attorney Martin Gang, psychologist Phil Cohen, and House Committee investigator William Wheeler prepared and supported those who chose to inform. They developed a technique that never failed once they had the full cooperation of the namer. It began with Wheeler, who visited all those who had been named. He brought a subpoena and asked them if they intended to cooperate and, if so, whom they would name on the witness stand. Bess Taffel remembered that he appeared at her door one summer evening in 1951: "Mr. Wheeler himself: Not your ordinary marshal. Everything became unreal. It was twilight and I didn't think to turn on a light. We sat in the half-dark and he told me ever so gently that I'd been named [by Leo Townsend and Martin Berkeley] and the Committee would like to ask me some questions. . . . He was sympathetic, sincere, sorry. He'd do his best to help me, except, of course, in the matter of work. He could do nothing about that. He gave me his card and said, 'We haven't informed your employers about this, and there's no need for you to do so either.'" However, the word got out, and she was approached by her producer, who urged her to contact Martin Gang. She said she could not, that Gang was the attorney used by cooperative witnesses, and she did not intend to cooperate.[3]

In his excellent chapter "The Reasons Why," Navasky profiles eleven namers, based on interviews with them. They are allowed to speak for themselves as to their decision-making process and afterthoughts. This material is far richer than what was available to Casty. Navasky then devotes a chapter to "The Reasons Considered." He begins with a cogent point made by Abraham Polonsky, an uncooperative witness, one not taken into account by Casty: Since the namers did not provide names prior to pressure being put on them by their employers or the House Committee, we can never know what their true motives were, noble or ignoble: "If you wait until they put a gun up against your head, it's too late to claim that you are doing it for moral-political reasons."

Navasky then examines the credibility of four of the usual explanations given by namers for their decision to name. The first rationalization is, "I didn't hurt anybody." That is, many of the namers claimed that they had carefully crafted their lists so as to only name people who had already been named or had died. But Navasky points out that many of those witnesses did name people for the first time. The second rationalization is, "They deserved what they got" (or, "They had it coming"). Third, the namer alleges, "I wasn't responsible for my actions," and, fourth, "I was acting in obedience to a higher loyalty." Navasky is much too dismissive of these claims. He is correct to point out the flaws in each, but that does not mean that those beliefs were not sincerely held. But it is clear that these rationalizations were post facto and that the actual, determining reason they all chose to become namers was economic—they wanted to go on working in the industry, and naming was the only path to that goal. Some of them, in effect, said as much: Why should I ruin my life for a cause I no longer believed in or for former comrades, with whom I no longer have any connection (and who excoriated me for leaving the Party)?

Navasky admits that he is unable to measure the extent of the damage caused by the friendly witnesses, but he is certain that the Cold War state "weakened American culture and weakened itself." Further, it deprived hundreds of Hollywood people of their "right to practice their art and craft." Finally, the namers polluted the public well, poisoned social life in general, and destroyed the very possibility of a community. He devotes a short chapter to the "Informer as Victim," noting that many of them had difficulty finding jobs after they testified, some experienced a loss of self-esteem, and some were ostracized.

Navasky does offer criticisms of the unfriendly witnesses, as well. They, like the friendly witnesses, erred by adhering to the rules established by the House Committee; in some way or another, all the witnesses played by those weird rules—rules, it should be noted, that were closely followed by the congressional investigation committees that came later, particular Joseph McCarthy's Permanent Subcommittee on Investigations. The uncooperative witnesses, Navasky declares, should have been more open about their politics, "since they would suffer the stigma anyway, no matter how they testified, had nothing to lose and society something to gain by a spirited, nonrhetorical, discriminating defense of their political pasts (or presents)." Except, that open admission of being a Communist could have left them open for prosecution under the Alien Registration Act. That said, they are, Navasky concludes, by dint of having taken a "personal risk for the common good," entitled to the label "moral heroes." The namers, however, have no legitimate claim on that title, and they wear it only because it has been conferred on them by cold warriors "to justify the unjustifiable."

The one serious weakness in the book is that Navasky does not explicate a moral standard by which the unfriendly witnesses can be judged. He judges them according to his own particular set of values, which denotes the informant as a "rat" or "stool pigeon."

Casty's bias is diametrically opposed to Navasky's. Whereas Navasky says nothing about foreign or domestic Communism, Casty opens by condemning the Hollywood Communists as part of an international criminal conspiracy: "The rhetoric of idealism, a golden crusade, was distorted into destructive ideological rigidity, into deceit and denial of fact and truth." Controlled from Moscow, "those who crusaded for free speech submitted to censorship, accepted the denial of the very freedom of speech that was the core of their political protests. In turn, they enforced thought control on others, to the ultimate point of personal vilification of those who had dared to disagree." (He should have written "tried to enforce thought control," because many resisted and left the Party, while others simply ignored Party dictates.) He then offers what he believes is a telling comparison of two Hollywood Party members put on trial by a Party tribunal, screenwriter Albert Maltz, for an article in a Party journal demanding more freedom for Communist writers, and writer-director Robert Rossen, for his movie *All the King's Men* (Columbia, 1949). Maltz became one of the Hollywood Ten; Rossen, one of the Nineteen, was recalled in 1951 and offered to talk about himself but not name names. After two years on the blacklist, he returned to the Committee, named names, and resumed his film career.

Maltz, as Casty summarizes, capitulated to a Party tribunal (wrote a second article recanting what he had said in the first), refused to testify at the October 1947 hearings (actually he refused to answer two questions), went to prison, was blacklisted, and his career never recovered. But, Casty continues, he "remained silent about the monstrous evils of the Soviet Union that he continued to defend," and he was subsequently (thirty years later, it should be said) "honored as an idealistic hero." Rossen, who stood up against the Party but then named names, "was subsequently castigated vehemently as a traitor" (by a few dozen blacklistees, it should be noted). In Casty's eyes, Maltz and Rossen "represent two emblematic extremes of action, consequences, and moral judgments. The consequences can be defined in two stages: (1) the immediate effects of their actions on their lives and careers and (2) the long-term moral paradoxes revealed in their actions and the enduring moral and character judgments based on their actions, shaped by the power of ideology and unrelenting feelings of betrayal." Yes, Casty acknowledges, Maltz suffered for his courageous and honorable stand against the Committee, but he remained a loyal believer in the ideals of the Communist Party and the accomplishments of the Soviet Union as well as a "persistent and often distorting critic [in Casty's view at least] of the policies and actions of the United States." By his silence, Maltz "evaded the immensity of [the Soviet Union's] assaults on humanity. Even when, much later, he admitted with obfuscation and limitation [again, in Casty's view] some degree of belated recognition, he expressed no regrets, saw no personal moral flaw in himself or his comrades for so belated a recognition of evil so long evaded and denied, allowed no recognition of any consequences of those years of active 'silence.'"

Rossen, however, in his second appearance before the House Committee, provided "thorough, thoughtful statements of principle and a detailed criticism of international Communism and the Soviet Union." And for this honorable stand, he was subject to "vituperative personal attacks" as a man and as a filmmaker. The attacks, however, had more to do with the number of names Rossen provided the Committee (fifty-four, the fourth-most among namers) than with his thoughtful comments on the Cold War. Casty, however, downplays the actual effect of naming names—"All those who were going to be named had already been a part of many lists," and "it was rare that someone's livelihood was any longer actually threatened." But each time a name was given, another nail was driven into the coffin of that person's career. Nor does Casty mention that only a tiny number of unfriendly witnesses were allowed to read prepared statements or to give "thorough, thoughtful statements." When they tried, they were gaveled into silence by the Committee chair. Casty does concede, however, that Rossen's desire to return to work influenced his decision to inform, and he did return to work as a filmmaker.

Casty, in his first chapter, posits the existence among historians of the blacklist of "an absolute moral dichotomy"—enshrining the "pure heroes and martyrs" who resisted and vilifying "the totally irredeemable untouchable informers." That dichotomy is a pure figment of his imagination. There was not, even among some of the "enshrined," such a dichotomy. For example, Dalton Trumbo, who had a much keener sense of moral ambiguity than either Navasky or Casty, told the members of the Writers Guild of America, after he accepted their Laurel Award for lifetime achievement:

> The blacklist was a time of evil, and . . . no one on either side who
> survived it came through untouched by evil. Caught in a situa-
> tion that had passed beyond the control of mere individuals,

each person reacted as his nature, his needs, his convictions, and his particular circumstances compelled him to. There was bad faith and good, honesty and dishonesty, courage and cowardice, selflessness and opportunism, wisdom and stupidity, good and bad on both sides. When you who are in your forties or younger look back with curiosity on that dark time, as I think occasionally you should, it will do no good to search for villains or heroes or saints or devils because there were none; there were only victims. Some suffered less than others, some grew and some diminished, but in the final tally we were all victims because almost without exception each of us felt compelled to say things he did not want to say, to do things that he did not want to do, to deliver and receive wounds he truly did not want to exchange. That is why none of us—right, left, or center—emerged from that long nightmare without sin.[4]

Casty begins his second chapter with statistics revealing the viciousness of the Stalinist regime and a series of quotations that state the case against those who did not bear witness to those crimes and challenge the criminals: "At the center of this sad and wide web of damage and loss were the party members who did not testify and people who were as close to the party and its shifting lines as the actual members." The flaw in this accusation is that the failure of the First and Fifth Amendment witnesses to bear witness had no impact whatsoever on the commission of any crime or the hiding of it. Nothing that these 150–plus men or women might have said would have changed the course of events in the Soviet Union or the Soviet bloc. Their repentant voices would have been a tiny section of the booming anti-Communist chorus of the postwar United States, which included, by the way, hundreds of former Communists. By the time the uncooperative witnesses testified, the crimes of the Stalinist regime were available to anyone who cared to know about them. Dozens of ex-Communists had written articles and books on the subject. That is, there was no direct consequential impact of their "silence," whereas there was a direct consequential impact of the informers' testimonies: prior to Larry Parks's appearance, there were ten people on the motion picture blacklist; in the two years following, another two hundred–plus names were added, all named by informers. (One, Martin Berkeley, named 155.) But Casty is after bigger fish: he wants to make the unfriendly witnesses "morally complicit in the ultimate, even if far-removed, consequences of what they defended and supported." That raises the question as to who is to be the judge of "moral complicity" and "ultimate" consequences. Certainly it cannot be the people Casty cites, anti-Communists all. It also raises the question of proximity—how close in time must a consequence be to make one morally complicit?

Casty also indicts the "silent" witnesses for having increased the clouds of Cold War suspicion and conspiracy theorizing, lessened the possibility of a united response to it, and created an atmosphere of confusion about the meaning of defense of civil liberties. There are several problems with these accusations. It was the congressional investigating committees that were mainly responsible for conspiracy theorizing in the United States. The possibility of a united response to the Committee had ended, not with what was said or not said at the hearings, but in the wake of the Communist Party's defense of the Soviet Union and criticism of the United States after 1945. Granted, there was an "atmosphere of confusion" sowed by the Ten's testimony, but it was about method, not substance. Yes, their secrecy and silence were harmful, but, as Trumbo pointed out in an unpublished manuscript of 1957, it harmed only them. (It is important to remember that the Ten's stand postponed the full brunt of the motion picture blacklist for four years.) Unlike Casty, Trumbo does not draw moral lessons from the policy of secrecy. Rather he condemns it on pragmatic political grounds. First, it made the Party appear to be "a conspiracy" and caused "secret" Communists to be driven from the labor movement. Second, it allowed numerous Hollywood people to join the Party without weighing their careers in the balance. "Their moment of choice was delayed until the illusion of secrecy collapsed— and by then the quality of choice was radically changed for the worse. Instead of voluntary choice between party and career, they now faced compulsory choice between informing and the blacklist. . . . That they were not given an opportunity to face the first and the real choice is a tragedy"; it robbed them of dignity and forced them to submit to a process "which separated them into informers, on the one hand, and professional and social exiles on the other. In a certain sense even the informers can be counted among the victims of a policy which gave them no realistic moment of choice." Trumbo did, however, value secrecy of another type: if one decided to leave the Party, one should do so quietly. First, to make a public announcement would undercut the main element of the Ten's fight against the House Committee: we will not allow it to force us to announce our political affiliations. Second, it would add to the tribulations and violate the secrecy of those who had chosen to remain in the Party.[5] Trumbo, unlike Casty, but like most of the informers, knew that those who remained represented no threat to national security; their exposure would not strengthen national security.

Casty then restates a perdurable anti-Communist mantra: the defense of Soviet Russia by the Communists laid the groundwork for the House Committee and Joseph McCarthy. Putting aside the counterfactual emptiness of that charge (the political value of anti-Communism laid the groundwork for the Committee and McCarthy), it simply ignores the rights of free speech guaranteed to citizens of the United States by the First Amendment. Further, it was not the Ten's silence that did them in; it was the behavior of several of them on the stand.

Casty leaves his moral high ground in chapters 3–5, in which he examines "The Birth of the Hollywood Party," "The Hollywood Party in Peace and War," and the strikes and interguild conflicts of the postwar period. Not a positive word about Communist activity can be found in these chapters. In chapter 6, Casty examines Rossen's life and work, and in chapter 7, he relates Rossen's battle with Communist screenwriter Abraham Polonsky and Communist producer Bob Roberts during the making of *Body and Soul* (Enterprise Productions, 1947). It is a diatribe against the efforts of those film historians like Paul Buhle and Dave Wagner to extol Polonsky and denigrate Rossen, the film's director. Casty argues that Rossen's ideas were far more cinematically sound, and he deprecates Polonsky's political and cinematic career. Casty then takes the reader through the 1947 hearings and the "Secret World of Communism."

In his chapter titled "Testimony and Silence: Jews, Free Speech, and the Degrees of Betrayal," Casty makes a valid point: The Ten, in their testimonies, condemned the House Committee for its anti-Semitism and attacks on freedom of speech while remaining either ignorant of or silent on the far more brutal anti-Semitism and lack of freedoms in the Soviet Union. Two more historical chapters follow, and then Rossen reappears. The "Testing of a Moral Life in Hollywood and in Films" traces Rossen's hegira from 1947 to 1953. Then, following his chapter on the 1951 hearings, in which Parks is barely mentioned, Casty makes his moral case.

In a chapter titled "What Is Behaving Decently? Those Who Testified and Named Names," Casty presents the statements of several of the more famous namers (Rossen, Edward Dmytryk, Elia Kazan, Clifford Odets, and Edward G. Robinson, et alia). In contrast to what he has described as the robotic, hypocritical, self-serving statements of the uncooperative witnesses, these select few are depicted as sincerely wrestling with their conscience and laying bare their honest thoughts and feelings. (He does not acknowledge that the unfriendly witnesses may have done their conscience wrestling in private. Albeit, many of them have said that they knew immediately that they would not cooperate.) In the following chapter, he pinpoints what he calls "the central moral paradox" of his project and reverses, in the process, the conventional wisdom concerning it. Those who refused to cooperate were morally strong (whatever their mix of motives) in attempting to defend their rights, and their beliefs, at the risk of losing their (often lucrative) livelihood. But their moral stance was ambiguously entangled with, and weakened and compromised by, the destructive righteousness of their pro-Soviet crusade that often betrayed truth—and betrayed those who were led to support and emulate them. Their righteous zeal led to denials and evasions of the immensities—and human cost—of the betrayals of their ideals by Communism and the Soviet Union, other Communist nations, and the Communist Party of America (CPUSA), as well as to evasions of any personal complicity, responsibility, or regret. The problem is that they were not complicit or responsible, and most of them, as Casty notes, did eventually express, if not regret, at least chagrin.

Those who named names, however, "whatever the mix of *their* motives," spoke thoughtfully of their principles and beliefs. (The unfriendly witnesses could not do so, for if they had, they would have forfeited their Fifth Amendment protection against naming names and laid themselves open to prosecution.) Their testimonies "were accurate about the state of the world and took place after painful inner debates about having to name names within the circumscribed world of choice that had been created." But, he acknowledges, "their moral stance was ambiguously entangled with righteous crusades of anti-Communism that also betrayed the ideals for which they testified." But he does not mention their ambiguous entanglement with their own economic well-being. It is interesting to note that Casty gives the unfriendly witnesses no credit for having principled beliefs. He seems to think they did not have a conscience to wrestle with. After all, the great majority of them were still Party members.

Casty concludes his book with chapters attempting to puncture two myths perpetrated by left-wing historians: the blacklist denuded films of the 1950s of substantive content; and McCarthyism severely undercut civil liberties and damaged the political culture of the United States. Those myths, he argues, have been used as "a shorthand and symbolic term for the alleged fascistic tendencies" of anti-Communism. As with Navasky's conclusions about the effect of his disfavored witnesses, these conclusions rest on unproved, subjective appraisals.

Missing from these two detailed accounts are two key aspects of witnessing. The authors do not examine the pressures felt by those subpoenaed to appear before a congressional investigating committee. That is, what factors determine their decision to cooperate or not cooperate? First and foremost is money. Hollywood people earned high salaries, much more than they could earn in other occupations (as many of them discovered). Though almost all of the witnesses were the main breadwinners for their families, this factor, for reasons unknown, weighed much more heavily with the informants (see chapter 5). The second, and more pressing factor was their identity as filmmakers. Rossen and Dmytryk, for example, could not imagine doing anything but directing movies. The uncooperative witnesses, for their part, every bit as tied to their crafts, preferred losing their film careers to being identified as informing actors, directors, and writers. Loyalty was a third factor. The informers decided that they owed their loyalty, not to their former comrades in the

Party but to a "higher" entity, their country. (Unlike E. M. Forster, who said, "If I had to choose between betraying my country and betraying my friend, I hope I should have the guts to betray my country.") A key element in this factor was their attitude toward the Communist Party and the Soviet Union. A number of the friendly witnesses, like Isobel Lennart, had been tepid members of the Party, joining as a matter of conscience rather than fidelity to Communism. A few, like Richard Collins, Budd Schulberg, and the Townsends, had been devoted Party members but had become disillusioned with Communism and the Soviet Union. Surely, they all did some sort of weighing of the factors, and clearly each assigned different weights to each. The question is, and Casty cannot answer it, did they then weigh their decision against a clearly articulable moral standard?

Which brings us to the second major lacuna: although the book is replete with the word "moral," Casty, like Navasky, never once defines what constitutes moral behavior or what it means to take a morally ambiguous position. They seem to have a clear idea in their own minds, but it never reaches the printed page. Thus, the reader is left at the end of Navasky's book thinking that it is almost always moral to refuse to inform on one's friends or former comrades. Casty, for his part, concludes that it is moral to condemn Communism and expose the identities of those who were Communists, and it is immoral to have defended the Soviet Union and to have refused, under oath and compulsion, to reveal their membership in a Soviet-dominated party and refuse to expose others who once belonged.

A number of philosophers have developed or argued for a large variety of moral systems. Neither Navasky nor Casty has taken the trouble to examine them and decide which best fits this era. Nevertheless, the systems they unwittingly use are identifiable: deontology (from the Greek word for duty) and consequentialism, respectively. According to deontologists, there is a categorical imperative at work in morality: you do nothing that you would not will others to do. It is a strict morality. A consequentialist holds that the consequences of one's conduct are the ultimate basis for any judgment about the rightness or wrongness of that conduct. Thus, from a consequentialist standpoint, a morally right act is one that will produce a good outcome.

Navasky is a quasi-deontologist. He fervently believes that no one should inform on any other person, except in certain circumstances (such as those faced by the members of the Nixon administration who related its criminal deeds; and whistleblowers who have witnessed violations of the public interest). A strict deontologist would not make exceptions. Deontology, however, provides no formula for balancing competing absolute values, such as informing is immoral and failure to protect the public interest is immoral. A deontologist is either too rigid to be useful or, as in Navasky's qualified case, unable to draw a clear line between acceptable and unacceptable informing.

Casty is a consequentialist. But he faces the dilemma of all consequentialists: to wit, how does one objectively define a good outcome? In Casty's subjective view, the friendly witnesses performed a good act in exposing a threat to national security; the unfriendly witnesses performed a bad act by covering up a vast criminal conspiracy. But he does not, perhaps because he cannot, demonstrate that a few hundred unexposed Communists threatened the national security of the United States or that a vast criminal conspiracy was covered up by the silence of a few hundred Communists. Further, a consequentialist is concerned only with outcomes; intent is not a factor. But if one is assessing good moral behavior, good intent is required.

The moral of the story of these two books about morality is that blanket judgments are useless to understand the complexity of a time that forced people to make decisions for which they had no training. One must evaluate each individual case to determine whether the individual did the necessary weighing of the values of human existence, tested, that is, their possible choices against a clear moral standard. Perhaps the best test is the one delineated by Aristotle, for whom moral virtue is a relative mean between extremes of excess and deficiency. Choice should be controlled by reason and the moral principles acquired by a combination of knowledge, habituation, and self-discipline. To act virtuously is to act consciously with a moral purpose in a social environment.

All the witnesses, even under the political, economic, and social forces pressing down on them, were free to choose, and, presumably, they partially grounded their choice in some nonpersonal set of moral values. But those sets differed between the unfriendly and friendly classes and among them. Examining the behavior of the witnesses, collectively, does not provide the historian with a coherent set of moral standards to guide future behavior.

But, when all is said and done, two crucial distinctions stand out. One, though both sets of witnesses wished to avoid being blacklisted, the unfriendly witnesses chose to sacrifice only themselves; the friendly witnesses chose to sacrifice others. One can question the friendly witnesses' strong (even purblind) adherence to an ideology and cause that did significant harm, but, and this is what makes them interesting cases, that adherence did not lead them to act harmfully. Outside of their Party allegiance, they supported positive social goals (civil rights, prominent among them). Two, the vast majority of the unfriendly witnesses and their families to whom I have talked or about whom I have read are certain that they did the right thing, and they would do so again should the situation arise; many of the friendly witnesses, however, are ambivalent and rueful.

4

Dashiell Hammett

The White-Haired Communist Ghost of Hollywood

Samuel Dashiell Hammett was unique among Hollywood Communists, proof positive that there is no one-size-fits-all profile of a Communist. He was likely the least educated, having left school at fourteen. He also had the least likely background—he worked five years (1915–1918 and 1920–1922) for the Pinkerton National Detective Agency, an organization notorious for its brutal union-busting methods, though there is no credible evidence that Hammett's work involved unions. He was also, arguably, the least healthy (suffering chronic tuberculosis and gonorrhea) and one of the most alcoholic (quite a feat among a very heavy-drinking crowd of male Communists in Hollywood). The combination of ill health, drinking, and smoking brought him close to death on several occasions. He was also the most guarded, reticent, and private of his generation of writers. His daughter wrote: "When Papa was sober, he kept to himself. He was in control, impenetrable, private." Drinking turned him "maudlin or sarcastic-mean. Not violent; he was never that. . . . But drunk he had a kind of lashing-out desperation about him that scared me to death."[1] He seemed half-ashamed of his fame as a writer and avoided the limelight as much as possible.

Hammett was born on a southern Maryland tobacco farm on May 27, 1894, the middle of three children, and was baptized and raised Catholic. (He later became a sharp critic of the church, which he considered "a political troublemaker and exploiter of the poor.")[2] Both his parents' families had been in North America since the seventeenth century: His paternal family came from England; his maternal family came from

France. His father was a drinker, a womanizer, a sharp dresser, and neer-do-well. His mother was a frail and sickly woman with a persistent cough. We know little more about his childhood. The forces that shaped and influenced him and the manner in which they did so are a matter of conjecture. The sources of his particular demons and contradictions are guesswork. We do not know how he was raised, how he was nurtured, how or what he was taught, or how he learned to deal with people. We do know that he emerged from his childhood a mass of contradictions. His younger brother, Richard, recalled that Dashiell was not a particularly remarkable child except for being quite stubborn at times.[3]

Hammett later said: "After a fraction of a year in high school [at age fourteen]—Baltimore Polytechnic Institute—I became the unsatisfactory and unsatisfied employee of various railroads, stock brokers, machine manufacturers, canners, and the like. Usually I was fired."[4] He began drinking heavily, and, at twenty-one, became an operative for Pinkerton's National Detective Agency. He worked mainly on financial fraud, swindles, robberies, etc. (Those writers who say otherwise are relying on Lillian Hellman's *Scoundrel Time*, which is now regarded as notoriously unreliable.) In 1917, when he contracted gonorrhea, his lifelong bout with chronic illnesses began. He took leave from the agency in 1918 to enlist in the US Army, where he was assigned to the Motor Ambulance Corps, at Fort Meade, Maryland. We do not know why he decided to enlist or why he waited until 1918, a year after the United States entered the war (April 2, 1917). (His delay may be attributed to the time it took to cure his venereal disease.) In any event, once enlisted, he contracted Spanish flu and tuberculosis and did not serve overseas. He was discharged from the army in May and resumed his work with Pinkerton's. He was sent to Spokane, Washington, where, in autumn 1920, he collapsed. He spent the next six months in public health hospitals in Tacoma, Washington, and San Diego, California. At the former, he met and fell in love with his nurse, Josephine Dolan. (She had trained and worked in Butte, Montana, and perhaps her account of the city influenced Hammett's rendition of Poisonville in *Red Harvest*.)

One wonders if Hammett, while lying in his hospital beds, had the same type of remorse about enlisting as did Joe Bonham in Dalton

Trumbo's *Johnny Got His Gun*. Of course, Hammett had not been in battle nor had he suffered the horrific maiming Joe did, but he had witnessed the postwar Red Scare and the failure of the peace conference to make the world safe for democracy and provide self-determination for the world's nationalities. It is possible that Hammett, like many wounded or sickened veterans, may have harbored the same types of thought as Joe: "No sir anybody who went out and got into the front line trenches to fight for liberty was a goddam fool and the guy who got him there was a liar."[5] Hammett's great fictional character, the Continental Op, who is, in some ways, modeled on Hammett, was also a war veteran,[6] and he, like Hammett, became disillusioned and cynical. They did not, however, go as far as Joe, who thinks at the end of the book: "we won't fight we won't be dead we will live we are the world we are the future and we will not let you butcher us no matter what you say no matter what speeches you make no matter what slogans you write."[7]

After his discharge, he moved to San Francisco and married Josephine. He returned to the Pinkerton agency, but another collapse forced him to quit the detective business. He attended a business college with an eye to becoming a newspaper reporter. The couple had two daughters (Mary, b. 1921; Josephine, b. 1926), but Hammett stopped living with them in 1926, after another health collapse. He was diagnosed with hepatitis, on top of his chronic tuberculosis, and a health worker advised the couple to live apart. They never reestablished cohabitation, but he helped support them and remained in regular contact via letters.

Money was always tight in those years, and he was constantly in debt. To support his family, he began to write, and he became very conscientious about the quality of his writing. He submitted articles to a number of publications: *Forum, Bookman, Saturday Review of Literature,* and *Sunset,* among others. In fact, about half of his output was noncrime.[8] Aside from his stories for magazines, he wrote advertising copy for a jeweler and reviewed mysteries for the *Saturday Review of Literature.* He slipped easily into a writing career, writing well from the beginning, and he did not seem to have experienced writer's block. He lacked a literary mentor, but he had read voraciously. Even his earliest letters display his facility with language and wit. He fully embraced the detective story form, hoping to make literature out of it, but he later said that it took him "some time getting the hang of the detective story."[9] He criticized other detective story writers for failing to do the obvious: "make some effort at least to learn something about [their] subject."[10] When one of his detective stories was rejected, he wrote to the editor: "The trouble is that this sleuth of mine has degenerated into a meal-ticket. I liked him at first, and used to enjoy putting him through his tricks; but recently I've fallen into the habit of bringing him out and running him around whenever the landlord, or the butcher, or the grocer shows signs of nervousness. There are men who can write like that, but I am not one of them."[11]

Literature, Hammett once stated, "is good to the extent that it is art, and bad to the extent that it isn't; and I know of no other standard by which it may be judged. . . . If you think that you have a story that seems worth telling, and you think you can tell it worthily, the thing for you to do is tell it." He quoted approvingly another writer who said, "Art knows no morals."[12]

His first published articles, sketches for *Smart Set,* appeared in print in 1922, and, in March 1923, the magazine published his "From the Memoirs of a Private Detective." It consisted of twenty-nine short squibs derived from his experience. On June 15, 1923, *Black Mask* published Hammett's first detective story, and four months later the first featuring the Continental Op. Between October 1922 and mid-1927, he published fifty-eight pieces (thirty-four of which featured the Continental Op). The Op was modeled on employees of the Pinkerton agency. Hammett told an interviewer in 1929:

I've worked with half a dozen men who might be he with few changes. Though he may be "different" in fiction, he is almost a "pure" type in life. I've always tried to hold him as close to the "type" as possible because I see him as a little man going forward day after day through mud and blood and deceit—as callous and brutal and cynical as is necessary—towards a dim goal, with nothing to push or pull him toward it except that he'd been hired to reach it—sort of a manual whose saying is: "The job's got to be done."[13]

According to Richard Layman and Julie M. Rivett (his granddaughter), Hammett absorbed a detective code of honor, which he imparted to the Continental Op: "According to this code, detectives maintain anonymity and resist publicity, sequestering themselves within a veil of secrecy." They are objective, dispassionate, and "steer by their own moral constellation."[14] That "moral constellation" was flexible, however, allowing use of what might be considered by many to be immoral actions to reach a "just" result. Of course, justice was always according to the Op's perspective. The Op is a significant literary creation, the first self-conscious detective. "Before Hammett," Dennis Dooley noted, "the emphasis—for all the eccentricities of character indulged for the amusement of the reader—was on the solving of the crime. With Hammett, the detective himself—his aches and pains, his motives, values, feelings, and needs, his fears of growing old—has become the real subject."[15] Hammett's Op, in Sally Cline's apt description, "lives a bleak existence in an indifferent universe. . . . Though the Op's job requires him to proceed in a methodical manner, he knows there is no order."[16]

The Op, a man with stern but flexible values, is depicted as the last bastion against the collapse of all civilized values. But he has no social vision. He is a not very introspective loner, for whom getting the job done is the sole concern. His world-weary cynicism is epitomized in Hammett's greatest creation, Sam Spade (*The Maltese Falcon*). It is of interest to note that the protagonists of his last two novels (*The Glass Key* and *The Thin Man*) are not dedicated, professional detectives. Rather they are reluctant participants in the murders to be solved. It is as though Hammett had concluded that the flood tide of corruption could not be stanched, or that he had taken his professional detective as far as he could. Perhaps because he is his own boss, not answerable to an agency supervisor, Spade is much crueler than the Op, and, by the novel's end, even his faithful, loving secretary looks at him with disgust. (According to several of Hammett's biographers, Hammett also possessed a cruel streak; like his detectives, he browbeat and physically hit or beat some of the women in his life.) Spade plays faster and looser with the rules and regulations than the Op did, but he does maintain a code of sorts: when a man's partner is killed, one is supposed to do something about it; when someone in a detective agency gets killed, it is bad business to let the killer get away; detectives do not capture criminals and then let them go. But even more important than the code is the personal commandment: Spade will not play the sap or sucker (he uses those terms five times in the final six pages), and, if he is going to bend the rules to save someone from prison, he must trust the person (he uses "trust" three times in the final six pages). "Spade," Hammett wrote, "is a dream man in the sense that he is what most of the private detectives I have worked with would like to have been." He is not an erudite solver of riddles, but "a hard and shifty fellow, able to take care of himself in any situation, able to get the best of anybody he comes in contact with, whether criminal, innocent by-stander or client."[17]

There is not much to be learned about Hammett from the Op stories and novels. There was no physical resemblance between the two. Hammett was tall (six feet, one and one-half inches) and thin (135 pounds): "I am long and lean and gray-headed," he said about himself.[18] The Op weighed 180–90 pounds and stood five feet, six inches tall. He was referred to in one story as a "little fat guy" and in another referred to himself as "thick through the waist." He said of himself, "Some of my hundred and ninety pounds were fat, but not all of them." The Op was about forty years old—in one story he referred to himself as "middle-aged"—and, in a 1924 story, he said he had been with the agency fifteen years.[19] He was very good with his fists, very tough and resilient, and not shy about using his gun. The Op did not believe in fighting fairly: "I'm not a kid fighting for the fun of it any more. If I've got to fight I want to win and I want to get it over quick."[20] He was not, as Hammett was, a drunk (though he occasionally tied one on), an extravagant spender, or a womanizer. Only in *Red Harvest* does the Op show strong interest in a woman. (Spade is strongly attracted to Brigid O'Shaughnessy.) He was, like Hammett, an army veteran.

We also learn very little about Hammett, as a person, though it is likely that the Op might have represented some of Hammett's aspirations. "My father," Jo Hammett remembered, "admired tough men and tough women. . . . Papa liked tough sports. Boxing was a favorite." And he "admired people who went too far, who did the crazily audacious."[21]

In one story, he writes: "I don't like eloquence: it isn't effective enough to pierce your hide, it's tiresome; and if it is effective enough, it muddles your thoughts."[22] The Op is also very pragmatic and flexible. Detecting, he states, "is a hard business, and you use whatever tools come to hand,"[23] and "sometimes just stirring things up is all right—if you're tough enough to survive, and keep your eyes open so you'll see what you want when it comes to the top."[24] He understands the need for the agency "to have its rules and regulations, but when you're out on a job you do it the best way you can."[25] In this story, he cold-bloodedly sets up the chief of police to be killed: "I looked at Noonan and knew he couldn't live another day because of what I was doing to him, and I laughed and felt warm and happy inside."[26] And yet, in one of his unpublished stories, he upheld rule-based conduct: "These men who refuse to—or for one reason or another are unable to—conduct themselves in accordance with the accepted rules—no matter how strong their justification may be, or how foolish the rules—have to be put outside."[27] He believed detectives should not take bribes and that they should wear "honestly won laurels easily, neither over-valuing nor under-valuing them."[28] He valued wisdom; one of his characters defined it as "a mystic science of knowledge behind and beyond known knowledge."[29]

Every so often, Hammett puts a quasi-philosophical statement in the mouth of the Op. In *The Dain Curse,* his second novel, the Op muses about people's belief systems:

Nobody thinks clearly; no matter what they pretend. People either don't think at all or they go about it exactly as you do. Thinking's a dizzy business—a matter of catching as many of those foggy glimpses as you can and fitting them together the best you can. That's why people hang on so tight to their beliefs and opinions; because, compared to the haphazard way in which they arrived at even the goofiest opinion seems wonderfully clear, sane, and self-evident. And if you let it get away from you, then you have to dive back into that foggy muddle to wangle yourself out another to take its place.[30]

Though Hammett did not, at this time, subscribe to any political or social ideologies, it might not be too big a stretch to see in these words the basis for his later, enduring commitment to the Communist Party.

There is little in the way of political or social commentary in Hammett's detective stories. No coherent political or ideological viewpoint is evident. Instead, corruption, the seedy side of institutions and people, lies at the heart of all the novels and most of the stories. Joan Mellen notes that even though Hammett did not entirely invent the hard-boiled detective genre, "no writer before him had offered so intense and unrelenting a vision of the corruption of America's social institutions." Though she has discerned "a profound political vision" permeating his fiction,[31] I see only a man dedicated to solving the particular problem with which he is confronted. The world is not necessarily a better place after the Op has solved a case. Only the corrupters have changed.

Following a dispute over salary with the editor of *Black Mask,* Hammett quit in 1926 and became an advertising copywriter. He returned to the magazine when a new editor was hired, and he began to write longer, more bloody tales. At the end of 1927, he wrote a four-part story he titled "The Cleansing of Poisonville." He sent it, unsolicited, to Alfred Knopf, whose wife, Blanche, accepted it. He agreed to make whatever changes she suggested, including changing the title to *Red Harvest.* Four other novels followed: *The Dain Curse, The Maltese Falcon, The Glass Key,* and *The Thin Man.* (His last Op story was published in November 1930.) All the novels were well received, and Hammett acquired a reputation as the best of the new school of "hard-boiled" mystery writers. He was contacted by Fox Film Corporation—"I have a request from William Fox Studio for material"—and he traveled to Hollywood in April 1928, but he did not secure a deal.[32] He also contemplated turning *The Maltese Falcon* into a play. Paramount did buy the rights to *Red Harvest,* but Hammett did not like the result, *Roadhouse Nights* (1930).

Hammett was by no means a movie buff. He does not appear to have gone to see many movies, and he does not say much about movies in his letters. In 1927, he said he was bored by *Don Juan,* starring John Barrymore, the first feature-length film to utilize the Vitaphone sound-on-disc sound system with a synchronized musical score and sound effects: "And now I am off movies for another couple of years. It was lousy—bad taste, bad acting and stupid ignorance can't go any further than last night's show carried them."[33] Nor did he like the movie colony. His work habits were lax, and he came to hate everything about the studios. His story "On the Way," written in 1932, is about a man who realizes and accepts the impermanence of Hollywood relationships.[34] And "This Little Pig" (1934) is sharply satirical about Hollywood. The protagonist is a cynical writer who cannot seem to complete a stage play but readily accepts all manner of movie script rewrites. On the set of one of his rewrites, he decides to play god: "I'm fixing things for everybody" by "simply doing what everybody wants. It's a beautiful plan." "Sure, I'm being malicious, but I've got to have some fun." He shows no remorse of the harmful effects of his scheming.[35] Hammett drifted in and out of Hollywood. He was there for most of 1934 and 1935, but following a massive mental and physical breakdown in January 1936, he returned to New York. He went back to Hollywood in the summer of 1937, spent a good part of 1938 there, and left after suffering another collapse. He returned briefly in 1940 to fulfill an assignment but abruptly left and never returned.

By the autumn of 1929, dead broke and dunning Knopf for advances and loans, he moved to New York City. One year later, David O. Selznick wrote to Paramount studio head B. P. Schulberg: "I believe that he [Hammett] is another [S. S.] Van Dine—indeed that he possesses more originality than Van Dine, and might very well prove to be the creator of something new and startlingly original for us." Selznick offered him a contract, but Hammett did not want to be tied to Hollywood, so he agreed to a three-hundred-dollar-per-week salary to write original stories for the studio.[36] One of them, "After School," became the basis for *City Streets* (1931). The following year, he sold *The Maltese Falcon* to Warner Bros. (who released it in 1931; and remade it in 1936 and 1941), and he went to work there on an original story, which was not made into a script. The 1934 RKO movie *Woman in the Dark* was based on one of his short stories, and *The Thin Man* series (M-G-M) were adaptations of and sequels (five in all) to his novel of the same name, for which he wrote some of the screen stories but none of the scripts. *Mister Dynamite*

(Universal, 1935) was another adaptation of one of his short stories, and two years later, Universal adapted his comic strip *Secret Agent X-9*, cowritten with Alex Raymond, into a film serial. He received a "based on the novel by" credit for *The Glass Key* (Paramount, 1942). His only screenplay credit was for adapting Hellman's play *Watch on the Rhine* (Warner Bros., 1943), albeit Hellman was credited for additional scenes and dialogue. In all, he worked for four or five studios. He earned a great deal of money, mainly from sales of his previous work, and he spent it all very quickly.

At a Hollywood party at the end of 1930, he met Lillian Hellman, with whom he would be romantically connected for many years (though fidelity was rare and reciprocal pain regular) and with whom he lived for many others. She would take care of him in his dying days. With his extensive assistance, Hellman emerged as a major playwright. She credited him with teaching her how to write. He provided plot ideas for some of her plays, tutored her in delineating her characters, and read and commented on every draft. When she would doubt herself, he always provided support. "He was," she wrote, "generous with anybody who asked for help. He felt that you didn't lie about writing and anybody who couldn't take hard words was about to be shrugged off, anyway. He was a dedicated man about writing. Tough and generous."[37] He worked closely with her on her first big success, *The Children's Hour*. According to Layman and Rivett, "Within a year of meeting Hellman, Hammett all but quit writing fiction for publication. . . . He concentrated instead on screenwriting and mentoring others, often young women."[38] He later said: "I stopped writing because I found I was repeating myself. It is the beginning of the end when you discover you have a style."[39]

Flush with cash and contemptuous of the movie people he met, Hammett began to spend lavishly and drink even more heavily. As he was completing *The Thin Man*, he wrote Knopf, in April 1931, "This will be my last detective novel: we'll try our luck with another genre."[40] He told Hellman the same thing. In August 1931, he became so depressed and suicidal that he had to be hospitalized in New York. He suffered bouts of recurring venereal disease and alcoholic collapses thereafter. At one point, he was charged with and found guilty of sexual assault against one of his lovers. In 1934, the last of his published short stories appeared. It is unlikely, as Diane Johnson speculated, that Hammett did so because he had a problem with authority figures, saw them as "evil and menacing," and perhaps stopped writing "as an unconscious means of defying the fatherly editors who so enthusiastically fostered and championed him."[41]

Though the Great Depression was in full flower, Hammett did not comment on it in his books or letters. Nor had he mentioned workers or unions much in his stories. One of his characters sings an Industrial Workers of the World (IWW) song, "The Preacher and the Slave,"[42] and the narrator of "Nelson Redline" had worked for a "worker's paper that had killed itself by a shortsighted policy of specialization upon the case of the unemployed who couldn't give it the material support it needed."[43] In *Red Harvest,* an organizer for the IWW, Bill Quint, plays a small role, but he is not depicted in a positive way. And yet, seemingly out of nowhere, Hammett became a very effective union organizer. He worked on behalf of the newly organized Screen Writers Guild (SWG), and, in late 1934, when the screen readers were trying to organize a guild, he spoke at a fundraising dinner for them. He participated in the massive enrollment drive launched by the SWG in 1936, and when the SWG petitioned the newly created National Labor Relations Board for a certification election, Hammett was selected as one of the representatives to meet with Nathan Witt, the board's executive secretary. Witt later said that Hammett was the most politically astute of the Guild's representatives.[44] After the SWG overwhelmingly defeated the company-backed Screen Playwrights, Hammett was elected to the Guild's executive board.

His major political work started in early 1935, when the Communist Party issued a call for an American Writers' Congress, to meet in New York City on May 1, and the delegates, in turn, created the League of American Writers. The call invited "all writers who have achieved some standing in their respective fields; who have clearly indicated their sympathy to the revolutionary cause; who do not need to be convinced of the decay of capitalism, of the inevitability of revolution." Hammett did not sign the call, but he did become a founding member of the League. It affiliated with the International Union of Revolutionary Writers; engaged writers in the fight against imperialist war and fascism and defended the Soviet Union against capitalist aggression; worked to develop and strengthen the revolutionary labor movement; fought against all forms of discrimination against or persecution of Blacks and against the persecution of minority groups and of the foreign-born; declared solidarity with colonial people in their struggles for freedom; exposed the influence of bourgeois ideas in American liberalism; and protested the imprisonment of revolutionary writers and artists, as well as other class-war prisoners throughout the world.[45] More than eight hundred writers joined the League. Communist writers dominated the executive positions, and the League closely followed the Party line.

The League also advocated support for the Loyalist cause in Spain, and, under the guidance of Donald Ogden Stewart, produced a pamphlet, *Writers Take Sides: Letters about the War in Spain from 418 American Writers* (1938). Hammett wrote a short paragraph for the pamphlet: "It is very difficult for me to believe that anybody can still have any honest doubts about Franco and fascism, either separately or as a team. However, I am against Franco and fascism; I am for the legal government and the people of Republican Spain."[46] The League also provided funds for the Medical Bureau of the American Friends of Spanish Democracy, the North American Committee to Aid Spanish Democracy, and the Spanish Societies Confederated to Aid Spain. Hammett, for his part, tried to enlist in the Abraham Lincoln Battalion (a component of the Soviet-created International Brigades), to fight on the side of the Republic, and he closely followed the course of the civil war, writing several detailed accounts of it to his daughter Mary. In one, he noted that the Republican government there was not Communist and that the Spanish Communist Party (Partido Communista de España) was not much stronger than the American one. He expected the war to continue for "a long, long time." And he prescribed for her a political rule: "be in favor of what's good for the workers and against what isn't."[47] He hoped, he wrote a few weeks later, "you are taking some interest in the war in Spain. It is tremendously important, since if the rebels win it will be a great setback for the cause of working people everywhere."[48] Hammett also supported the Motion Picture Artists Committee to aid the Spanish Loyalists and the Chinese resistance to Japan. When the Loyalists were defeated, he worked for the Joint Anti-Fascist Refugee Committee (1939) to supply aid to Loyalist refugees interned in French relocation camps and those who had immigrated to South America. And he helped raise funds for the returning members of the Abraham Lincoln Battalion.

He kept a close eye on Germany, but his analysis was not very perceptive. He stated that Hitler was not as strong a man as other Nazi leaders and German generals "and has only stayed in power this long because he has played along with them." He predicted a split between Hitler and Joseph Goebbels, on the one hand, and Hermann Göring and the generals, on the other, but he did not think that the German Communist Party (Kommunistische Partei Deutschlands) would be able to take advantage of it.[49]

It is not clear when he joined the Communist Party of the United States. Martin Berkeley, in his 1951 testimony to the House Committee on Un-American Activities, claimed that Hammett and Hellman were present at the June 1937 meeting that founded the Hollywood branch of the Communist Party. But it is likely that they had joined either in 1935 or 1936, and they had been placed in a special category, freeing them from the usual Party duties and meetings. (They were not named by any other informer.)

The major question that looms above all others is, why would a loner, a flaneur, a louche individual, a man who rejected authority and dogma, join, and remain a member of, such a highly disciplined and doctrinaire organization? It would be too facile to say, as some biographers do, that he was compensating for his disappointment in himself, for his writer's block, for a life without purpose. Joan Mellen, who criticizes him for virtually every aspect of his being, concedes that "he was infused with compassion, and became a man with too much integrity not to aspire to justice for other people."[50] Hammett himself told a New York State legislative investigation committee in February 1955: "Communism is to me not a dirty word. When you are working for the advancement of mankind it never occurs to you whether a guy is a Communist."[51] Which answer simply sharpens the question, when and why did he decide he should take a role in the advancement of mankind? The best answer is probably the simplest: he was a radical patriot; a man who enlisted in two wars; someone who likely would have subscribed to Paul Jarrico's apothegm: "Not my country right or wrong, but my country right the wrong." Hammett was well-informed; he had been writing and thinking about corruption and unfairness and justice for a long time; and world and domestic affairs in 1933–1934 were ominous. In those years, if someone who believed in progressive change and feared the spread of fascism wanted to be active and effective politically, the Communist Party was a good choice. In addition, as Julie M. Rivett suggests, he had the financial means to devote himself to political activity.[52] He stayed a Party activist for as long as he did because he derived satisfaction from Communist-backed political activity. He probably never formally quit the Communist Party, but his political life ended ten years before his death, due to imprisonment and illness.

Whatever the catalyst, he demonstrated great skill at organizing, administering, fundraising, and speaking on behalf of the many organizations with which he would become affiliated. Though he signed virtually every Party-line letter, petition, and call, he never became a doctrinaire, ideologue, or apparatchik, nor did he socialize with other Communists. Like most of the Hollywood Communists, Hammett did not espouse a revolutionary line. He worked, rather, for political and social reform within the system. He told his daughter Mary that the Communist Party, "so far as I know, does not now and never has advocated the overthrow of the United States government by force or violence. Their stand on overthrowing governments is pretty much the same as Lincoln's—that you only use force and violence when *most* of the people want a change and the *few* in power won't give it to them peacefully."[53]

He cannot be labeled a "Stalinist." Though he was loyal to the Party line when it came to supporting the Soviet Union, he did not advertise himself as a believer in Stalin as leader or exemplar, nor did he look closely at what was happening in the Soviet Union. He did not declare it a workers' paradise, and he did not evince any desire to travel there. Lillian Hellman called him "a critical Marxist" who was often "contemptuous of the Soviet Union" and "bitingly sharp" about the CPUSA.[54] Charles Glenn, a columnist for the Party's West Coast newspaper, *People's Daily*

World, recalled that Hammett had read "the Marxist stuff . . ., and when you could get him sober, he sort of knew what he was talking about theoretically."[55]

In one of his letters to his daughter Mary, he addressed two arguments used by anti-Communists against Communism and Socialism. Their first argument, that Communism does not take into account human nature, is a joke, he wrote: "The most optimistic thing communists and socialists do is taking 'into account human nature.' Jesus, they dote on it! Their argument against capitalism is that it doesn't 'take into account human nature.'" Under capitalism, "man has been turned into a machine for making money for somebody else." To the second argument, that a leveling of incomes will not provide incentives for people to work, he countered with three points: (1) there is not necessarily a leveling of income in the Soviet Union; (2) in a country where there are so many unemployed, as in the United States, any kind of income that constituted a living wage would be an incentive; and (3) the worst incentive is the knowledge that the more you produce, the more the market is flooded, and the sooner you will be laid off.[56]

Hammett's list of political activism is a long one. In the main, his support for most of these groups was financial, and the loan of his name. He participated in money-raising activities on behalf of the Scottsboro Boys, nine Black southern males falsely accused of raping two white women. He did not, however, support the 1936 reelection campaign of Franklin D. Roosevelt, telling his daughter Mary: "There's no truth in the statement that the Communists are supporting Roosevelt. . . . They've been against Roosevelt from the beginning and, though, they'd rather have him elected than [Alf] Landon [the Republican candidate], it's only because they think he'd do less harm." They are working hard, instead, to gather votes for their own candidate, Earl Browder: "The idea is that if the Communists and Socialists and Farmer-Labor interests make a pretty good showing this time, the Democrats will try to win their support by doing something for the workers between now and the next election."[57]

In Hollywood, he supported the United Studio Technicians Guild effort to dethrone the mob bosses of the International Alliance of

Theatrical Stage Employees and to introduce democratic unionism and local autonomy to studio unions. In 1937, he cofounded Contemporary Historians to support a documentary on the Spanish Civil War, to be written by Ernest Hemingway and directed by Joris Ivens. *The Spanish Earth* was completed in October and, with a narration by Orson Welles and music by Marc Blitzstein, was shown in many places to raise money and consciousness. In 1938, he became president of the Motion Picture Democratic Committee, an organization dedicated to electing progressives to political office, starting with the successful gubernatorial campaign of Culbert Olson. Hammett commented that Olson was "just about as 'red' as Roosevelt, which in my book is hardly red at all."[58] When it appeared that Congress was on the verge of enacting an anti-Communist law (the Alien Registration Act), he worked with the League of American Writers' National Federation for Civil Liberties (October 1939) to establish a Civil Liberties Committee to defeat the act.

Surprisingly, given the strong statements about being nobody's patsy he put in the mouth of Sam Spade, Hammett failed to see anything wrong with the Soviet purge trials. (Of course, it is entirely possible that he did know that the trials were bogus, and that he also knew he would be expelled from the Party if he spoke out.) In any event, in April 1938 he signed a statement in defense of them, calling on liberals "to support the efforts of the Soviet Union to free itself from insidious internal dangers, principal menace to peace and democracy,"[59] which was published in the *Daily Worker*. In the case of the German threat against Czechoslovakia, in the fall of 1938, he wrote: "The present trouble is largely the fault of that group of British capitalists which backs [Prime Minister Neville] Chamberlain. They have been building Hitler's Germany to weaken France."[60] Two weeks later, he continued on that theme, stating that Chamberlain and his backers want to promote a war between the fascist countries and the Soviet Union that may result in the two sides destroying one another or at least inflicting considerable damage to both sides, "leaving England sitting pretty, holding once more the balance of power."[61]

After Kristallnacht, the Nazis' murderous attack on Jews and their synagogues, homes, schools, and businesses in November 1938, his political activity heightened. He served on the editorial boards of two pro-Semitic journals, *Jewish Survey* and *Equality,* a magazine dedicated to fighting racial and ethnic prejudice. He also spoke at a mass meeting in New York City organized by the American Sponsoring Committee against Nazi Outrages. In fact, he told Mary, "Your old man is becoming a talking fool: he spoke four times last week, at an afternoon affair at the Commodore for Spain, at a dinner for the League of Peace and Democracy, at a Mecca Temple anti-Nazi mass meeting, and over the radio for Jewish refugees." He did not enjoy public speaking, "but there is, as usual, so much to be done and so few people to do it."[62] He worked as well for the People's Forum and the National Committee for People's Rights.

Hammett, along with virtually every other Communist, was stunned by the August 1939 signing of the German-Soviet Nonaggression Treaty, which instantly put into question all his antifascist activities. But he and other Communists quickly got their new bearings. Eighteen days after the German invasion of Poland on September 1, and two days after the Soviet invasion of Poland, on September 17, the CPUSA's National Committee announced: "The war that has broken out in Europe is the Second Imperialist War. . . . It is not a war against fascism."[63] When the Soviet Union invaded Finland on November 30, Communists fully supported it. And, when all the New York theaters were asked to offer one night's receipts in a benefit to aid Finland, Hellman and Hammett refused to allow her play *The Little Foxes* to be involved.[64] He was actively involved in the Keep America out of War committees created by the League of American Writers. (He had been elected League president two weeks before the announcement of the Nonaggression Treaty.) The committees produced an *Anti-War Bibliography* (a sixteen-page list of antiwar music, drama, poetry, fiction, memoirs, film, art, periodicals, and pamphlets), linked up with other antiwar groups, organized an "America Declares Peace" rally in Los Angeles, and sponsored numerous speeches and manifestoes. He also joined the American Peace Mobilization, a national Communist front organization, and he solicited well-known authors, such as Theodore Dreiser, to join a committee to sponsor a statement titled "In Defense of the Bill of Rights." Those rights, the committee stated, are presently endangered by "war hysteria" and "witch hunts," in the form of the House Special Committee on Un-American Activities investigations, vigilante activity against labor unions, minority radical and religious groups, and repressive measures against the foreign-born. In particular, "serious efforts are being made to silence and suppress the Communist Party."[65] He helped Robert Ingersoll establish the non-Communist left-wing periodical *PM* and worked on it for the next two years. He supported the cause of German refugees and the League of American Writers' Exiled Writers Committee. And he chaired the Committee on Election Rights—1940, which wrote an open letter to President Roosevelt, urging him to take immediate steps to halt the states' attacks on the voting rights of minorities. He also spoke at a "For Free Elections" rally.[66] Roosevelt did not receive the open backing of the Party in that year's election, but a significant number of Communists likely voted for him.

An interesting conflict of interest occurred at the end of 1939, when Hellman completed her first draft of *Watch on the Rhine,* a play glorifying the struggle against fascism. Party critics faulted aspects of the play, and Hammett did not attend rehearsals, the out-of-town opening, or the postplay party in New York. Yet Hellman lobbied for him to get the job of adapting it for the screen. Warner Bros., however, demanded that Hellman oversee the project and paid her $11,500 to do so. She did a significant amount of rewriting, and she also, when the Production Code Administration (PCA) tried to neuter the anti-Nazi elements of the script, threatened to go public with her objections to this censorship. The PCA backed down.[67]

When the United States entered the war, in December 1941, the Party line again shifted. The League of American Writers became pro-war, and the American Peace Mobilization was renamed the American People's Mobilization. (The League was dissolved in January 1943.) The war, Hammett noted accurately, is "primarily a killing war rather than a geographical one, . . . and victory will come to the side that succeeds in destroying the other side's armies."[68] He worked on the campaign to free Communist Party leader Earl Browder, who had been jailed for passport fraud.

At the age of forty-eight, Hammett, in September 1942, enlisted in the army. His daughter thinks his enlisting was "an act of defiance against age, and decline, and sensible behavior." And he might have thought this was a chance to make up for getting ill and not contributing to the war effort in 1917–1918.[69] Unlike many other Communists who tried to join the war against fascism, and most men his age, he was accepted. He was assigned to the Signal Training Unit at Fort Monmouth, New Jersey. (Ironically, Senator Joseph McCarthy [R-WI] would later make that unit the target of one of his most obsessive investigations, and his committee would subpoena Hammett, though on another matter.) There, he took lessons in cryptography. In July 1943, Hammett was sent to Adak Island in the Aleutians and wound up editing an army newspaper. E. E. Spitzer, another soldier on Adak, recalled: "Having taken him as a volunteer, the Army decided he was a radical and not to be trusted. By the time it decided that, Sam was working in cryptanalysis on the island of Umnak in the Aleutians. What to do with him? The Army transferred him to the island of Adak, attached him to Headquarters Company and gave him nothing to do." He asked the company commander if he could start a newspaper. When he received permission, he set up a city room, in which his usual position was "lying in his sleeping bag on the wooden counter that served as the staff's desks," his head resting on a mimeograph machine, reading a book on materialist philosophy.[70]

The newspaper was a serious effort to inform soldiers on the island about world events.[71] In late summer of 1944, he was assigned to deliver a series of lectures on the importance of the noncombat duties of the soldiers stationed there. He cowrote a pamphlet, *The Battle of the Aleutians*, which was published by "the intelligence section" of Adak.[72] He loved the cold weather. He said, toward the end of his tour, "I have been having the best time I've had in years. I feel tip-hole most of the time."[73] Jo Hammett concurred: "He was as happy there, or at least as contented, as he would ever be again."[74] He, did not, while on Adak, take a drink of alcohol.

He wrote hundreds of letters, mainly to Hellman, but his letters contained little about politics and only occasional comments on the war. Bernard Kalb, who worked on the newspaper, remembered that Hammett rarely spoke about political matters.[75] He read voraciously and requested that Hellman send him clippings from the *Daily Worker* and *New Masses*. He did caution Hellman in May 1944 not to be overwhelmed by burgeoning political events. With the war favoring the Allies, the anti-Communists were beginning to reorganize and launch new attacks on Communist subversion.

> There's no question that a great deal of trouble is looming, but—what the hell!—history railroaded us into an approximately ideal set-up (if you look chiefly at its possibilities and don't pay too much attention to some details) and you have to pay for that sort of thing sooner or later. You can't beat the spiral and there are few shortcuts to the third step [synthesis] in the dialectical process. But so long as there is a spiral and there is the process, then the rest of it's more or less a matter of paying a high price or a little lower one, of having to wait until tomorrow or till the day after.[76]

He became a target of this resurgent Right when the *Chicago Tribune* denounced him and a few other Signal Corps people as Communist propagandists, "inferring that I was up here scouting Alaska for the Soviet Union in case they wanted to take the Aleutians away from us, and there is a little to-do over it in Congress, but I'm not in the guard-house and nobody's taken away my dog tags."[77] A few months later, in July, *Stars and Stripes,* the official daily newspaper of the armed forces of the United States, carried a story that a House Military Subcommittee had made public the names of sixteen army personnel, including Hammett's, alleging that their backgrounds "reflect Communism in some form."[78] Again, there were no repercussions.

In another of its spectacular turnarounds, the Communist Party backed Roosevelt's 1944 reelection campaign, and, when Roosevelt decided to jettison Henry Wallace as the Democrats' vice-presidential nominee, Hammett approved. He told his daughter that Wallace would have "become the focal point of the Democratic anti-FDR forces. I love him as much as you do, but you simply can't make a politician out of him and a politician is what you've got to have in that second-place spot."[79] Shortly before his discharge, he delivered a history lesson, his version of dialectical history, to his daughter Mary.

In all periods of history there has been, among the ignorant, this same silly confidence that their mode of life was the final, fixed, everlasting ideal civilization towards which all earlier modes had been but steps. That *every* stage is only a step to another stage, and that this will always be true as long as man is capable of advancement is, I suppose, a little tough on people's vanity and maybe makes them feel less secure in themselves . . . but that doesn't keep it from being the most obvious and the most unmistakably true lesson that, not only history, but also most of the sciences, have to teach. We've only had three hundred years of this kind of social structure and that's far from being long enough, as time runs in history, to be considered even semi-permanent.

He then mused about how people who considered themselves liberals or revolutionaries when they were young move rightward as they get older. Then, clearly referring to himself, he notes how some people as they get older have moved left: "Their efforts may be a little weaker because of age and often their viewpoints may be dated, but those who were honest and straight when they were young stay honest and straight when old."[80]

Following his discharge in September 1945, Hammett plunged back into political work. He served on the board of the Hollywood Independent Citizens Committee of the Arts, Sciences and Professions, a progressive group dedicated to sustaining Roosevelt's policies and to struggle against the rising wave of conservative and reactionary politics. (It was a merger between the Hollywood Democratic Committee, the successor to the Motion Picture Democratic Committee, and the Independent Citizens Committee of the Arts, Sciences and Professions.) In late September or early October 1946, he attended a meeting of progressives in Chicago. He reported to his daughter Mary that even though the conference did not go "as far to the left as some of us would have liked to see it, it didn't, on the other hand, go as far to the right as some of us were afraid it might. I think we came out of it with a pretty good set-up for trying to goose the Democratic Party back into the footsteps of the late FDR . . . the rest is a matter of a lot of hard work between now and this fall's election and still more work between then and the '48 elections."[81] (Progressives were torn between those wanting to stay with the Democrats and those advocating a third party.) In the spring of 1947, he spoke at a meeting of the American Youth for Democracy and became active in the Progressive Citizens of America (formed in late 1946 by former members of the Independent Citizens Committee of the Arts, Sciences and Professions and the National Citizens Political Action Committee). It was not created or controlled by the Communist Party at the outset, but eventually it was dominated by Communists. He did not, however, for reasons that remain unclear, involve himself in Wallace's campaign for the presidency in 1948. (Hellman worked hard on Wallace's behalf.)

He joined or supported the American Labor Party, a committee to protest the arrest of the Chilean poet Pablo Neruda, the American Peace Crusade (to protest the Korean War), the United Negro and Allied Veterans of America, and the Consumers Union. He also began teaching a course on mystery writing at the Party's Jefferson School in New York City and served on its board of trustees. He served on the editorial board of *Soviet Russia Today,* and on its behalf sent out a fundraising letter, referring to it as "one small American magazine, courageous, determined, carrying on the fight for sanity and truth in American-Soviet relations."[82] He cofounded the Negro Publication Society, and he, along with hundreds of others, signed on as a cosponsor of the Communist-organized Scientific and Cultural Conference for World Peace, held in New York City in March 1949.

By far his most important position was president of the Civil Rights Congress of New York (CRC). The CRC, the result of a merger of three Party-organized defense groups, the International Labor Defense, the National Federation for Constitutional Liberties, and the National Negro Congress, was dedicated to funding litigation and publicity on behalf of those fighting racial injustice in the United States—mainly Communists, it turned out—who had been arrested for their efforts. It numbered ten thousand members and more than sixty chapters. Hammett, who had been a member of the National Federation for Constitutional Liberties, built the CRC New York into the most successful American Communist organization of its time. He was also one of the trustees for the

CRC's bail fund, which collected nearly $800,000, to be used for those arrested and convicted for political reasons. In 1947, the House Committee on Un-American Activities branded the CRC a Communist-front organization and named Hammett as one of those individuals whose name is linked to the CRC. He was also listed as an individual who had contributed five hundred dollars or more to the organization.[83] The CRC was also added to the attorney general's list of subversive organizations. As chairman of CRC New York, Hammett penned a "Progressive Protest," condemning a congressional bill that would have outlawed the Communist Party. He called the planned proscription "a direct assault on American democracy, on American tradition of civil rights and freedom and of electoral freedom."[84] And, under his auspice, the CRC held, on October 11, 1947, a Conference for the Abolition of the Committee on Un-American Activities and drafted a petition to abolish it.

In 1949, the domestic Cold War caught up with him, when the CRC fund came under intense scrutiny by the US government. The CRC's bail fund had disbursed $260,000 to free eleven Communist Party leaders who had been convicted for violating the Alien Registration Act. When they lost their appeal, four of them went underground to avoid imprisonment. On July 9, 1951, Hammett and the other trustees were called before Sylvester J. Ryan, chief judge of the United States District Court of the Southern District of New York, to answer questions about the fugitives and produce CRC financial records. It was the position of the prosecutor that one or more of the contributors to the bail fund might be harboring the fugitives. The night before his appearance, according to Hellman, she asked him, "Why don't you say you don't know the names?" "No," he replied, "I can't say that. . . . I guess it has something to do with keeping my word. . . . [I]f it were more than jail, if it were my life, I would give it for what I think democracy is and I don't let cops or judges tell me what democracy is."[85]

The trustees refused to answer any questions, and they refused to produce the fund's books and records. Hammett cited the Fifth Amendment thirty-three times. They were charged with contempt of court, arrested, tried, convicted, and sentenced to six months in prison. Ryan refused Hammett's request for bail while the appeal was being heard. In fact, Ryan said he had been inclined to sentence Hammett to a longer prison term, because "I felt his claim of privilege was especially unwarranted and unjustified." He was, after all, the trustee of the fund, the chair of the CRC, and he knew, from observing the testimonies of the previous trustees, what would happen if he did not answer.[86] He served five months (with time off for good behavior) in the Federal Correction Institute in Ashland, Kentucky (recently vacated by two of the Hollywood Ten, Dalton Trumbo and John Howard Lawson). Ironically, he had just written an introduction to *The Communist Trial: An American Crossroads*, a self-published book written by George Marion, a former *Daily Worker* reporter. On the day he was sentenced, he learned that the Internal Revenue Service had levied an income-tax lien against him for failure to pay his taxes. The IRS billed him for slightly over one hundred thousand dollars.

At the time of the court hearing, Hammett was already on the media blacklist, as the result of being one of 151 "subversives" listed in *Red Channels: The Report of Communist Influence in Radio and Television* (June 1950). A mere eleven of his myriad "subversive" activities were enumerated, but this was sufficient to lead to the cancellation of three radio shows based on his characters. Walter Winchell took to calling him "Dashiell Hammett and sickle" and "Samovar Spade."[87] On September 9, 1951, two months after his incarceration, and six months into the House Committee's renewed investigation into "Communist infiltration of the motion picture industry," Hammett was named by Martin Berkeley. He was not, however, subpoenaed, and he remained active in Communist Party activities. He was chairman of the Committee to Defend V. J. Jerome, who had been the Party's literary commissar and was currently on trial, with sixteen other Party leaders, for violating the Alien Registration Act. Hammett authored a letter of invitation to several prominent left-wing journalists, inviting them to a rally-tribute on Jerome's behalf and another asking them to sign a petition regarding freedom of expression. (One of the addressees, I. F. Stone, declined because, he wrote accurately, Jerome had "tried to ride herd on the intellectuals in a way most offensive to anyone who believes in intellectual and cultural freedom.")[88]

Anti-Communists continued to dog Hammett's path. He was subpoenaed to appear on March 24, 1953, before an executive session of the Senate Permanent Subcommittee on Investigations of the Committee on Government Operations, chaired by Joseph McCarthy. He was one of dozens called to testify about the Department of State's purchases of "Communist" books for its overseas libraries. McCarthy was not present, and committee chief counsel Roy Cohn posed most of the questions. He began by asking whether Hammett knew that "a considerable number of your works are used in the State Department Information Program?" Hammett said that he did not until Cohn had told him in a telephone call prior to the hearing. After flippantly asking if the government had given him "a good civil suit for royalties," Cohn popped the big question: "Are you a member of the Communist party today?" Hammett declined to answer, "on the ground that the answer would tend to incriminate me, pleading my rights under the Fifth Amendment." Were you, Cohn continued, "a member of the Communist party in 1922?" Hammett again declined to answer. When Cohn asked how many books Hammett had written between 1922 and the present time, Hammett said "five." "Just five?" "Yes, and many short stories and stuff that has been reprinted in reprint books." What would your answer be, Cohn then asked, "if I were to ask if you were a Communist party member at the time you wrote the book." Hammett said it would be the same. Did you, Cohn continued, "write a story which could be classed as other than a detective story?" "Yes," Hammett replied, "I have written quite a number of short stories that were not detective stories." "Any that deal with social problems?" "I don't think so. Yes, I remember one, if you take it as a social problem"— "Night Shade," which had to do with "Negro-white relations." "When you wrote this short story, 'Night Shade,'" Cohn asked, "were you a member of the Communist party?" Hammett again declined to answer, but when Cohn asked, "Did that story in any way reflect the Communist line?," Hammett did answer. "That is a difficult—on the word 'reflect' I would say no, it didn't reflect it. It was against racism." At that point Senator Karl Mundt (R-SD) interjected a question: "Would you say that it resembled—whether it reflected or not—the Communist line with respect to race problems?" Hammett replied: "I would have to say no. I think the truth would be that it didn't reflect it consciously or solely." Cohn resumed questioning, asking if Hammett ever had any contact with the publications commission of the Communist Party? When Hammett said "no," Cohn asked if he knew any members of the Party's publications commission. When Hammett asked for some names, Cohn provided three. Hammett declined to answer the first two, but when asked about Alexander Bittelman, he said he thought he was in the West Street Jail at the same time I was. Cohn then asked a series of questions about royalties, which Hammett answered. But when Cohn asked if Hammett had contributed any of that money to the Communist Party, Hammett declined to answer. Mundt then asked a few questions about the sale of book rights to a movie studio, all of which Hammett answered. That concluded the questioning. Hammett was only on the stand for a few minutes. (Only one other Hollywood writer—Arnaud D'Usseau— was subpoenaed for these hearings, and he also was on the stand only for a few minutes.)[89]

Hammett was recalled two days later to testify at a public session, and this time McCarthy was present. As in the executive session, Cohn began the questioning, basically repeating the questions he had previously asked, and Hammett made the same replies. McCarthy interjected a question as to whether Party members, under Party discipline, "would propagandize the Communist cause, normally, regardless of whether he was writing fiction books or books on politics?" Hammett replied: "I can't answer that, because I honestly don't know." When asked if he knew the whereabouts of the four fugitives, Hammett replied that he had read that one of them was in jail but that he did not now know, nor ever had known, where the other three were. Hammett denied having ever engaged in espionage or sabotage, and, when McCarthy asked a series of questions pertaining to Hammett's regard for the Soviet form of government, Hammett said that he could no more say that Communism was better for the United States than he could say if imperialism is better. But he did say that he did not think Communism should be adopted in the United States—"it would seem to be impractical, if most people didn't want it." In response to McCarthy's final question—if you were in charge of a program to fight Communism, would you purchase the works of some seventy-five Communist authors and distribute them throughout the world? (as McCarthy alleged the Department of State was doing)—Hammett said: "if I were fighting communism I don't think I would do it by giving people any books at all."[90] He would be subpoenaed one more time, in 1955, by the New York State Joint Legislative Committee, which was investigating philanthropic organizations.

Hammett did secure one victory in a court of law, in 1954. Warner Bros., claiming that it had exclusive rights to the title and characters in *The Maltese Falcon,* had sued Hammett and Columbia Broadcasting System, in 1946, after the radio station aired a program based on that book. The studio lost at the trial level and appealed. A three-judge panel of the Ninth Circuit Court of Appeals of the United States upheld the verdict, setting a very important precedent for future sequel writers. Justice Albert Lee Stephens Sr. established two rules of law: (1) Without a specific contractual grant of an exclusive right, it does not exist; (2) the copyright law does not foreclose the original creator's continued use of his/her characters in subsequent works.[91]

By then, Hammett was a dying and impoverished man. The years of heavy drinking and smoking, the years in the Aleutians, and the five months cleaning toilets at Ashland had severely weakened him. The Internal Revenue Service had increased his tax arrears to $140,000 and placed a lien on any income he earned, which, he told an FBI investigator in 1957, amounted to thirty dollars.[92] His books were no longer in print. When Hellman sold the farm on which they had lived for many years, he moved into a small house in Katonah, becoming a virtual recluse, in Hellman's words "a hermit, and the ugly little country house grew uglier with books piled on every chair and no place to sit, the desk a foot high with unanswered mail. The signs of sickness were all around."[93] A reporter who interviewed him wrote, "Three typewriters stand mute as tombstones in a wooden caretaker's cottage outside New York." Hammett told the reporter, "I keep them chiefly to remind myself I was once a writer."[94] He started a new novel, "Tulip," but left it unfinished, perhaps because he was too ill or too worn out. When it became obvious he could no longer live alone, Hellman took him in, and he spent the last four years of his life with her. He died on January 10, 1961, and is buried at

Arlington National Cemetery. But even then, the US government could not let him rest. One week after his death, an interoffice FBI memo stated: "Dashiell Hammett is dead and to be buried at Arlington." A short summary of his "subversive" activities followed. The memo writer suggested that the assistant to the director "might wish to call the attention of one or more of his press contacts to the incongruous situation which exists wherein one who has been a member of an organization which believes in the overthrow of the government by force and violence receives a hero's funeral among those who gave their lives to support this government."[95]

Hellman contrived to get full control of Hammett's estate and kept tight control over it. She rebuilt his literary reputation, but she also made it difficult for biographers to study Hammett's letters and manuscripts. Eventually, she did allow a few biographers access, but she always tried, sometimes very creatively, to keep control of his image.

Annotated Bibliography of Works on Hammett

Bruccoli, Matthew J., and Richard Layman, eds. *Hardboiled Mystery Writers, Raymond Chandler, Dashiell Hammett, Ross Macdonald: A Literary Reference.* New York: Carroll and Graf, 1989.

The section on Hammett includes some of his hard-to-get articles as well as contemporary reviews of his writing. It also includes transcripts of Hammett's appearance before investigating bodies.

Cline, Sally. *Dashiell Hammett: Man of Mystery.* New York: Arcade, 2016.

Well-researched and well-written account that weaves the life through the writing, finding clues about the life in the writings.

Dooley, Dennis. *Dashiell Hammett.* New York: Felix Unger, 1984.

Dooley traces Hammett's evolution as a mystery writer, setting him securely in his cultural milieu and focusing on Hammett's philosophy of life. One-half of the book is devoted to the short stories.

Fuller, Ken. *Hardboiled Activist: The Work and Politics of Dashiell Hammett.* Glasgow: Praxis, 2017.

The most thorough discussion of Hammett's politics. Fuller presents Hammett as a nihilist turned Marxist. Although Fuller is sympathetic to

Hammett's politics, he disdains his writing and clearly does not like the persona.

Hammett, Dashiell. *Selected Letters of Dashiell Hammett*. Edited by Richard Layman and Julie M. Rivett. Washington, DC: Counterpoint, 2001.
A wonderful collection of his letters. They provide the reader with the best perspective available on Hammett.

Hammett, Jo. *Dashiell Hammett: A Daughter Remembers*. Edited by Richard Layman and Julie M. Rivett. New York: Carroll and Graf, 2001.
This is the most personal account of Hammett. Though Hammett left his wife and two daughters, Jo Hammett has fond memories of him as a father. But, and this is what makes the book so valuable, she does not flinch from revealing his faults and weaknesses, particularly his drinking.

Johnson, Diane. *Dashiell Hammett: A Life*. New York: Random House, 1983.
The first biography written with the cooperation of Lillian Hellman. It is well, almost novelistically, written. She is very speculative about what Hammett might have been thinking or learning from his experiences. She quotes extensively from his writings but provides no literary analysis.

Layman, Richard. *Shadow Man: The Life of Dashiell Hammett*. New York: Harcourt Brace Jovanovich, 1981.
The first in-depth study. Layman is scrupulously factual, eschewing all speculation. The result is a plodding, just-the-facts-ma'am book that does not bring Hammett out of the shadows. It is, however, factually reliable and the template for the many biographies to come.

Mellen, Joan. *Hellman and Hammett: The Legendary Passion of Lillian Hellman and Dashiell Hammett*. New York: HarperCollins, 1996.
A well-researched, gossipy, often vicious account of the pair's intertwined years. Mellen takes more than 450 pages to convince the reader to dislike the pair as much as she seems to. She frequently puts thoughts and motives in their heads and words in their mouths, without references. She also does not cite her evidence for some of Hammett's activities.

Metress, Christopher, ed. *The Critical Response to Dashiell Hammett*. Westport, CT: Greenwood, 1994.
Hammett has been the subject of a raft of literary criticism. This anthology is an excellent introduction to the criticism.

Nolan, William F. *Dashiell Hammett: A Casebook*. Santa Barbara, CA: McNally and Lifton, 1969.

Primarily bibliographical, a basic reference to Hammett's writings.

Nolan, William F. *Hammett: A Life at the Edge*. New York: Congdon and Weed, 1983.

An attempt at a personal study, to bring Hammett out of the shadows. It is sympathetic, well researched and well written, but Nolan accepts Hellman's statements uncritically.

Panek, LeRoy Lad. *Reading Dashiell Hammett: A Critical Study of the Fiction prior to* The Maltese Falcon. Jefferson, NC: McFarland, 2004.

Exactly as advertised, an in-depth appraisal of Hammett's work up to 1930.

Thompson, George J. "Rhino." *Hammett's Moral Vision*. San Francisco: Vince Emery Productions, 2009.

An in-depth examination of the five novels, to ascertain how the Continental Op engages with his sordid world without himself being too tarnished by it.

Ward, Nathan. *The Lost Detective: Becoming Dashiell Hammett*. London: Bloomsbury, 2015.

In his long, highly detailed account of the first half of Hammett's life, Ward thoroughly mines the stories and novels. (The reader may learn more about the Pinkerton agency than he/she desires.)

Story Collections by Dashiell Hammett

The Big Book of the Continental Op. Edited by Richard Layman and Julie M. Rivett. New York: Vintage Crime/Black Lizard, 2017.

A collection of all his writings featuring the Continental Op, the protagonist/narrator of his groundbreaking detective output. It contains twenty-eight stand-alone stories, the introductions to two novels, and one unfinished story.

The Big Knockover: Selected Stories and Short Novels. Edited by Lillian Hellman. New York: Vintage, 1989.

Nine short stories and the beginning of his unfinished novel "Tulip."

The Continental Op. Edited by Steven Marcus. New York: Random House, 1974.

A collection of seven stories, with an introduction by the editor.

Crime Stories and Other Writings. Edited by Steven Marcus. New York: Library of America, 2001.

Contains all the pulp fiction, using original story texts.

The Hunter and Other Stories. Edited by Richard Layman and Julie M. Rivett. New York: Mysterious, 2013.

A collection of seventeen published and unpublished stories, three screen stories, and an unpublished Sam Spade story. These demonstrate Hammett's ability to write excellent non-Op stories.

Lost Stories. Edited by Vince Emery. San Francisco: Vince Emery Productions, 2005.

Twenty-one stories not featuring the Continental Op.

5

Isobel Lennart and the Dynamics of Informing in Hollywood

In 1950, the informer subculture in the Hollywood motion picture industry began to emerge in fits and starts. It became full-fledged in the spring of 1951, when the House Committee on Un-American Activities announced a new set of hearings into "Communist Infiltration of the Motion-Picture Industry." Prior to October 1947, when the first set of hearings was held, the studio heads and industry associations had made no public announcement regarding the fate of uncooperative witnesses, but after those hearings they initiated a blacklist of the ten uncooperative witnesses and a graylist of those who continued to defend them. In addition, between 1947 and 1949, a new subindustry appeared, consisting of three firms, one individual, and the American Legion. They all publicized the names and purportedly subversive associations of hundreds of motion picture industry employees, and some then offered to clear those named for future employment. Finally, in March 1951, the Motion Picture Industry Council urged full disclosure by all witnesses, and the Motion Picture Association of America announced that uncooperative witnesses would find it difficult to get movie jobs in the future.[1]

The dozens of witnesses subpoenaed in early 1951 faced a clear choice: to invoke their Fifth Amendment privilege, refuse to answer the Committee's questions, and be blacklisted; or unhesitatingly answer every question and remain employed or employable in the industry. The most difficult part of the latter choice required naming people who the witnesses knew had been members of the Communist Party. Actor Sterling Hayden was probably the first industry employee who faced that choice and decided to inform. On his own initiative, he met with Federal Bureau of Investigation (FBI) agents three times in the late summer and autumn of 1950. He was followed to the FBI's Los Angeles office by writer Richard Collins (who had been subpoenaed in 1947 but had not testified) and director Edward Dmytryk (one of the Hollywood Ten, who had just finished serving his prison sentence for contempt of Congress).

The first witness at the new hearings was actor Larry Parks (who had also been subpoenaed in 1947). He appeared on March 21 and tried, without success, to convince the Committee to allow him to talk only about himself. When asked to give names, he pleaded with his questioners not to insist. In an executive session, later that day, he "provided" twelve names.[2] The following day, Parks's contract with Columbia Pictures was terminated, and writer Paul Jarrico, who had also been subpoenaed, issued a press statement: "If I have to choose between crawling through the mud with Larry Parks or going to jail like my courageous friends, the Hollywood Ten, I assure you I'll choose the latter."[3] (Hayden appeared on April 10; Collins on April 12; Jarrico on April 13; and Dmytryk on April 25.)

What separated the informer from the resister? What factor or factors impelled forty-some people to salvage their careers at the expense of the careers of former friends and colleagues? Though the informers were a diverse lot in terms of their ages, personalities, and stature within the industry, the majority of them were male screenwriters. Of the nineteen unhesitant informers who testified at the height of this set of hearings (March 1951 to May 1952), fifteen were men, and ten of these men were writers. (Three of the women were also writers.) Six of these witnesses were longtime, active Party members; four were longtime, inactive members; and nine were short-time, inactive members. Although their alleged motives for informing varied, the basic determining factor for all of them was their fear of being blacklisted and their fear of the effect the blacklist experience would have on them and their families. In contrast, the two hundred–plus witnesses who chose to resist were unwilling to save their careers at the expense of others. Actor Howard Da Silva, who testified right after Parks, later said that his decision "to take a principled stand" was made long before he received his subpoena. It was something he had known he would do for as long as he could remember. The only decision he had to make, in 1951, when he was subpoenaed, was the manner of his refusal.[4]

On the witness stand, only one of the unhesitant friendly witnesses, Isobel Lennart, testified that she had undergone serious soul-searching as to whether or not to give names. Later, she was one of the few informers who publicly repented for having done so. At the time of her testimony, she was one of the most successful screenwriters, male or female, in Hollywood, and she remained so until her death in 1971. Unlike Elia Kazan, the only other informer who ranked with her in terms of pay and quality screen credits both before and after their respective testimonies, her life and her decision to inform have not received the attention they merit.[5]

Lennart's father, Edward M. Hochdorf (d. 1996), was a Jewish dentist who lived in Brooklyn. He married Victoria Lennart Livingston (1889–1924), a member of the Church of England, and when she died from a ruptured appendix, he married his first cousin, Hattie Satz (1896–1996). Two children were born during the first marriage, Stanley (1911) and Isobel Fredrika (1915). Isobel had red hair and freckles, like her mother. Her childhood was negatively impacted by two events. When she was five years old, she contracted polio, and she spent almost ten years in leg braces. She believed that this illness caused her to have stocky legs and a weight problem, both of which preyed on her mind for the rest of her life. Four years later, her mother died suddenly. Isobel's daughter, Sarah Harding, recalled: "My mother seemed to carry that trauma with her always . . . and I believe she grew up thinking that everything would have been okay if only her mother had not died." Isobel also grew up thinking that her father's second marriage was neither romantic nor sexual but rather a marriage of convenience on his part, which he had undertaken mainly as a means of procuring a caretaker for his children. Isobel did not have a smooth relationship with her stepmother. In a journal entry, in 1932, Isobel wrote: "long talk with Hon [Hattie]—about the real thing [love]—why did she marry father? Just looking for a husband, and reaching the dangerous time. When I think of how she's changed. I could have loved her so—it was a normal affection—why didn't she let me? Why those months of coldness and why am I afraid when I've run up bills—why have I to have these stupid pride things hanging over my head?"[6]

Isobel attended Lincoln Junior High School from January 1927 to January 1928, and Girls High School from January 1928 to January 1931. She then matriculated at Smith College, where she spent two years. She majored in English and worked on the college newspaper, but her grades were low. Her journal entries reveal that she was a deeply insecure person, desperate for some self-discipline. During her first month there, she wrote: "I begin to lead a life suffocating with good resolutions—the control of my temper—a little reserve—the to-hell-my-dear-with-your attitude to people." But one month later, she noted, in despair: "My resolutions are all broken. . . . Why do I have to live? No happiness is ever evident. I'm living in a black hole. . . . I wish my mother and father were dead—I want to be dead so much, so very much."

And in December 1932, she asked herself: "Why can't I obtain peace and a quiet kind of happiness? Is it because I'm a Jew? Because I'm so consumed by my stupidity? Because I don't have any center—any starting point—any god and any self? O God, help me! Let me be good, God! Just a person . . . or let me die."

She left Smith, for health reasons, in June 1933, and transferred to New York University. At the end of 1933, she noted that "it was not bad really. Must work harder. Dad is disappointed in me. It kills me. Hon? I don't know how she feels, but I love her. . . . It's going to be a good year anyway. I won't let anything spoil it." But one year later, in one of her last entries in this particular journal, she wrote: "Am determined to make a new life for myself. I live now without dignity—without interest. Each day should be exciting—new—instead: in the midst of life I am in death. I never understood that before. I will try. Especially with Hon. I love her so. And with myself. My past must no longer be in flames behind me and dust in my mouth today."

She had long harbored a dream of becoming a movie director, and, in 1934, she started her climb to it when she went to work at the fan-mail department at M-G-M's New York office. She was paid thirteen dollars a week to answer letters. There is no indication in any of her surviving papers when or why she began to develop a leftist consciousness or radicalism. However, the FBI claimed to have information that she had been a member of the Young Communist League when she was sixteen. She told the agent that she had "forgotten."[7] In any event, she decided to organize a union at M-G-M. She was summarily fired. She then worked as a secretary at the Brooklyn YMHA and as a secretary at Universal Pictures. She also enrolled in a film course.

She moved to Los Angeles in 1937 and rented an apartment there with Laura Sward. She also changed her last name to Lennart and was hired by M-G-M as a script girl. She wrote in her journal: "New people . . . and now what looks like a new kind of life—and frankly—in spite of my gladness at getting a job quickly—a pretty disappointing beginning." She told the Committee on Un-American Activities in 1952 that the job had "brutal working hours. My normal day was leaving my house at 6:30 in the morning and I seldom got home until midnight." She prepared the shooting sequence for the director, and she matched all the details of sets, costumes, movements of actors, dialogue, and so forth, for the editor. She worked on B pictures: Mr. Moto and Charlie Chan series, and Westerns. Those were, she recalled, "18-day, 18-night pictures. You shot all day and most of the night and the key crew remained the same."[8]

During her time off, she and Sward wrote a twenty-seven-page treatment titled "A Boy Comes Home." It concerned a boy of good breeding and birth, being raised by a widowed father, who is turning into "a swaggering, unsocial brat." After stealing a car, for which a homeless boy is arrested, he goes with his psychology class to a prison. A prisoner on death row tells the class about his progression from a child who told a lie to an adult who committed murder. The boy, profoundly shaken, returns home and confesses to stealing the car. The judge places him on probation and releases the other boy into his father's custody.[9]

In 1938, Lennart decided to join the Communist Party (CP), probably the only script girl to do so. She told the Committee: "When I was first out in Hollywood . . . it was the first time I had ever been away from home, except for college. I knew nobody in the entire town. I was feeling completely useless as a human being. I wasn't doing anything for anybody but myself. This was during the rise of Nazism which terrified me as it did many other people, and I talked about it a great deal and I felt as if I wanted to do something about it, not just talk."

Communists seemed to be the only people she met who were leading active and useful lives, and Jessie Burns, a reader at the studio, convinced Lennart that the Communist Party was the only group trying in an organized way to do something about Nazism. Burns told her about a studio group that was being formed that would consist of people who were not members of the Communist Party, although it would be under the auspices of the Party, and that its purpose was to discuss current events, economics, and so on, including the whole question of Hitlerism and what could be done about it.

Lennart joined this group of about seven or eight white-collar studio workers. Because she lived alone, the first several meetings were at her apartment, but when the meeting place was shifted to another location, she dropped out of the group. (She did not drive, and she was too tired after work to take a long trip on public transportation.)[10]

Several months later, at the beginning of 1939, she joined the Communist Party. She was assigned to a writers' group, but though she attended meetings on a regular basis, she claimed she was not a very active member. She also claimed that she did no recruiting, held no office, and did not participate in Party fractions. The only CP-front group she joined was Associated Film Audiences, where her sole activity was to lick envelopes.[11] In August, she resigned from the Party because of her opposition to the German-Soviet Nonaggression Treaty.

She continued to write scripts on her own time, but she believed that she was treading water. In December 1940, she wrote in her journal: "I've been here 3½ years and . . . I've found that I can if I must make my own way—work with people—have them like me—but am still irresponsible, still fantasizing, still dreaming my life away. I have a rather constant feeling of emptiness and despair. . . . Whether or not I can write or not is still unresolved. I have my laziness to thank for that. Anyway boys and girls it's been a bad year and I'm getting older. If I want to get better I have to make it get better."

The following year, she moved into her own apartment, and, in June, following the German invasion of the Soviet Union, she rejoined the

Communist Party. She continued to be, in her words, "a passive member," and, she told the Committee:

> I never asked myself what I was doing in it at all. And that seems fantastic to me now, but I think I can explain it. I think I joined for good motives but my joining was unexamined, uncritical and emotional, and something to regret. However, once I got in, I found a number of people who seemed to be there for the same reason I was, for nothing more vicious than that. You must remember that my knowledge of people was quite limited, I did not know the really active people in the party, and some of the information that has been divulged at other hearings of this committee has been startling to me, too. To me, and to many others, it was a place to gather to talk about what was going on around us, who was writing and what, what we could do about things that seemed unjust. But the atmosphere in the party is strictly a hot-house atmosphere. You all read the same things, you talk about the same things, you hear nothing but one point of view. You don't realize this when you are in. You don't realize you have blinders on. . . . I know now that I had absolutely no right even from a Communist point of view to be where I was, because I had no understanding of what that might imply.[12]

The first FBI report identifying her as a member of the Party was written five years later. It read: "Subject was a member of Group A-2 of the Writers' Branch, Northwest Section, and held 1943 CP Book No. 25171, and 1944 CP Book No. 48636. Subject presently a member of Group A-1 of the Writers' Branch, and holds 1944 CPA [Communist Political Association] Card No. 46816." A later report described her as a twenty-nine-year-old female, single, five feet, three inches tall, weighing 130 pounds, light complexion, brown hair, and brown eyes.[13] Subsequent FBI reports indicated that she was a sponsor of the Actors Laboratory, subscribed to *People's World,* and was a member of the Hollywood Arts, Sciences and Professions Council. Sylvia Jarrico, who was in the writers' branch of the Party, remembered Lennart as very driven, ambitious to be successful and well paid.[14]

In September 1941, Lennart received her first screenwriting job. Twentieth Century-Fox hired her to revise the script for *On the Sunny Side,* a comedy-drama about an English boy who is sent to live with an American family to escape the German air attacks on Great Britain. Meanwhile, she and Lee Gold (who was also a Communist) were trying to sell their script, a comedy about a maid who pseudonymously writes an autobiography. When the book is published, the town is convulsed, because every family thinks its maid wrote the book. After six months' effort, M-G-M bought the story and hired her and Gold to write the script. She was paid $150 a week. When *The Affairs of Martha* opened, in August 1942, the *Hollywood Reporter* reviewer termed it "one of those minor gems that captivate and charm an audience" and congratulated the writers on their "high humor." It did exceptionally well at the box office.[15]

Then she and another writer, William Kozlenko, devised a story about a Supreme Court justice who, while on vacation, helps expose corruption in the small town where he is staying. They told it to Dore Schary, who was in charge of B movies at M-G-M. Schary liked it, bought it for the studio, and put Lennart and Kozlenko to work on the script. It was released as *A Stranger in Town.* The critics agreed it was "entertaining." M-G-M subsequently hired Lennart on a full-time basis, and she began to amass screen credits, mainly for what she called "very light and frothy pictures."[16] In 1943, she wrote the script for *Lost Angel* (a youth, comedy-drama based on an idea by another writer) and for *Anchors Aweigh* (her first musical, and the first of many scripts she would write for producer Joe Pasternak). The *Hollywood Reporter* reviewer of *Lost Angel* called the script "charming," and the reviewers for *Hollywood Reporter* and *Variety* raved about *Anchors Aweigh* (released in 1945).[17]

Lennart apparently did not seek (nor was she assigned) any scripts with a political or social theme, nor did she attempt to insert political or social messages into her scripts. She was mainly concerned with story coherence and dialogue. Because she possessed a good sense of structure, she generally did not write outlines or treatments. She usually wrote only a story and then the screenplay, and she mainly worked without a collaborator.[18] Probably no writer, male or female, worked as hard at her craft as Lennart did. Her daughter remembered her being "driven, driven, driven." Lennart herself told Philip Scheuer of the *Los Angeles Times:* "I always say, my trouble is that I don't have a wife to come home to! I need more help than most people. And I feel guilty in both areas most of the time. Maybe my experience explains why there are not many women screenwriters around anymore."[19]

She never believed that she worked hard enough. In a journal entry dated January 28, 1957, she wrote: "Do I like it—writing—the act itself—or do I like 'having written.' Why the *laziness*—the vast sitting and having coffee and cigarettes—why the peeing away of energy." And she was her most severe critic. But she confided to Fay Kanin, also a writer: "I moan, and groan, and torture myself. But I love every agonizing hour of it. I want to sit in my room and write. And then I want those damned actors to say every word *exactly* the way I wrote it." Philip Dunne remarked that Lennart would become furious when actors changed the dialogue she had written and directors allowed the changes. In fact, she told him that she was happy when a director would get 70 percent of her intention on the screen. Usually she had to settle for 30 percent.[20]

At some point during World War II, she met John B. Harding, a writer (for the *New Leader,* among other publications), who was married (with one child) and serving in the US Army. He divorced his wife, and he and Lennart married on August 24, 1946. Their daughter, Sarah, told me that her father was the only radical in an arch-Republican family and that he defied it whenever he could. He dropped out of Harvard, flirted with the Trotskyists, moved to Hollywood, became an actor, married two Jewish women, etc. After the war he tried, with little success, to become a screenwriter and a screen actor. Although he had a great stage voice and was, in Sarah Harding's estimation, "an amazingly gifted stage actor," he never came across on the screen. He wrote and acted in a number of stage plays, many of which were performed at the Stage Society Theater he and Steve Brown ran from 1958 to 1968. Lennart's screenwriting salary supported their family (and the Stage Society Theater.)[21]

Harding did not approve of Lennart's membership in the Communist Party. Though he did not ask her to leave the Party, he posed many questions about the reasons for her membership, which she could not answer to her own satisfaction, and which convinced her that she was in an organization about which she knew nothing. She told the Committee: "He asked me how much Marxist literature I had read, and 'very little' had to be the answer. He asked me how much I knew about the actual set-up of the party itself, who the actual leadership was, where the money came from and mostly for what purpose it was used, and I didn't know."

She claimed that her breaking point occurred in the spring of 1945, when the so-called "Duclos letter," sharply criticizing Earl Browder, was published. When she realized that the Party would conform to the dictates of the letter, she resigned. She told the Committee: "I joined the CP without the critical examination of it which I should have made. . . . I believe I was too young and too politically ignorant. I stayed in it as long as I felt certain I was doing nothing wrong. When I was no longer certain, when I realized I didn't understand the nature of communism or the party, sufficiently to be sure of the relationship of what I was doing to a possibly larger plan, I got out. . . . I wish it was sooner."[22]

Meanwhile, she received sole credit for *Holiday in Mexico* (M-G-M, 1946) and *It Happened in Brooklyn* (M-G-M, 1947); gave birth to a son, Joshua, in 1948; and cowrote, with her husband, *The Kissing Bandit* (1947), a very silly historical musical comedy set in Spanish California, which was one of M-G-M's biggest flops that year and represented the low point in the careers of its stars, Frank Sinatra and Kathryn Grayson. It was the last time Lennart and her husband collaborated on a screenplay. Her next two scripts for M-G-M, *East Side, West Side* (1949) and *A Life of Her Own* (1950), were tear-jerking melodramas, both of which received mediocre reviews for the writing.

In July 1950, Darryl F. Zanuck, the head of Twentieth Century-Fox, asked to borrow her from M-G-M, to write the script for a project entitled "It's a Man's World." The readers at the studio were very impressed with what she wrote, and, after several revisions, it was released as *The Girl Next Door*. Some critics liked the story, whereas others thought that the plot was limp and the story a cliché. Six months later, Fox borrowed her again to rewrite a script her husband had written (*My Wife's Best Friend*). During this assignment, she became pregnant, and, in her opinion, this condition affected her writing. She decided that she was not giving the studio its money's worth and asked to be taken off salary, but she informed Zanuck that she intended to finish the script on her own. Two weeks later, she delivered a first-draft continuity to the studio and, four weeks later, a final draft.[23] The finished product received tepid reviews. In between, at M-G-M, she wrote the script for *Skirts Ahoy!* (1951), a female version of *Anchors Aweigh*, and one of the eight episodes ("Rosika the Rose") for *It's a Big Country* (1951), the studio's epic paean to Americanization.

In the summer of 1951, in the midst of a new set of hearings by the Committee on Un-American Activities investigating "Communist Infiltration of the Motion-Picture Industry," she was visited by Committee investigator William Wheeler. She had been expecting him (or a subpoena), had discussed the situation with her husband, and was, in her words, feeling "very brave at this point." She had decided, she later told actor Robert Vaughn, that when Wheeler returned, she would talk about her Party membership but that she would not give him any names. "I really steeled myself," she remembered. "I was miserable, but I was still very close to having been in the Party. . . . I loved these people." She told the Committee:

> I thought it was more than likely that many of the people I had known once [in the Communist Party] had changed as much as I had, and I couldn't bring myself to damage anyone in a way that I felt I was going to be damaged because I thought that when I testified, that career I had worked hard at for a long time would be over.
>
> They [the Committee investigators] came back about a week later, and they had been told by somebody that I was pregnant. Which I was. Which I hadn't mentioned—I didn't think it was relevant. I was about three or four months pregnant, and they felt that for a pregnant woman to test them on this ground would be bad publicity. They buzzed around. Somehow, through M-G-M, I think, they found out who my obstetrician was and went to him. They wanted an affidavit saying that I could testify

without danger to my health. My obstetrician, who was a very wise man, said certainly not. He would sign an affidavit saying it would definitely endanger my health. I didn't know that was going on at all. This was all very subterranean. I was Rh negative, which was a big thing in those days. . . . They came back two weeks later and said, "We withdraw the subpoena." I said no. By this time I felt I was going to get away with it too. But I said no because it had been hanging over my head for a year or so. . . . They said that was it, and they wouldn't be back.

(An FBI informant reported that Lennart was definitely out of the Party and opposed to what it was doing, but she had expressed "some coolness" about former Party members who had testified and given names to the Committee.)[24]

On September 19, 1951, Lennart (along with more than one hundred others) was named by Martin Berkeley. She went to an executive at M-G-M, probably Eddie Mannix, and offered to resign. Mannix told her to wait and see what the public reaction would be to the movies based on her most recent scripts. If no groups picketed the theaters showing movies for which she had written the script, her tenure at M-G-M would remain secure.[25]

The day after she returned home from the hospital (November 1951), FBI agents came to her house and asked her "a million questions. . . . They came back twice, and my husband said, 'Stop harassing my wife.'" When they asked her for names, she decided to provide them, because, she naively told Vaughn: "I had a different feeling about the FBI than I did about the Un-American Activities Committee. The FBI was not in the business of stopping people's employment and ruining their lives." On December 14, she agreed to be interviewed, at her home, by two FBI agents. She told them that if she had appeared the previous summer, "she would have freely admitted her own CP membership but would have refused to identify other individuals as having been CP members," because doing so "would have in many instances unduly injured individuals who are possibly today out of the Party and in some instances against the Party." She was, however, willing to cooperate fully with the FBI, because, she told her interviewers, she believed that the FBI "would treat any contact with her in a confidential manner and would use the information thus obtained to investigate persons who are considered dangerous to the internal security of the United States." She told the agents the names of those people who had been in her Party branches.[26] (Lennart did not reveal to Vaughn why she had so much confidence in the FBI.)

She then volunteered to appear before the Committee, and she told Wheeler that she would provide names. She claimed that two things had changed her mind: M-G-M executives had told her that they could not protect her if she did not testify in a cooperative manner; and she claimed that she had experienced "a tremendous reversal of feelings about the Party," although she did not say why. (She might have been reacting to the manner in which local Communists were treating former members, like her friend Richard Collins, who had informed.) In any event, she told Vaughn that she decided to cooperate mainly for "quite selfish" reasons: "My father had died, which made me know I would now be responsible for my stepmother and my brother. . . . On a personal level I had to come to feel that people don't sustain you, your work sustains you, and I knew how to do absolutely nothing else but screen write. I didn't know how to live if I couldn't work."[27]

She felt sure that she was "rationalizing," but she also felt that

there was an enormous difference in the situation for me. Every name that I knew had been mentioned by this time. The first time I would have hurt other people; this time I felt I could hurt only myself. I had weeks of debate about what effect it would have on me, because I felt it was wrong to cooperate. To the extent that I did talk [to the Committee] it *was* a deal. It was very important for them for me to testify; they told me so. My studio felt that if I could testify and still continue to be employed, it would prove that [the Committee] did not necessarily ruin lives. They were having a lot of trouble with people who had cooperated who could not find employment. . . . [But] my criterion was that I would mention no name that had not been mentioned before. . . . [Committee counsel Frank Tavenner] said, "There is one name we will ask you that has not been mentioned," and they said the name [probably William Kozlenko], and I said that he had been my collaborator and closest friend. I said that I knew he was in the army, and that most people who were in the army were asked to leave the Party in this community. I said he had been thinking of joining the Party when he went into the army, and that altered it; he did not; and by the time he came back I was out. Tavenner and Wheeler said, "We don't believe that," and I said, 'That's your problem.' . . . They came to my hotel room [in Washington, DC] the night before I testified, and said again that they had to have his name, and they would ask me on the stand and what would I do? I said, "I will get up and say you are trying to corrupt my testimony, since I told you I don't know about this man." Wheeler said, "You're lying," and I said, "Prove it."[28]

On May 20, 1952, Lennart appeared before the Committee. Tavenner did not ask her about this man, and she did not mention him, but she named twenty-three people (though she later told Vaughn it had been ten or twelve).[29] She also claimed that every name that she provided had been mentioned by this time. In fact, two people, Nora and George Hellgren, had not been previously named. When a Committee member asked why she had changed her mind about providing names, she replied that when she returned to M-G-M, in the spring of 1952, she began to hear rumors about herself that

were very shocking to me and horrifying to me. This one I didn't hear directly, but I was told that it was commonly supposed that the reason I was still able to work even though I had been mentioned at the last hearings last year was that I had made a deal with someone, and this was pretty revolting for me and for this committee, too, I felt. The other rumor, this opposing rumor was that I was the last active, powerful Communist in Hollywood, that for some reason I was such a powerful Communist I couldn't be touched. This rumor was appalling to me, too. . . . It is pretty horrifying to hear that I alone was working because I possibly had paid out a great deal of money, and you can imagine that this was a very upsetting thing to hear.

She was also told that she had become a source of embarrassment to her friends who had not been Communists. In addition, she had to take into consideration that she had three children (her son, daughter, and stepson): "I don't think it is fair that they grow up under a cloud which is none of their doing and which there is no reason for today, since I have no brief or affiliation in this organization." Finally, she believed that she owed loyalty to the motion picture industry. "I am working in a field which I love, and which has been very good to me. I realize now that there is a great deal of public opinion on this point, and that public opinion is important to the industry for which I work; rightly so. If that public opinion wants to know where I stand and what I do aside from the pictures I write, I think they have a right to know and I have to answer them. This is what changed my mind about coming here today."[30]

Although Lennart had consoled herself that she had not mentioned any new names, that she had not ruined anyone, she did have one major regret: "I was cut off from all the people who went in [the Party with me], some of them my closest friends, for a very long time. I cut myself off because I was so overcome with shame and guilt. The few nasty letters I got I felt were justified. I felt tremendous misery about it as the years went on." She was not, however, subjected to the "terrible kicking around that other people like [Richard] Collins got—probably because I was a woman."[31] Lennart did not write for a year after her testimony, though she remained under contract to M-G-M. She told Vaughn:

I had a very peculiar relationship with Metro. . . . I had the most intense child-parent relationship with them, especially [with executives Eddie Mannix and Louis Sidney]. It was like I was one of their kids. . . . I spent my life there, and so it wasn't so much [a matter of] how good a writer I was. These were tough but very sentimental men, and they wanted me to work, and I was good at my job. . . . [Mannix and Sidney] really were people with some heart. They tried to protect all of us who were involved there—they really did and when they let us go, it was only after a struggle. It was a family thing.

Harding told Navasky: "I was always trying to get her away from screenwriting to write a book or play. But she had a certain security at MGM. It was her place, like a school. It was murder even trying to get her to go on loan-out to other studios."[32]

In September 1953, M-G-M assigned her to revise Daniel Fuchs's script about the life of the singer Ruth Etting. She received cocredit (with him) for *Love Me or Leave Me* (1955), and they were nominated for an Academy Award for Best Screenplay. (Fuchs was also nominated for, and won, the Award for Best Screen Story.) They won the Writers Guild of America (WGA) Award for Best Written American Musical.[33] Her original story and script for *Meet Me in Las Vegas* (M-G-M, 1955) was also nominated for a WGA award. And *This Could Be the Night* (M-G-M, 1957) received very good reviews.

At the end of 1957, she was taken off a script for the first time in her career. The project, *Merry Andrew,* a comedy to feature Danny Kaye, was a classic nightmare of the screenwriting craft. It began its life as a Paul Gallico serial ("The Romance of Henry Menafee"), which had been published in *Good Housekeeping.* Gallico wrote a screen story, and then eight other writers, separately or in combination, wrote six scripts between 1944 and 1949. Thereafter, it sat on the shelf of the story department for four years until, in July 1953, Lennart was assigned to the project. She wrote a step outline, and once again the project was postponed. In an intrastudio memorandum written in June 1954, an M-G-M executive wrote: "The story just isn't there! . . . The studio at this time would never buy this story. Why not just put it back on the shelf?"[34] But in May 1956, Lennart was put back to work on it, and she wrote five drafts. In December, the studio replaced her with I. A. L. Diamond, with whom she shared credit for the finished film. It received generally good reviews. (She was paid $2,250 per week, for forty-two weeks' work.)

Lennart wrote in her journal: "Off Merry Andrew—canned! Misery, then enormous relief and then weeks of laying around, off salary, for once not panicked. Waiting to hear about 'Small Woman' [*Inn of the Sixth Happiness*] with Mark Robson at Fox." A few days later, she wrote: "Slight panic setting in. Whether over the fact that I might get Small Woman or that I might not. I don't know." She was given the assignment, and worked on it for nine months. In January 1958, as she was working on what would be the final shooting script, she wrote in her journal that she had endured the

> nine strangest awful months in which the only good thing was the work itself. . . . Plagued during writing. . . . The compulsive delays—agonizing deadlines, usually self-imposed, and the feeling that it's not the pure job I would have done. In talking to Amanda [Dunne] today, I said that Phil [Dunne] and I have same problem—still looking for an authority figure to say, "great big wonderful you!" And that we have to face that we are either too old or too good at our jobs to accept that approval from anyone but ourselves, and much disapproval ditto. In other words, we've *got* to learn to concentrate on the job itself . . . in my case to write with *pleasure* the story I decide I want to write. And to assume that the interference of others—Mark [Robson, director], Buddy [Adler, producer], etc.—is well meant—they want a good film too—and to deal gently and infrequently, and without shoulder chips, on personal feelings. I have still the ghastly nonsense of wanting too much from each working relationship.

She was also, in her words, "desperately in need of money." Though *Inn of the Sixth Happiness* (1958) received generally good reviews, which mainly centered on Ingrid Bergman's performance, it was one of her scripts that she thought the director had ruined. (Years later, she viewed the movie again and publicly repented about Robson's work.)

She worked steadily from 1959 to 1962, accruing plum credits for *Please Don't Eat the Daisies* (M-G-M, 1959), *The Sundowners* (Warner

Brothers, 1960), *Two for the Seesaw* (Mirisch Brothers, 1962), and *Period of Adjustment* (M-G-M, 1962). In 1960, she was nominated for two WGA awards: *Please Don't Eat the Daisies* for Best Written American Comedy, and *The Sundowners* for Best Written American Drama. *The Sundowners* was also nominated for an Academy Award for Best Screenplay based on material from another medium. Two years later, she received another WGA nomination for Best Written American Comedy for *Period of Adjustment.*

And then along came the Fanny Brice project. She had been asked to write a screen story based on the life of Fanny Brice. Lennart later said that the director, Vincent Donahue, "read some pages at my house in Malibu one day and went wild about them. He called Mary Martin and later Ray Stark (Brice's son-in-law), and the thing just snowballed. Ray wanted to do it as a play and I agreed just to please him. Well, not altogether. My vanity entered into it; I didn't want anyone else messing around with my idea."

But the production proved to be fraught with problems. It went through four directors, Jerome Robbins, Bob Fosse, Garson Kanin, and then Robbins again. She had to rewrite the script for each; in fact, she claimed that she had rewritten each scene hundreds of times. At one rehearsal, Barbra Streisand read a scene in which she was supposed to cry. When Robbins asked her why she did not, she replied that she could not cry with those words. According to Jule Styne, Lennart stood up and said: "I don't blame you, Miss Streisand. They're terrible words. And they're mine." When all the revisions had been made, Lennart said that it had been "a deflating, ego-crushing experience."[35]

Once it opened, it was, of course, a smash. (It played on Broadway for more than 1,300 performances.) Lennart's agent, Lucy Kroll, wrote to her: "Again I salute you, darling, for a brilliant job that you did, although it was a gigantic effort and a tremendous physical and emotional sacrifice on your part. As I had told you once when you were ready to check out, I knew you could not bear to desert this work and it would kill you if it had been done without you—and so we have a happy ending." Lennart told Scheuer: "And yet, now I've done one play, I can't wait to do another. There's a kind of excitement and absorption . . . that doesn't happen in pictures." She thought that playwriting might provide her with the opportunity to learn whether she, as a writer and person, had something to say. *Funny Girl* may also have been the first script into which she poured her personal feelings. She later said to her friend Fay Kanin: "Ray thinks 'Funny Girl' is Fanny. And Barbra [Streisand] thinks it's her. But it's really me."[36]

Though Lennart contemplated several play projects, her finances dictated that she focus on the certainty that screenwriting provided. She still commanded $100,000 per picture. She wrote a script titled "The Old Man and Me" (M-G-M), which was not produced; a comedy, *Fitzwilly* (Mirisch Brothers, 1967); and adapted *Funny Girl* for the screen (Columbia, 1968). After viewing the first cut of *Funny Girl,* she sent a six-page, single-spaced memo to producer Ray Stark. "I think," she began, "we have a hell of a fine picture." But, she continued: "There are a few overall things I don't like, and a great many small and possibly unimportant ones. Perhaps some of the small points bother me and no one else, but I have to look at things through my own narrow writer's eyes. So here goes." Her two overall big points concerned the big musical numbers, which did not seem as good on-screen as onstage; and the excessive number of close-ups, particularly of Streisand. Her small points concerned the pauses and emphases of the actors when they spoke her dialogue.[37] Very few of the changes she suggested were incorporated.

Funny Girl was her last movie credit. Though she remained very much in demand and continued to command $100,000 a script, her projects did not reach the screen. In 1966, she was given the Laurel Award for career achievement by the Writers Guild of America West (WGAW), but looking back on her career, she regretted that she had not done more substantive, original work. She once asked Dunne why they continually agreed to adapt mediocre books and rewrite others' scripts. "We're both of us," she said, "better writers than the guys who wrote the material we're adapting. Why do we always have to start with someone else's ideas? Why can't we write something that's original with us from start to finish?"[38] The answer, of course, was that they were paid a very high salary for those adaptations.

In 1970, eighteen years after her testimony, Lennart was interviewed by the actor Robert Vaughn, who was writing a doctoral dissertation on the motion picture blacklist. She told him:

> I believe with all my heart that it was wrong to cooperate with this terrible Committee in any way, and I believe that I was wrong. I believe I did a minimum of damage, but I still believe it was wrong. I had a much bigger reaction to it than I thought I would. . . . It was shame and guilt and nothing else. I've never gotten over it. I've always felt like an inferior citizen because of this. . . . I am able to comfort myself by saying I hurt nobody, but I'm aware that this is a comfort device.

After her death, John Harding told Navasky: "Her final decision was one she regretted all her life. [It] was based on pressure from me and her lawyer."[39]

On January 25, 1971, she was killed in an automobile crash. Charles Champlin wrote about her: "She was a quietly intense craftsman who agonized toward perfection—and who then fought like a tigress to protect the words she knew were at last the right ones."[40]

6

Ring Lardner Jr. and the Hollywood Blacklist

Ring Lardner Jr., scion of a distinguished author and himself a successful screenwriter (winning an Academy Award for *Woman of the Year*), joined the Hollywood section of the Communist Party and participated in a number of political and labor activities prior to 1945. Subpoenaed by the House Committee on Un-American Activities in 1947, he was imprisoned and blacklisted when he refused to answer the Committee's questions in the required manner. While blacklisted (1947–1962), he wrote a novel, several forgettable movies, and many scripts that were not made into films. He also, with Ian Hunter, wrote dozens of scripts for the television series *The Adventures of Robin Hood, The Adventures of Sir Lancelot,* and *The Buccaneers.* Finally off the blacklist, he won a second Academy Award (for *M*A*S*H*), wrote another novel, a family memoir, and a personal memoir; and he was cited and awarded many times as a man of heroism and courage. His speeches and articles on the blacklist helped educate a younger generation. "Hundreds of lives have been scarred by the blacklist," he wrote, "and even I, who have managed to survive it more successfully than most, would not claim that being on it has any compensations to outweigh the penalties and frustrations."[1]

Ring Lardner Jr.'s official path to the blacklist began on October 30, 1947, at 10:30 a.m. At that appointed half hour, he, as a subpoenaed witness, one of nineteen "unfriendlies" subpoenaed, and the ninth, and, along with Adrian Scott, the most low-key and soft-spoken of the eleven who would testify, faced the first question from Robert E. Stripling, chief investigator of the House Committee on Un-American Activities.

Because Chairman J. Parnell Thomas (R-NJ) had been juggling the previously announced lineup of witnesses, Lardner was caught by surprise when his name was called: "I was not pleased with this turn of events. For one thing, I am not a particularly articulate person and do not seek opportunities to speak in public. I was worried about what kind of presence I would make before the Committee."[2] He told me, during an interview: "I had no confidence in my capacity to outduel the Committee verbally."[3]

After a few biographical queries, Lardner intervened to ask permission to read a statement. He was told he could do so at the end of his testimony. Lardner's statement consisted of two parts: a defense of his Americanism and an attack on the Committee's un-Americanism. In the first part, he equated one's attachment to democracy to one's true Americanism and evoked his family as exemplars: "My father was a writer in the best tradition of American literature. That tradition is very closely allied to the democratic ideal in American life." Two of his brothers, he continued, "were killed in separate chapters of the same great struggle to preserve that democratic ideal," one in the Spanish Civil War and the other in World War II. He did not make any claim to his father's genius or his brothers' courage, but he did maintain that everything he had done or written "had been in keeping with the spirit that governed their work, their lives, and their deaths. . . . My record [in Hollywood] includes no anti-democratic work or act, no spoken or written expression of anti-Semitism, anti-Negro feeling or opposition to American democratic principles as I understand them." He then compared the atmosphere in allegedly "Communist-riddled" Hollywood to that of the witch-hunting atmosphere in Washington, DC: "Compared to what I have seen and heard in this room, Hollywood is a citadel of freedom. Here un-American sentiments are freely expressed and their spokesmen heartily congratulated. Here there is such a fear of free speech that men are forbidden to read their statements and are cut off in mid-sentence lest they expose too much of what is going on here to the public." As a result of what he had seen and heard, he concluded, he feared the coming of a blacklist and censorship.[4] (Fifty years later, on the fiftieth anniversary of the hearings, Lardner read his statement for the first time.)

After he had, in accordance with the Nineteen's prearranged strategy, side-stepped the first key question—"Are you a member of the Screen Writers Guild [SWG]?"—he was told he would not be allowed to read his statement if he continued to refuse to directly answer the Committee's questions. Impatient with Lardner's avoidance of a simple "yes" to Stripling's question about membership in the SWG, Thomas began to badger Lardner. Failing to get the answer he wanted, Thomas told Stripling: "All right, put the next question. Go to the sixty-four-dollar question." Stripling asked Lardner if he was a member of the Communist Party. Lardner, in his reply, neatly summarized the position of the Nineteen: "It seems to me that you are trying to discredit the Screen Writers Guild through me, and the motion picture industry through the Screen Writers Guild, and our whole practice of freedom of expression." An angry Thomas again intervened, saying: "Anybody would be proud to answer [that question]—any real American would be proud to answer that question." In perhaps the most quoted lines from those hearings, Lardner quietly responded: "It depends on the circumstances. I could answer it, but I would hate myself in the morning." Thomas ordered Lardner to leave the witness chair, and, when Lardner did not immediately do so, Thomas ordered the sergeant-at-arms to remove him. Committee investigator Louis J. Russell then introduced into evidence a Communist Party registration card, allegedly issued to Lardner in 1944.[5] Lardner told me that he had, prior to taking the witness stand, something like that phrase in mind, but he was not sure he could use it. In a later interview, Lardner commented on his memorable phrase:

I waited until he [Thomas] drew a breath, determined to get one parsible sentence into the record in order to justify the efforts of my childhood English teachers. What I meant, therefore, was that I would subsequently reproach myself if I ever yielded to the committee's terms entirely. I have always associated the words "I'll hate myself in the morning" with a situation in which a previously chaste woman is succumbing to the indecent blandishments of a scoundrel and very likely launching herself on the road to prostitution. That is the analogy I wished to suggest.

In that interview, he emphasized that he had not refused to answer any questions: "The transcript shows that I was interrupted every time I started to speak, sometimes after only one or two words. What I did do was refuse to submit to a yes-or-no limitation after the committee had given its 'friendly' witnesses absolute latitude."[6]

The next month, Lardner was fired from his screenwriting position at Twentieth Century-Fox and, along with the nine other uncooperative witnesses, charged with contempt of Congress and blacklisted from the motion picture industry. Three years later, he and the other members of the Ten were found guilty of contempt of Congress, and Lardner was sentenced to a one-year term of imprisonment and fined one thousand dollars. (The eleventh "unfriendly" witness, Bertolt Brecht, answered all the Committee's questions, was not cited for contempt, and immediately departed from the United States.)

An Apologia

Why does the world need another look at a member of the Hollywood Ten, especially one who has written extensively on this phase of his life? Why is it valuable to recall this ancient history? I can provide no better answer than the one Lardner gave when asked the same question: "Because our nation has moved through two centuries in a continuous cycle from liberty to repression and back. And there is no more reason now to relax our vigilance than there was in the days when many people thought we had then a Roosevelt revolution culminating in a grand alliance and the unconditional surrender of the forces of hate, intolerance and aggression."[7]

Different personalities offer different perspectives on the blacklist, and Lardner's experience is, in its own way, as illuminating as Dalton Trumbo's.[8] While writing Trumbo's biography, I was struck by the steady, rational, thoughtful voice of Lardner, his close friend. I then reread the summary of my impressions of Lardner after I interviewed him in 1976, in which I noted that he was "the most intelligent interviewee so far. He has a fine memory and excellent insights. He is not a very emotional person; he is detached and seems impersonal. There was no apparent bitterness." (I had had an appointment to interview Trumbo two weeks earlier, but he died a few days before we could meet.) I then reread the family biography he wrote and his own memoir, and I came to the belated conclusion that Lardner, in his quiet way, played a significant role in creating the Hollywood Ten, exposing the blacklist, and preserving, in his writings and speeches, the essence of what the Ten had tried to do.

Trumbo and Lardner were complete opposites. They faced the same blacklist but responded to it differently. Trumbo fought it tooth and nail and broke through triumphantly, getting screen credits for two hugely successful 1960 films (*Spartacus* [Universal, 1960] and *Exodus* [United Artists, 1960]). Lardner did it more quietly, when he wrote the second insider account of the blacklist experience (1961),[9] but he had to wait another three years for a screen credit. Both saw the humorous sides of the world in which they lived, but Lardner's commentaries were drier and more ironic. Both wanted to free themselves from screenwriting to write novels, but neither could survive financially with any other form of writing. Finally, their backgrounds were utterly different. Trumbo emerged from a lower-middle-class Colorado family and clawed his way to the top of his profession. Lardner's ascent was much easier.

The Path to Hollywood and the Communist Party

A chubby, garrulous child, Lardner grew into a tall, slender, bespectacled man, taciturn and witty. Following his prep school years, he was, he wrote, "described as laconic, reserved and less than articulate," and some of his friends in Hollywood called him "the Indian." His father and namesake was a highly regarded writer, the descendant of an English family that had settled in colonial Pennsylvania in 1740. The Abbotts, the family of his wife, Ellis, had arrived in the Massachusetts colony in 1642. She graduated from Smith College, began a teaching career, and met her future husband in 1907. They married four years later. They had four sons, and all four became writers. The senior Lardner bequeathed to his four sons, Lardner wrote: "intellectual curiosity with a distinctly verbal orientation, taciturnity, a lack of emotional display, an appreciation of the ridiculous. It was a matter of course that you mastered the fundamentals of reading and writing at the age of four, and by six reading books was practically a full-time occupation." Indeed, reading was "the main leisure-time activity" of the Lardner family. In addition, the senior Lardner provided his sons with "informal guidance" in newspaper writing.[10]

Lardner's unofficial path to the blacklist began at Princeton University, where he joined the Socialist Club and campaigned for Norman Thomas, the Socialist Party candidate for president. He then dropped out of college and in the summer of 1934 traveled to the Soviet Union, where he enrolled in two sociology courses at the Anglo-American Institute at the University of Moscow. He told his mother, "I have never been so enthused about any place in my life" and that he found the academic work much more interesting than at Princeton. He also noted, "It is much too trite to be a communist around here."[11]

When he returned to the United States, he became a reporter for the *New York Daily Mirror*. There he met Ian Hunter, who would become his closest friend and frequent collaborator. Hunter was British-born, and those who knew him describe him as charming, fun, and sophisticated, with a quiet charisma.[12]

Lardner joined the movie industry when the father of a friend secured him a job in the publicity department of Selznick International, and in 1936 he moved to Hollywood, where he was drafted as a screenwriter. He joined the Screen Writers Guild, which was fighting for its existence against a company union, and Budd Schulberg, one of his traveling companions in Russia, recruited him for the Communist Party. Lardner carefully studied the works of Marx, Engels, and Lenin. He later said that his conversion to Marxism was "a purely intellectual process."[13] And he wrote to his mother, "I wish that you along with many millions [of] others would at least take the trouble to understand what Marxism-Leninism is and then dislike it from a more proper point of view."[14] Members of the Hollywood Left spoke highly of Lardner's knowledge of Marx. He also served on the executive board of the SWG and on the editorial board of its journal, *The Screen Writer*. For that journal, he wrote a scathing article attacking director Cecil B. DeMille, the doyen of Hollywood reactionaries.

When his mother informed him that Jim, his youngest brother, was going to Spain as a war correspondent and bemoaned the war, Lardner replied: "Who, in the long run, is the pacifist, you or Jim? I say Jim, because he is doing his share to hold off the next world war until you and all those Americans who want to isolate this country from world affairs until it is too late, realize that we can stop the war now without striking a single military blow. How? By adopting a policy of collective security."[15] A few months later, in response to his mother's criticism of Stalin, he wrote, inaccurately, "He has devoted his whole life to speaking, writing and acting for peace, democracy and socialism."[16]

Lardner worked for Selznick International, Republic, Warner Brothers, RKO, M-G-M, and Twentieth Century-Fox. He began his career with uncredited contributions to *A Star Is Born* (United Artists, 1939) and *Nothing Sacred* (United Artists, 1939). For the first, he and Schulberg came up with the famous closing line, "I am Mrs. Norman Maine." For the second, he and George Oppenheimer devised the final scene. After that, he earned eight cowriting credits. Three were with Hunter; two with Michael Kanin; and one each with Leopold Atlas, Philip Dunne, and Albert Maltz. It is interesting to note that all of Lardner's cowriters were liberals or Communists: Hunter and Maltz would be blacklisted; Schulberg and Atlas would become informers; and Kanin and Dunne were liberals who publicly opposed the Committee on Un-American Activities in October 1947.

Lardner not only had partners who were politically congenial, his first seven assignments all had amenable social content. The first two, *Meet Dr. Christian* (RKO, 1939) and *The Courageous Dr. Christian* (RKO, 1940), told about a doctor who cared about the poor. In *Arkansas Judge* (Republic, 1941), a lawyer saves a poor scrubwoman from the machinations of a venal banker's daughter. He and Michael Kanin shared the Academy Award for Best Original Screenplay for *Woman of the Year* (M-G-M, 1942), which told the story of a woman who put her career ahead of her marriage, until, that is, the studio had the ending rewritten to depict her trying, by cooking breakfast, to become a more conventional wife. (Lardner and Kanin strongly objected, to no avail.) Three war films followed: *The Cross of Lorraine* (M-G-M, 1943) about French prisoners of war who escape and join the resistance; *Tomorrow the World* (United Artists, 1944), about a German member of Hitler Youth who is brought to the United States and taught to reject Nazism; and *Cloak and Dagger* (Warner Brothers, 1946), about the Organization of Secret Services. (He and Trumbo wrote, on speculation, another script about the French resistance, *The Fishermen of Beaudrais,* which did not sell.) He was working on a melodrama for Twentieth Century-Fox, titled "Britannia Mews" (released in 1949 as *Forbidden Street*) when he was subpoenaed. It would be his only sole screen credit until *M*A*S*H,* twenty-one years later.

He told me that he and his screenwriter friends were very aware that they could not get too much realism into their scripts, but they realized that film was an important medium, one in which a comparatively small number of Communist writers would have a greater influence than they could have had working, say, in the automobile industry. Besides, he enjoyed the creative process of script writing.

His FBI dossier indicates that prior to the war he was very active politically, and, as a result, he was not successful in finding a civilian war job. After several failed efforts, he was hired by the Photographic Division of the Signal Corps, for a ninety-day trial period, but just as it was expiring, he received an offer from Twentieth Century-Fox to write a script for Otto Preminger, based on the diary of former US ambassador to Germany William E. Dodd and his daughter's memoir, *Through Embassy Eyes.* While he was writing it, Preminger drafted him to rewrite the dialogue for Clifton Webb's character in *Laura,* to make that character wittier. By the time Lardner returned to the Dodd project, Darryl F. Zanuck had lost interest in historical films and aborted the movie, but he liked Lardner's script and raised his salary.

In the spring of 1945, he and his first wife decided to separate and divorce. One year later he signed a lucrative contract with Fox and married the widow of his brother David. He now had two families: his former wife (Silvia) and their two children (Peter and Ann); and a new wife (Frances) and her two children (Kate and Joe). A fifth child, James, was born to Ring and Frances in 1948.

The Domestic Cold War, Committee on Un-American Activities, and the Hollywood Ten

Lardner was one of several writers, directors, and actors in Hollywood who, after the war, wanted to find a vehicle for making socially relevant movies. In 1946, he, Dalton Trumbo, Allan Scott, Richard Collins, Hugo Butler, and John Garfield purchased stock in Xanadu Film Corporation, founded by Bob Roberts. When the company folded the following year, Roberts, in partnership with Garfield, founded Roberts Productions, Inc. Lardner, who was under a presumably exclusive contract with Fox, signed a contract with Roberts Productions, Inc., to write an original story and screenplay titled "The Great Indoors." He was to be paid $40,000 ($510,000 in today's dollars), in two installments, and receive 5 percent of the net profits of the finished film. It is a romantic-comedy-triangle, along the lines of the Cary Grant/Katharine Hepburn screwball comedies of the 1930s, which satirizes the natural food/hearty physical exercise fad and demonstrates the superiority of the man of intellect over the man of action. He completed the script, was paid, but the movie was never made. Periodically, over the years, Roberts would contact Lardner about updating it, but Roberts could not find a financial backer for the project.[17] Lardner also made occasional efforts to peddle it.

Everything changed for Lardner and the other left-wing activists in the spring of 1947, when the Committee on Un-American Activities held executive-session hearings in Los Angeles, as the opening wedge of its investigation of the "Communist Infiltration of the Motion-Picture Industry." A few months later, dozens of subpoenas were issued, including nineteen to those with "subversive" histories. These Nineteen were a diverse group in terms of their personalities, relationships, and success. They were all men, mainly screenwriters. They were of different generations, and few could be called close friends. Two of the closest, Trumbo and Lardner, had been moving away from the Party, but, given the prominent positions they had held in the SWG, they deemed it likely they would be subpoenaed. They discussed their situation and concluded that if they were called, they could not admit Party membership, because the studios would surely fire those under contract, and had they admitted membership, they could not, then, refuse to answer questions about other Party members. They could not deny membership, because fifteen were or had been members of the Communist Party, and there were sufficient informers around to make them liable to a perjury charge. They decided that the best strategy was to refuse to answer that question (and the prior question about membership in the SWG) and to challenge the right of the Committee to ask it. They believed that using the First Amendment protection of the right to freely associate and speak was superior to invoking the Fifth Amendment privilege against self-incrimination. The use of the latter amendment would have put them in the position of saying that it was a crime to be a Guild member or a Communist, and it would not have given them the platform to challenge the Committee's right to exist and ask questions about people's political affiliations. So, they convinced the other subpoenaed men to say: "I refuse to answer your question because it violates my First Amendment rights." Such a response would have been neat and clear. However, at a subsequent meeting of the group, Robert W. Kenny, one of the attorneys, argued that an outright refusal would work against them at their jury trial for contempt of Congress. He suggested that they prepare statements challenging the Committee, ask to read them, sidestep the direct questions about affiliation, and, when challenged as unresponsive, claim that they were answering the question but in their own way. In retrospect, of course, Lardner and Trumbo saw that this tactic made them seem argumentative and evasive, undermined their liberal supporters, and left them open to anti-Communist critics for their lack of "candor."

After he was fired by Fox, Lardner sued the company for breach of contract. (The suit was finally settled in 1955, for $10,000. Lardner netted $4,867.16.) While that case dragged through the courts, he found that some independent production companies were willing to hire some of the proscribed Ten. Two liberal actors, Burgess Meredith and Franchot Tone, engaged him to work on an adaptation of John Steinbeck's story "The Pastures of Heaven," but they could not secure financing. Lardner, however, was paid $10,000 (in cash) for his work. He rewrote the dialogue for *Up Front* (Universal, 1950), based on Bill Mauldin's

World War II cartoons of GI Willie and GI Joe. His new agent, Ingo Preminger, then secured a deal for Lardner with Lazar Wechsler, a Swiss producer, and Lardner traveled to Europe to work on *Four Days Leave*, for which he received a dialogue credit. (After 1951, the US Department of State routinely denied blacklisted people permission to leave the country.) He also did some work for the King Brothers, who provided much work on the black market, particularly for Trumbo. They were not, Lardner said, "unpleasant people to work with," but they did not seem particularly sympathetic to the situation of the blacklistees.[18] Lardner also wrote a script for Joseph Shaftel, "Star in the Wind," about the Israelis' war against the Arabs after the creation of the Jewish state. It is interesting for the ongoing debate within it between the realists and the idealists. In the end, the realist accepts the need for idealism.[19] It was not made.

Those clandestine jobs enabled him to feed his new family until April 1950, when the Supreme Court declined to review the convictions of the Ten. To maintain the family while he was in prison, he was forced to sell his newly purchased home, at a net loss of $9,000. His wit extended to the advertisement he wrote: "House for Sale/Owner Going to Prison! One of the taciturn Ten offers 10-room house for immediate sacrifice sale. . . . $26,000 in direct sale by owner; $11,000 cash required." Lardner gave part of the proceeds to Silvia, but for many years he was unable to provide her with much in the way of financial support. She voluntarily waived all legal claims stemming from the divorce settlement and supported herself and their two children from her income as a full-time contractor.

Between the hearings and prison, Lardner spoke and wrote on behalf of the Ten. In one interview, he stated that he took the position he did because he wanted to tell the Committee that no one has to reveal what trade union or political party he belongs to, and because "I hate the purposes and methods of men like Thomas and [John] Rankin [D-MS], and I wanted in the course of my answers to challenge the committee at the very foundation of its existence: its asserted power to enforce answers in violation of the Bill of Rights."[20] On his way to prison, in June 1950, he spoke in New York City at a gathering sponsored by the National

Council of the Arts, Sciences and Professions. He told the audience that the Ten were being punished for holding opinions "which the government considers dangerous to its purposes, especially when they exist in the minds of writers and directors with a measure of influence on popular attitudes." And he concluded: "The real crime for which we face imprisonment is an honorable one, and I would like to be given full credit for having committed it."[21]

Prison

During his prison term (at the Federal Correctional Institution, Danbury, Connecticut), Lardner contemplated his future prospects. He was certain that he would not be welcomed back to his prescreenwriter occupations, journalism and advertising. He had no experience writing novels or plays. And writing for magazines seemed to be too difficult, because he would have had to use an assumed name, one without a list of prior publications. "The situation," Lardner wrote, "clearly demanded a readjustment for which my background had done nothing to equip me. When you are descended from a Lardner who sat on the Governor's Council in colonial Pennsylvania, and an Abbott who fought with the minutemen at Lexington and Bunker Hill, you find it hard to accept the 'un-American' designation. And the fact that I bore, through no fault of my own, a well-known name in American letters simply made it the most easily remembered among the 'Hollywood Ten' by people who read about the case in the newspapers."[22] Ironically, one of the Ten's many critics made the same point: "Here is an American citizen who enjoyed advantages far beyond those which are the lot of the average young man; he came from a talented family and showed unusual talents himself; he received the best possible education and used it to acquire profitable jobs; he had every reason for following the political philosophy shared by the vast majority of American citizens. But like a few others of his generation, young Ring decided that this philosophy was not for him."[23]

His ten months in prison were, he claimed, marked by an "absence of any marked degree of pleasantness or unpleasantness," and "the conversation is good, if one is selective."[24] He was assigned the job of clerking in the parole department. As with the other members of the Ten, his letters are mainly filled with his thoughts about getting a parole, family news, and what he will do once he is released. But the parole possibility, narrow to begin with, was dealt a fatal blow when one of the Ten, Edward Dmytryk, shortly after being incarcerated at Mill Point (in West Virginia), broke ranks with the others and issued an affidavit stating that he was not, at the time of the hearings, a member of the Communist Party and pledging his allegiance to the United States. (Six months later, he began his rehabilitation process, which required him to reappear before the Committee and name names. Lardner was not one of them, but he was named by fourteen others.) When he heard the news, Lardner wrote to Frances: "Eddie's manifesto was a blow which will serve to fortify my cynicism for the future. . . . But this is so craven—and so injurious to those who, with much more time at stake [Dmytryk and Herbert Biberman had been sentenced to six months], won't go along with his surrender."[25]

But, when he learned that the newly released Biberman had reestablished the Hollywood Ten defense office, Lardner reacted negatively, writing to Frances:

> I want you to convey an earnest message to Herbert, who I hear is still keeping office hours and organizing Heaven-knows-what activities in behalf of a nonexistent cause. . . . [T]his is not the first time I have advocated a cease-fire of energies but at least this time there can be no even remotely plausible argument in rebuttal. Now that the parole issue no longer exists and neither, I maintain emphatically, do the Hollywood Ten, there is no constructive direction activity can take. . . . I am resolutely against agitation for agitation's sake. Take publicity for example. It is the one thing we have all had a serious overdose of and the thing most devoutly to be avoided from here on.[26]

As for himself, he was determined not to make any public appearances or take any political action "until my own estimate of my professional (or artistic) standing seems to justify it."[27]

In terms of his professional or artistic standing, he devoted a great deal of thought as to whether he should continue to pursue a screenwriting career. He had, he told Frances, come to the conclusion that "through inheritance, circumstance and my own bad judgements, I got to be something of a public figure before becoming a writer instead of the other way around, and I propose to make a belated effort to restore the proper balance." That meant dedicating himself to becoming a writer of novels and giving up screenwriting:

> I think I would have abandoned movie writing by now even if I hadn't been pushed out of it. One reason I clung to it was that I couldn't accept the stock formulation that movie work was all prostitution in contrast to the virtuous respectability of "serious" writing. I still don't accept it. But the catch about Hollywood is that you have to be extremely good at it . . . in order to surmount the restrictions and limitations. And I was never, nor I think could be, better than a fair screenwriter, though money success and a natural hesitancy to face facts obscured this realization for a long time.[28]

He began work on a project he had previously researched, a witty satire of the Catholic Church and true-believers of all sorts. He asked Frances to send him his research notes, and using a pencil and a pad of paper—a prison typewriter could not be used for personal work—Lardner began to write. It was an unusual subject for him, one that may have been, to some degree, inspired by his thoughts on Communist Party membership. He said he was curious about ways in which some Catholics followed the church's doctrines faithfully, whereas others adhered to some, going to mass, taking holy communion, and not adhering to others, virginity, contraception, divorce, and abortion. What if, he thought, I paired "a nominal Catholic with an idealistic and utterly sincere convert?"[29]

Lardner served nine and a half months of his sentence, getting time off for good behavior and "meritorious good time"—his reward for his typing, spelling, and grammar skills. On his release, he was given a seventy-two-dollar railroad coach ticket to Los Angeles. When he returned to Hollywood in the spring of 1951, he found an altered atmosphere. The new round of Un-American Activities Committee hearings had everyone running for cover, and black-market offers had become extremely rare. He did get one job, rewriting the script for the Joseph Losey–directed noir *The Big Night* (United Artists, 1951).[30] But pickings were slim, and Ring and Frances and their three children, along with the Trumbos, Hunters, and Butlers, moved to Mexico. Shortly after arriving, he wrote to his children Peter and Ann: "I think we will probably stay here for a while anyway, perhaps moving to a smaller house in a less costly neighborhood. I have been doing some good work on my book but I haven't made a penny since I've been here and this is a situation which must be corrected soon."[31] He received news that he had won his breach of contract suit but that Fox was appealing the decision.

Life and Work on the Blacklist

Lardner did not play a role in the effort, led by Trumbo, to break the motion picture blacklist by exploiting the black market for movie scripts, nor did he join in any of the class-action suits by blacklistees against the studios. He did, however, remain politically active, supporting groups dedicated to abolishing the Committee and those fighting for civil rights for Blacks. Though the FBI kept Lardner under surveillance until 1970, issuing periodic reports on his activities and whereabouts, the Bureau regularly reported that they were unaware of any Communist Party activities or connections.[32]

The Lardners stayed in Mexico for six months, departing for Connecticut, where they lived with his mother for two years, before moving to New York City. There, the Lardners became part of an Upper West Side community of blacklistees, including the Marzanis, Hunters, Mostels, Kaplans, Krafts, and Rapfs. He adapted two of his father's stories for television, fronted by his older brother, and a magazine article, fronted by a friend, but none succeeded. Frances was able to continue her work as an actress on the stage and, for a while, on television, but she soon found herself blacklisted. Her past politics might have explained this proscription, but her name had not appeared on any list nor had she been named in any testimony. Lardner thought that she had acquired her unemployability by marriage. There was no black market for blacklisted actors, and she never regained the career she had lost. Her daughter, Kate, thinks she suffered far more from blacklisting than her father did; it shook her confidence in herself.

Lardner spent his first two years out of prison writing his novel, and the family lived on the proceeds from his brother's life insurance policy. *The Ecstasy of Owen Muir* was rejected by seven or eight publishers before it was accepted by the small firm of Cameron and Kahn and published in 1954. An English edition was published by the well-known Jonathan Cape. Though the novel was translated into several languages, it did not provide a satisfactory income, and he could not afford to devote another two years to another novel. When he realized that the book was not going to receive a positive response from the critics, he wrote his daughter Ann: "in the U.S. nowadays, books are treated according to who wrote them, who published them and whose toes they step on, rather than according to whether they are good, bad or indifferent in themselves."[33]

The novel could also be called the odyssey of Owen Muir. Owen is an earnest but hapless man, yearning for an end to doubt, but has difficulty finding a principle or doctrine to live by. He goes from pacifist, to capitalist, to Catholic convert. The book is replete with lengthy, albeit witty, debates between Owen and his father, the prison warden, his wife, and a variety of political and religious types about principles and doctrines. Ultimately, Owen finds love and the Catholic Church in the person of April, who picks and chooses which church rules she will obey. Owen, who can never do anything by halves, becomes more devout than the pope. Owen and April's conflicts over intercourse, birth control, and abortion widen the chasm growing between them. Meanwhile, in the background, Lardner is offering a severe critique of the Cold War United States and a rogues' gallery of anti-Communists, all of whom are portrayed as opportunists, hypocrites, or dogmatists. There is one seemingly dogmatic Communist who turns out to be an FBI infiltrator, and a dedicated left-wing activist who is willing to go to jail in defense of her beliefs. Lardner's research into the church and its spokespeople is impressive, and he condemns them out of the words of their own mouths. And, though he does not directly satirize the Communist Party, it is not too difficult to discern that he is not just talking about the Catholic Church when he has one of its spokesmen say that whatever "the true church" says must be true. And the church is "true" because "the Lord made it very clear."[34] Simply substitute "party" for "church" and "history" for "the Lord," and the implication is clear. (Lenin once said, "The Teaching of Marx is all powerful because it is true.")[35] Unable to find a sustainable moral footing, and to free himself from any more doubt and debate, Owen becomes a Trappist monk.

The book was not widely reviewed, but it did receive favorable comments in three left-leaning journals: *Frontier, Nation,* and *New Republic.*[36]

Lardner managed to keep himself financially afloat during the 1950s by writing dozens of televisions scripts and several movie scripts. He was fortunate in his television work, earning a steady income and mainly writing about heroic figures fighting against evildoers, albeit, as he once noted, they tend to use "extra-legal" means to right the wrongs.[37] He was much less fortunate in his movie projects, being saddled mainly with forgettable topics and projects that aborted. The black market of the 1950s was replete with honest producers looking for a discount, would-be producers without reliable financing, and outright scoundrels. Lardner encountered all three types. He found that he had even less control over content than he had during his years in the studio system, and he had to expend a great deal of time and effort trying to collect what was owed him.

In 1954, Lardner and Hunter were approached by Hannah Weinstein, an American leftist, who had just formed a production company and who was very friendly with a number of blacklistees. She had employed several of them to write and direct her first expatriate series, *Colonel March of Scotland Yard.* Her new company, Sapphire Productions, planned to produce several adventure series for British television, and she ended up employing sixteen blacklisted writers.[38] Albert Ruben, the script editor for Sapphire, told me that this employment policy was not an attempt to break the blacklist: "Hannah hired a number of blacklisted writers because they were available, good, and she was pleased to be in a position to offer them employment when they needed it. They benefited as did she."[39] They enhanced, pointed out Tise Vahimagi, the sociological subtext of what would have been simply a "tales of the greenwood series."[40]

Lardner wrote the pilot episode for the first show, *The Adventures of Robin Hood,* and he and Hunter wrote thirty-nine in all. They wrote ten scripts for *The Adventures of Sir Lancelot;* three for *The Buccaneers,* three for *Four Just Men;* and three for *Sword of Freedom.*[41] (They also wrote the pilot episode of *The Highwayman* for George King Productions.) They used a half dozen pseudonyms, and they were paid $1,250 for each *Robin Hood* script. (Though there was no blacklist in the United Kingdom, the pseudonyms were necessary to avoid the network and ad-agency watchdogs when the programs appeared on television in the United States.) Lardner wrote Ann: "For all its failings the Robin Hood show is a great success in terms of its percentage ratings and will probably be renewed for another year, which means steady work if we want it."[42] They quickly discovered that an elaborate series of precautions were required to keep from being discovered, from regular pseudonym changes to a series of bank accounts. As Lardner noted, "Cashing a check made out to an imaginary person is not a simple matter when your own name cannot appear as an endorser. You have to open a bank account under your alias."[43] And, as Trumbo discovered, one had to keep very precise records to avoid being charged with tax fraud.

Lardner and Hunter's first encounter with the movie black market was not a happy one. In 1957, they adapted Robb White's *Our Virgin Island,* a fairy tale about a couple that buys a small island and attempts to live without the comforts of modern life, starring John Cassavetes and featuring Sidney Poitier. According to Lardner, "Everyone, including the director [Pat Jackson], professed to be delighted with our script, and then he proceeded to rewrite every scene and roll up an astounding record of 5% improvement to 95% damage."[44] He did not like the finished product, released as *Virgin Island* (British Lion, 1958).

In January 1958, Lardner and Hunter were paid $15,000 to adapt Harold Flender's novel *Paris Blues* for Sam Shaw. It was a congenial project, a romantic drama involving two expatriate jazz musicians, but there was a series of misunderstandings on both sides, including the producer's claim that Lardner and Hunter had refused to do rewrites. They claimed that they were ready and willing to do so.[45] (It was rewritten by, among others, former blacklistee Walter Bernstein, directed by former blacklistee Martin Ritt, and released by United Artists in 1961.) Lardner and Hunter had no better luck writing a script for M-G-M, "See No Evil," about a deaf boy on the run from a crime he did not commit. It was to be directed by Nicholas Ray, and they were to be paid $15,000. It was not made.[46]

A fine example of what Lardner termed the "sleeveless errands" (deals with unreliable producers) of the black market occurred in 1958. It began with a letter from Trumbo, who was by this time receiving many more offers than he could undertake. He had recommended Lardner for a comedy laid in Mexico, for a Mexican producer, Pedro Galvan. Galvan telegraphed Lardner with an offer of $20,000 plus 5 percent of the producer's gross to adapt a novel (*Casa El Paraiso*) about a phony crown prince who dupes Mexican society. Interested, but wary, Lardner wrote to Albert Maltz, who was living in Mexico and had had some dealings with Galvan. Maltz replied that Galvan seemed "straight and good" but that he tended to overenthusiasm. Do not come here, Maltz warned, unless you are absolutely certain he will pay your expenses. When Galvan did guarantee expenses, Lardner procured a tourist card, was vaccinated, hired a woman to read the still-untranslated novel and give him an oral synopsis, and made an airplane reservation. He then received a telegram from Galvan telling him to postpone the trip until further notice, but Galvan did send a translation. Lardner, after reading the translation, replied that he could not faithfully adapt the novel to the screen, he would have to be given a free hand to create a new screen story, the deal must be made immediately, and he must receive the bulk of the $20,000 up front. He did not hear from Galvan again until 1962, when the producer offered him another project about the Ballet Folklorico.[47]

Two more reputable producers, Marcello Girosi and Carlo Ponti, contracted with Lardner in 1959 to adapt Ferenc Molnar's play *Olympia* as a vehicle for Sophia Loren. It is a portrayal of the Austrian-Hungarian Empire at its peak, focusing on a love affair between an Austrian princess and a captain in the Hungarian army. While writing it, Lardner wrote Hunter: "the most stimulating thing is that I'm almost making it up as I go along; I'm not at all clear on how it's going to end up but I'm the only one who seems to care a hell of a lot about it; the constant injunction is 'Don't try for perfection; make that deadline.'"[48] Lardner finished the script in early June and traveled to Europe in August to make revisions. He wrote to his wife, "I haven't licked the story and I still think it can be licked." The producers, however, "insist that we have enough of a story and all I have to do is write it in such a way as to camouflage the loopholes. But this isn't true and if I wrote it they would see that as clearly as I do now, or else they would just think I had written it badly." He did not think he had solved the major problems.[49] The next year, when the movie was being filmed in Vienna, Lardner could not get away, so he asked Walter Bernstein to front for him. (Bernstein had been blacklisted, but his name had been cleared.) Bernstein was not happy with the assignment. He hated Vienna, and he thought the director, Michael Curtiz, "is insane and, I suspect, senile." The script had to overcome several problems, including rejection by the Production Code Administration, because it included a premarriage seduction scene and a nude scene. In addition, all concerned thought that the last thirty pages were weak. Bernstein rewrote those pages. Lardner responded with a six-page critique. Bernstein attempted to incorporate those suggestions but concluded: "I have no idea how the script is and don't care very much. It seems to me fairly tight, some of it seems funny, and I have no desire to hear of it again for the rest of my life." Released as *A Breath of Scandal,* it bombed at the box office. In a letter to Ann, Lardner called it a "disaster."[50] And, when, during the 1990s, the Writers Guild of America West established a committee to investigate and restore credits to blacklisted writers, Lardner assured the members that they need not bother doing so for *A Breath of Scandal.*

Prospects seemed to be looking up for Lardner in early 1959, when Malcolm Stuart of the Preminger/Stuart agency asked to represent him. Lardner accepted the offer, but nothing significant resulted from it. For one thing, Lardner did not have a number of unproduced scripts to circulate. Stuart did send around "The Great Indoors," but Lardner rejected his idea to propose it as a vehicle for Jerry Lewis. In August 1960, Stuart wrote Lardner that times were still tough for blacklistees, especially those living in the East. "On the other hand," Stuart said, the "lack of activity for you is not at all based on people turning you down. Your reputation here is still excellent and I don't think the barrier is insurmountable."[51]

The number of stymied possibilities and aborted projects, the built-up pressures of the blacklist, the frustrations of trying to collect money owed, financial worries, and the sudden deaths, in early 1960, of his mother, his last surviving brother, and a very close female friend pushed Lardner, at least in his own mind, from serious drinking to alcoholism. He told his daughter Kate: "There was a whole difference between when I drank in my twenties, thirties, and forties and later. . . . I did get drunk quite a bit but I didn't drink every day until [1960]."[52] After that point, he wrote a friend, his attitude toward his drinking altered: "I've regarded myself as at least semi-alcoholic for years but always qualified it in some such phrase as 'responsible drunk' because I've never allowed drinking to interfere with my work or get me in any more serious trouble than sounding foolish at a party."[53] Kate told me that her father was clueless about his alcoholism: he came from a long line of alcoholics, and he had been one since the 1930s, but because of his self-reliance, he would not seek help. (All of Lardner's close friends drank heavily. Hunter had an especially severe problem, often going on benders that rendered him incapable of completing assignments.)

In the depths of despair, Lardner, like dozens of other blacklistees, seriously considered writing a letter to the motion picture industry stating that he had not been a Communist since 1950. He discussed it with Trumbo and with Ingo Preminger, and authorized Preminger to investigate the possibilities. Two weeks later, when he met with Malcolm Stuart, Preminger's partner, Stuart proposed that Lardner might want to write a clearance letter. Apparently, Preminger had not told Stuart about his conversation with Lardner. Lardner was furious: "This sort of thing is almost the ultimate frustration. Desperation drives you across a barrier of conscience and then you find that what is so urgent for you is not pressing enough for one partner to remember to impart it to the other."[54] He ultimately decided not to write such a letter.

Lardner made a significant contribution to the campaign to expose the blacklist when, in the summer of 1961, the editors of the *Saturday Evening Post* asked him to write an article detailing his life on the blacklist. "It seems," he wrote his uncle, "that their readers are dying off at a rapid rate and they've decided that one of the elements they need to attract younger readers is DISSENT. That's where I come in."[55] In the article, he discussed the Ten's response to the Committee, acknowledged his membership in the Communist Party (and stated that he left it in 1950), and reviewed his experiences writing on the black market. Lardner offered a judicious appraisal of what it meant to see the blacklist weakening: "With these various chinks appearing in the iron screen, I find myself increasingly confronted with the social problem of persuading acquaintances outside the movie business that the blacklist still exists for me and all the others who have not made their peace with the industry. In earlier years people were generally too tactful to ask what I was doing; now they are astonished to hear that I am still obliged to respect the confidential nature of the agreements I made with employers." And, he wryly concluded: "if there is an occasional craving for the satisfaction of seeing my name attached to a piece of work, there is always the solace I share with those on the blacklist. We can look at our old movies on television. It is a rare night that you cannot find one of the proscribed names on the still-unaltered credits. Some factor, very likely the smaller screen, has deprived them of the power to subvert."[56]

The editors received nearly four hundred letters in response, most of them uncomplimentary. They printed them in three issues. In the first, seven of ten were negative; in the second, all four were negative; the third consisted of only one letter, from Congressman Francis E. Walter, the chairman of the Committee on Un-American Activities. In fact, Walter had written a very lengthy reply, but the editors printed only a portion of it. (Walter read the entire letter into the *Congressional Record*.) In the printed version, Walter cited six activities that proved Lardner was still a Communist: a letter to *The Worker;* attendance at a dinner honoring Paul Robeson; a book review in *Mainstream;* endorsement of a book about the Abraham Lincoln Battalion; and support of two organizations. Lardner responded only to Walter's letter, noting: "I did not say that I had ceased all political activity or that I had taken the path of contrition prescribed by the committee." As for Walter's allegation that the two organizations—New York Council to Abolish the Un-American Activities Committee and the Emergency Civil Rights Committee—were Communist, that was "utter and easily disprovable nonsense." [57]

Another anti-Communist watchdog, Roy M. Brewer, the ranking anti-Communist in Hollywood, also wrote a lengthy critique, but the editors declined to print it. In it, Brewer stated that Lardner's article was only his latest performance in the service of the Communist Party, and he denied that a blacklist was in operation. Movie studio bosses were simply refusing to hire members of a "world-wide organization of gangsters which is irrevocably dedicated to destroy every government which it does not control." [58]

Most of the other letter writers condemned Lardner for having been a Communist. Some accused him of whining about his reduced standard of living and loss of screen credits. In an unpublished response, Lardner focused on the harm being done to the national interest by people's obsession with the conspiratorial image of Communism. Instead of facing the reality that Marxism is "an intellectual and emotional force that has captured, for good or evil or very possibly a blend of the two, the imagination of half the world, and brought about the greatest social upheavals in history, we think in terms of sinister superhuman plots that somehow lure the Chinese or Cuban masses, like so many lemmings, to their own destruction." This misapprehension is the result of propaganda "as one-sided in its own subtle way, as anything Mr. [Nikita] Khrushchev has been able to devise over his own people." [59]

Dozens of left-oriented people wrote laudatory letters directly to Lardner. Trumbo applauded Lardner's openness: "It is a real coup, and its impact on the present situation can be almost shattering. I really don't think it is possible to overestimate the good it will accomplish, and your approach to the material is, as always, exactly right." [60]

Shortly after the article appeared, Harry Belafonte signed a contract with Lardner and Hunter to write an original screenplay, "a dramatic story set in a locale in the Caribbean to be determined by us, and shall be suitable for the inclusion of musical numbers." It was tentatively titled

"The Girl in the Glass Cage," and they were to be paid $25,000. Belafonte liked the script but not for himself, and the movie was not made.[61]

Despite the article and Trumbo's breakthrough, Lardner's future as a screenwriter remained up in the air. At the end of 1961, however, Robert Whitehead approached Lardner and Hunter to adapt Ben Jonson's *Volpone*, to inaugurate the restored Dawson City opera house, the centerpiece of the Canadian government's plan to revive the Klondike region as a tourist attraction. Afterward, Whitehead intended to move it to Broadway. The project began under bright auspices: Johnny Mercer wrote the songs; David Merrick produced; Bert Lahr and Larry Blyden starred. But Merrick switched his time and attention to *Hello, Dolly,* and his successor, Billy Rose, proved unenthusiastic. Lacking a line of credit and an advertising campaign, *Foxy* closed after nine weeks.

Unblacklisted at Last

In November 1962, Otto Preminger announced that Lardner had been contracted to adapt Patrick Dennis's novel *Genius,* but it was not made. Lardner then did an uncredited rewrite for Preminger's *The Cardinal* (Columbia, 1963), and in 1964 he wrote the first draft for *Ice Station Zebra* (M-G-M, 1968). The tide turned for Lardner in 1964, when Martin Ransohoff hired him to write the script for *The Cincinnati Kid* (M-G-M, 1965), for which he received a cocredit. Though only two other screen credits followed, one, for *M*A*S*H* (Twentieth Century-Fox, 1970), garnered him his second Academy Award. (The other was for his adaptation of Muhammad Ali's autobiography, *The Greatest* [Columbia, 1977].) Lardner continued to write scripts, and he wrote a second novel (*All for Love* [1985]). He was quite well paid for his screen projects, allowing him, according to his son Joe, "to put off selling the house in New Milford [Connecticut], where working on anything was pleasant, to take trips, and to move from a low, dark apartment on West End Avenue in New York to a high, sunny one on Central Park West."[62]

He received many invitations to speak and write about the blacklist, and, in his later years, awards for his stance in 1947. He wrote a biography of his family (1976) and completed his own memoir a few months before he died. In notes he prepared for an appearance at the John Bard Seminar Program in March 1976, he acknowledged his continuing "academic interest in the McCarthy period and the lessons we can learn from it," but he wanted "finally to free my identity from that particular association to whatever extent I can."[63] In 1978, in an essay in the *New York Times*, he reviewed, once again, the Ten's strategy before the Committee, and he denied that the Ten were heroes: "we weren't volunteers and we thought we were going to win."[64] Congressman Henry A. Waxman (D-CA) inserted it into the *Congressional Record*, calling it an example of "a sensitive and compelling essay."[65]

He received many honors in the last years of his life: Laurel Award for distinguished achievement by the Writers Guild of America West; the Ian McLellan Hunter Award for lifetime achievement by the WGA East; Nantucket Film Festival's First Annual Writers Tribute. But, as he told several interviewers over the years, his very best scripts did not make it to the screen. In the Lardner archives there are copies of thirteen unproduced scripts written between 1966 and 2000, including "The Boys of Summer" (about the Brooklyn Dodgers), "The Cradle Will Rock" (Marc Blitzstein's opera), "Death Row Brothers" (lawyer saves two falsely accused half brothers from death penalty), and "The Volunteers" (about the Spanish Civil War). In addition, he worked on three other produced movies without receiving credits. Perhaps his most successful project, and one closest to his heart, was the script he wrote in April 1986 for the fortieth anniversary of the Spanish Civil War, held at Avery Fisher Hall (Lincoln Center, New York City).

Near the end of his life, on the fiftieth anniversary of the 1947 hearings, the four talent guilds that had supported the blacklist honored him, the only surviving member of the Hollywood Ten, at their gala presentation "Hollywood Remembers the Blacklist." When he and Paul Jarrico were presented plaques engraved with the First Amendment, in recognition of their devotion to those words and their fifty-year struggle to uphold them, he said, "It is almost worth fifty years waiting for."[66] He died three years later.

This life of early success and late trial, tribulation, and disappointment may not appear heroic, but the ability to combine financial success with social activity; to withstand the trials of the Committee and the district court with grace and wit; to overcome proscription by the government, the movie studios, and the culture at large; and to emerge successful again as a writer and earn the plaudits of a younger generation, reveals deep reservoirs of courage, tenacity, and a powerful sense of rightness and rectitude. Both Trumbo and Lardner denied they were heroes, but those who watched them endure, day after day, week after week, year after year, believed they were heroic warriors who fought the good fight, paid a huge price for doing so, and resolutely continued the battle. Only a few blacklistees, Trumbo and Lardner among them, regained their status as well-paid, highly regarded screenwriters. But when a new generation of historians came of age in the 1970s and 1980s, all the blacklistees were accorded the respect they deserved for their stance against the Committee, censorship, and blacklisting.

Shedding Light on *Darkness at High Noon*

Fourteen years ago I wrote an article entitled "The Squishiness of Current Blacklist Documentaries." In it I criticized the makers of those documentaries for failing to ask and answer serious questions about their topic. I also noted, though I did not explore, the one-sidedness of those documentaries, that they treat former blacklisted people as heroes. I, too, think of them as heroes. But there is another side to the blacklist: the anti-Communist side. And it is virtually nonexistent in these documentaries.

Darkness at High Noon: The Carl Foreman Documents is the latest in this series of one-sided, heroicizing efforts.[1] But it is unique in two ways: (1) Its target is not the anti-Communists or the studios but an independent producer (Stanley Kramer) who not only played no role in the blacklist but hired a blacklisted writer before the blacklist ended and attacked, on several occasions, the blacklisters; and (2) it was produced and directed by Lionel Chetwynd, one of Hollywood's most conservative figures.

Karen Kramer, Stanley Kramer's widow, has taken sharp issue with Chetwynd, and they have conducted a sparring match in several publications. I have spoken with both of them, and both have provided me with access to relevant documents in their possession.

Chetwynd's clearly stated purpose is to furbish the reputation of Foreman, a screenwriter who was blacklisted in 1951. Based almost exclusively on a lengthy letter Foreman wrote to *New York Times* movie critic Bosley Crowther, in 1952, *Darkness* announces up front: "This is the story of how one man's producing credit [for *High Noon*] was taken from him." The narrator labels this taking "an act of apparent betrayal by the colleagues this man loved most." A few minutes later, the narrator reiterates this accusation, calling the documentary "a tale of betrayal and destruction" by people Foreman believed he could trust.

The documentary's thesis is that Foreman was the auteur of *High Noon*, that indeed he was the genius behind all of the previously successful films made by the Stanley Kramer Company (*Champion*, *The Men*, and *Home of the Brave*), but that when Foreman honorably refused to cooperate with the House Committee on Un-American Activities, Kramer forced him out of the company, deprived Foreman of a producing credit, and then took credit for a movie he (Kramer) had practically disowned. My research has led me to the conclusion that the documentary makers' uncritical acceptance of Foreman's viewpoint led them to damn Kramer from the outset and thus inadequately research his side of the story. If one looks at the complete record, it becomes clear that the Foreman-Kramer episode resulted from conflicting, but not dishonorable, loyalties and principles; no credit was "taken," and Kramer was not indifferent to *High Noon*.

In the early months of 1951, the House Committee on Un-American Activities delivered a new flood of subpoenas to Hollywood studio employees. Movie industry executives immediately offered their "strength and support to any legally constituted body that has as its object the exposure and destruction of the international Communist party conspiracy." Studio employees who had been or still were members of the Communist Party faced a difficult choice. They could either cooperate with the Committee, by apologizing for their political past *and* giving the Committee the names of other Communists (they had to do both), or they could refuse to answer the Committee's questions, citing the Fifth Amendment. All who took the former position continued to work; all who took the latter position were blacklisted.

On March 18, three days prior to the opening of the new hearings, it was announced that the Stanley Kramer Company had signed a major production contract with Columbia Pictures. Kramer's other company, Stanley Kramer Productions, Inc., still owed one movie to its previous distributor, United Artists. Foreman, a partner in both companies and the script writer for both, was assigned, according to an undated production data card shown in the documentary, as producer of that movie, *High Noon*.

On June 13, Foreman received a subpoena from the House Committee on Un-American Activities, ordering him to appear on September 6. (His appearance would later be postponed to September 24.) There is no reliable account of what Foreman told his partners between June 13 and September 24, regarding his Party membership or the position he would take when he appeared before the Committee. Foreman told me, in 1977, that he had wrestled for months with the form "my cooperation would take," until he found a lawyer "who worked out a diminished Fifth position with me." Until then, he believed his partners would support his decision not to cooperate with the Committee by informing.

And yet, one month later, fully two months before Foreman would be called to testify, the Kramer Company (at Columbia) decided it could not employ an unfriendly witness. Vice President Sam Katz learned in July that director Joseph Losey, who had just been offered a three-picture deal, was going to receive a subpoena. Katz told Losey he would first have to sign an anti-Communist oath. Losey decided to leave the country before the subpoena was served.

Kramer told me, in 1977, that Foreman had never honestly or fully revealed to the partners his (Foreman's) political past or his strategy regarding the Committee. (Though Kramer's version may be found in his autobiography, *A Mad, Mad, Mad, Mad World,* and in Victor S. Navasky's *Naming Names,* the documentary makers do not include it.) Raymond C. Sandler (an attorney for and a shareholder in the Kramer companies, who was not interviewed by the documentary makers) told me that Kramer had asked Foreman, "Are you a Communist?" and Foreman had answered, "No." Ms. Kramer has in her possession letters from two other members of the companies (neither interviewed by the documentary makers) stating that Foreman had denied he was a Communist to the cast and crew as well as to the partners. (This statement was technically true. Foreman had, according to Stanley Roberts, left the Party in mid-1946. And, it should be noted, Foreman was under no obligation to disclose his political past to anyone.)

High Noon began filming on September 5. Two days later, *Variety's* Film Production Chart listed Stanley Kramer as its producer. Shortly thereafter, Foreman told his partners about his decision to use a "diminished Fifth." According to him, they "blanched" when they heard the words "Fifth Amendment." When the documentary begins to describe what ensued, it begins to telescope events, placing within a few days what occurred over several months. The voice reading Foreman's letter states that George Glass, one of the vice presidents, was subpoenaed and became a cooperative witness. Actress Marsha Hunt, signed to appear in *The Happy Time* for the Stanley Kramer Company, reports that Glass urged her to compose an open letter stating she had never been a Communist. Richard Fleischer, signed to direct *The Happy Time*, reports that Kramer had urged him to sign a similar letter for Columbia. But Glass testified on January 21, 1952, and the circumstantial evidence indicates that he would not have decided to "cooperate" until at least September 17. (His widow's testimony might have been useful here, but she was not interviewed.) Fleischer was signed to direct on September 13. *The Happy Time* began filming on January 10, 1952.

In any event, Kramer and the other partners had decided to separate themselves from Foreman. On September 12, by letter, Kramer (on behalf of the Stanley Kramer Company), "relieved" Foreman "of any and all assignments heretofore given you by this Company" and ordered him not to appear at Columbia Pictures. (This letter is displayed in the documentary.) A second letter from Kramer (on behalf of Stanley Kramer Productions) "relieved" Foreman of his assignments on *High Noon* and ordered him to stay away from its shooting location. (This letter is not displayed.) No reasons were given in either letter. (Karen Kramer, it should be noted, does not have copies of these letters. Copies were provided to me by Lionel Chetwynd.)

Foreman and the documentary makers believe that Kramer, fearing the repercussions on his companies and himself of Foreman's coming testimony, had issued a preemptive strike. But an equally plausible scenario is that Columbia Pictures' boss Harry Cohn, when he learned that Foreman would be invoking the Fifth Amendment, told Kramer to keep Foreman off the Columbia lot. (Howard Hughes had done the same thing to Paul Jarrico at RKO, several months earlier.) Or that Kramer, believing Foreman had not been forthright about his political past and future stance with the Un-American Activities Committee, decided to fire an untrustworthy associate. Or that company policy toward subpoenaed employees had been established in July and Foreman had refused to follow it. Or it could have been a combination of all four.

But because Foreman was an officer and a stockholder and had not previously signed a deferral agreement crucial to the companies, he possessed the leverage to get himself partially reinstated. On September 13, a document signed by both men stated that Foreman agreed "to continue to render [his] services to [Stanley Kramer Productions, Inc.] as writer and associate producer" in connection with *High Noon*. (It is not clear—no document has come to light on the matter—whether Foreman was also reinstated in the Stanley Kramer Company, at Columbia.)

When he testified on September 24, Foreman readily answered all questions about his life and career, but he invoked the First and Fifth Amendments when asked about his membership in the Communist Party. (The documentary omits this crucial point.) Instead, he told the Committee: "on September 11, 1950, I voluntarily signed an oath as a member of the executive board of the Screen Writers Guild that I was not a member of the Communist Party."

Pressured by Cohn, and by spreading rumors of a sharp rift between him and Foreman, Kramer reneged on an agreement he had made with Foreman to make no public statement until sixty days after Foreman's appearance before the Committee and then only by mutual consent. Kramer told the press, directly after Foreman's appearance: "There is total disagreement between Carl Foreman and myself. Interests and obligations involved are far greater than his or those of the company. Therefore, at the earliest possible date permitted by our by-laws, a meeting of shareholders and directors, of which Mr. Foreman is one of several, has been called. Necessary action will be taken at that time."

Following the completion of shooting on *High Noon*, in early October, a special stockholders' meeting was called. It convened on October 22. Raymond Sandler, who was at the meeting, told me that Foreman agreed with the other stockholders that it would be in the best interest of the company to terminate "by mutual consent" all Foreman's previous employment agreements with the Kramer companies, including that of September 13. Paragraph 6 of the settlement agreement stated: "In connection with the picture *High Noon,* Foreman waives and, therefore, need not be accorded credit as producer thereof, but he shall, however, be accorded screen credit as writer of the screen play." (This document is not cited in the documentary.) Foreman publicly declared himself satisfied with the financial settlement, reported to have been $250,000, but the documentary does not mention this payment. Nor does it note that no other blacklisted screenwriter obtained anywhere near that amount as a contract settlement. (Marguerite Roberts received $100,000 from M-G-M.)

Two questions remain, though. First, why did the partners decide not to give Foreman credit as associate producer? The documentary fails to provide an answer. (And I confess the question puzzles and troubles me.) Second, why is there no "Produced by" credit? All the previous Kramer films for United Artists carried a "Produced by Stanley Kramer" credit, but for *High Noon,* the phrase "A Stanley Kramer Production" appears just before "The End." (It should be noted that there are no industry or Academy of Motion Picture Arts and Sciences rules governing the assignment or placement of producer credits.)

The second count in the documentary's indictment is that Kramer, who had nothing to do with the making of *High Noon,* indeed hated it, took credit for it when it became a major hit. Yet Foreman admits that Kramer watched the rushes on a daily basis and that they fought about them regularly. Fred Zinnemann, the director, has publicly stated and written in his autobiography that Kramer had worked on the script with Foreman, was deeply involved in casting the movie, and that he had "brilliant original ideas about the musical style of the movie, especially the use of a theme song." And Elmo Williams, the film's credited editor, whose testimony supports the documentary's anti-Kramer viewpoint, admits in the documentary (and in his somewhat different account for Rudy Behlmer in *Behind the Scenes*) that Kramer was deeply involved in the editing process.

In sum, the documentary makers have selected a few documents and a few interviewees to transform a complex episode into a melodrama. For those who know little or nothing about the period, their technique is persuasive, especially the intercutting of "betrayal" scenes from *High Noon* with "betrayal" accusations in Foreman's letter to Crowther and newsreel footage of the Committee's hearings, albeit that footage is from the 1947 hearings.

Stanley Kramer may not have behaved with exemplary steadfastness in 1951, but he did not blacklist Foreman, and nothing Kramer could have done would have saved Foreman from the blacklist. (Indeed, Robert Lippert, another independent producer, could not fulfill the producing deal he signed with Foreman in late October 1951.) Blacklisted, Foreman made the best deal he could for himself. There were no heroes, no villains, simply two colleagues, decent men both, confronted with indecent circumstances over which they had little control.

Addenda: Karen Kramer reread this chapter and, via email, answered two of the questions I had posed. As to the first, why did Foreman not receive an associate producer credit?, she wrote: "That couldn't be given because Foreman did not complete any work on the film." As to the second, why is there no "produced by" credit?, she wrote: "Starting with HIGH NOON he [Stanley] dropped the producer credit and went above the title which said, 'Stanley Kramer Productions Presents . . . HIGH NOON.' That was true of all of the 15 films that Stanley made while at Columbia Pictures. He never took a producer credit again while at that studio—his name always went above the title and at the end of the film. When he finished his contract with Columbia, he went back to United Artists and started producing and directing. During that time until the end of his career he took 'produced and directed by' as his title."

For an in-depth analysis of the making of *High Noon*, see Glenn Frankel, *High Noon: The Hollywood Blacklist and the Making of an American Classic* (New York: Bloomsbury, 2017).

8

Looking Ahead

From my perspective, we should have learned several lessons from all these books, films, and articles on the blacklist: the fragility of the First Amendment protections of free speech; the fragility of the Fifth and Sixth Amendment guarantees of due process; the predatory nature of congressional investigating committees; the necessity of clearly stating the basis for your opposition to encroachments on constitutional rights; the necessity of coming to the aid of those whose First and Fifth Amendment rights are being undermined, even if you do not agree with their politics; silence in the face of a suppressive state is the greatest crime.

Whether or not we have learned these lessons, a major question must be posed: Can a 1950s-type movie/television blacklist recur? The short answer is "improbable, but not impossible." Several Supreme Court decisions have strengthened civil liberties and due process protections, but the court actions brought by the Hollywood blacklistees charging the producers with a conspiracy not to hire, failed, leaving no legal precedents on which to rely. Statutory safeguards are in place in some states (twenty-nine states have enacted antiblacklist laws, and a number of state agencies investigate the practice), but statutory language is notoriously vague (witness the antiblacklist clause of the National Labor Relations Act discussed in chapter 1). The House Committee on Un-American Activities no longer exists, but the Senate Permanent Subcommittee on Investigations (the one chaired by Joseph McCarthy) still functions, and there are Homeland Security committees in both houses of Congress. The Red Scare has ended, the Soviet Union has collapsed, and the Communist Party of the United States is a mere shadow of its former self (enrolling, perhaps, five thousand people). But a prolonged span of hysteria and anxiety over an imagined national security threat remains a distinct possibility. The attacks on Muslims (after 9/11), immigrants and refugees (during the Trump administration), and Asians (during the Covid pandemic) illustrate that nativism is alive and well in the United States. As such, a relatively large, well-disciplined, revolution-oriented organization with close ties to a perceived foreign enemy is not required to stoke fears of "subversion from abroad" or "strangers in the land." Finally, though there have been major structural changes in the entertainment industry, a new behemoth, social media, has emerged.

In any case, blacklisting, as a proscriptive device, has not gone away. It has proven effective over the centuries because it is difficult to prove. In the contemporary United States, blacklisting of individuals proceeds unabated. Virologist Peter Duesberg was subject to loss of grants and publishing venues, and almost fired from the University of California in 2009, because he publicly challenged the medical-establishment belief that the HIV virus caused AIDS.[1] No pro football team has signed Colin Kaepernick since he took a knee to protest the police killing of Black men in 2016. In the field of linguistics, 550 academics signed a letter, in 2020, demanding that the Linguistic Society of America remove Steven Pinker's name from its list of distinguished Fellows because, they alleged, six of his tweets and a two-word phrase from a book minimized racial injustice. Though many of those targeted for individual blacklisting have successfully pushed back, the very threat of getting caught in a "tweetstorm" may be causing academics and public intellectuals to, in effect, blacklist themselves by censoring their thoughts.[2]

In addition, there are several collective quasi-blacklists in operation in the entertainment/media industry, among them "deplatforming" and the "cancel culture." The first is the work of Twitter, YouTube, and Facebook, which have banned some ultraconservative and alt-right podcasts and accounts, most notably that of former president Donald Trump, his former aide Steven Bannon, and Trump zealot Congresswoman Marjorie Taylor Greene (R-GA), although plenty of their supporters and other conspiracy theorists still hold forth, especially on the dark web. Spotify has censored several of Joe Rogan's podcasts. Right-wing commentator Alex Jones and Black Muslim leader Louis Farrakhan have been expelled from

Facebook, as has QAnon. On February 14, 2019, Congressman Adam Schiff (D-CA) sent a letter to Sundar Pichai and Mark Zuckerberg, the chief executive officers of Google and Facebook, respectively, to express concern that the company's platforms including YouTube, Facebook, and Instagram are trafficking in information that discourages parents from vaccinating their children. He asked them to answer four questions, including: "What action(s) do you currently take to address misinformation related to vaccines on your platforms? Are you considering or taking additional actions?"[3] Shortly thereafter, YouTube announced it will no longer serve ads on channels that espouse antivaccination rhetoric. Several months later, Barbara Loe Fisher, head of a radical antivaccination organization, National Vaccine Information Center, alleged that antivaxxers are being blacklisted.[4]

In the second, cancel-culture proponents currently support two blacklists: the first includes men in the media industries and professional sports alleged to be sexual predators, abusers, or harassers; the second targets anyone, past or present, who is perceived as racist. Those on the first list are generally targets of "weaponized social media" and may be fired from their jobs or forced to resign. Their "trials" may take place in the press or on television long before a court appearance. In book publishing, Hachette reneged on a contract to publish Woody Allen's memoir (*Apropos of Nothing*) after two of his children raised the issue of his having abused them, and Norton ceased publication of Blake Bailey's biography of Philip Roth when allegations of sexual assault by Bailey were aired. (Both books were acquired and republished by Skyhorse Publishing.) Chris Cuomo's book was pulled by HarperCollins after reports surfaced of his involvement with his brother's sexual harassment situation. The executors of Theodore Geisel's estate announced that it would no longer publish six of his Dr. Seuss books, in the wake of criticism that they contain racial caricatures.[5] And food writer and blogger Alison Roman had her column discontinued by the *New York Times* after she criticized two Asian food writers, though she maintains that their ethnicity was not a factor.[6] The second list is composed of historical figures who have had their statues taken down and their names removed from streets and schools.

What is most interesting about cancel culture is that it is supported by both the Right and the Left. Conservatives are convinced that we live in "a world in which the corporate elite, the media elite, the political elite, and the academic elite have all coagulated into one axis of evil, dominating every institution and controlling the channels of thought."[7] The Left, for its part, criticizes this behemoth as the protector of systemic, institutional racial and gender bias, and, perversely, given its history of struggle against blacklists, now supports a variety of cancellations.[8]

And, recently, a new type of list has emerged, what I would call the secret white list. The first such list involved Facebook. When the company executives promised to cut down on the sites Facebook data-mined, a number of companies were excluded.[9] The second was adjudicated in a recent California case that reached the Supreme Court of the United States. In it, a conservative white advocacy group, Americans for Prosperity Foundation, sought an injunction to avoid turning over its list of donors to the California attorney general (Rob Bonta). California requires that all nonprofit organizations that raise tax-deductible funds within the state must disclose their largest donors. The attorney general claims that his office needs this information to investigate fraud in the nonprofit sector. The lists are supposed to remain confidential, but they do leak out from time to time. The United States District Court decided in favor of the plaintiffs and issued an injunction. The US Court of Appeals for the Ninth Circuit vacated the injunction. The Supreme Court of the United States granted certiorari, and, during the oral argument, two of the conservative justices expressed alarm at the potential threat to the donors if their names were to be so disclosed. Justice Clarence Thomas repeatedly suggested that the Court must provide constitutional protection to any advocacy organization that is accused of being "racist" or "homophobic." Justice Samuel Alito warned of "vandalism, death threats, physical violence, economic reprisals, [and] harassment in the workplace" directed against donors to an anti-LGBTQ campaign. By a 6–3 decision, in *Americans for Prosperity Foundation v. Bonta*, the Supreme Court reversed the circuit court's decision, as not narrowly tailored to the state's interest in investigating charitable misconduct.

In addition, many companies now use more sophisticated methods, such as do-not-hire lists, master lists of prospective job candidates that human resources or recruitment departments flag in the hiring process. These departments add the job candidates to an applicant tracking system to ensure they do not get hired within the company.[10] However, there is no evidence that these lists are shared with other employers in the same business, although rumors constantly circulate about a Silicon Valley blacklist, but the evidence is mainly anecdotal. (A Google search on that topic turned up more than four and a half million hits.)

All that said, does the entertainment/media industry have an incentive or capability to blacklist now or in the future? Since movie and television production companies are much smaller and much more numerous than they were during the 1940s and 1950s, it is difficult to see how they could effectively organize and police a blacklist. Social media companies, however, are significantly larger and more monopolistically inclined than were the major movie studios. But control of content is not for the social media companies the bugaboo it was for the movie and television studios of the 1930s, 1940s and 1950s. Indeed, the social media companies are hungry for content, any content, the more controversial the better. They do not want to appear biased; they do not want to piss off anybody; their mantra is "level playing fields"; they resist fact-checking and drawing lines. But they will, like most major corporations, "yield to activist pressure. Just a bit. Enough to get them off your back. Companies caught in the scorching light of a social-media outcry are like politicians caught lying or cheating, who promise a 'judge-led inquiry': They want to do something, anything, to appear as if they are taking the problem seriously—until the spotlight moves on."[11] Indeed, since most Americans now get their news from social media, misinformation and hate speech are much greater problems than restricted information. But if, as in Russia and China, Google, Facebook, and Twitter come under pressure from the government or public opinion to block dissident voices or opinions, they could simply tweak their algorithms; a blacklist would not be necessary. Nor would it be effective, given the huge number of independent production companies, cable television, the proliferation of easy-access media platforms (podcasts and blogs), and the ease of self-publishing.

And with technology surging far ahead of anyone's capacity to predict the consequences of developments in that field, the future may strongly replicate the present in the People's Republic of China: security cameras with face-recognition software on every corner or edifice; identity chips for everyone; highly invasive algorithms and data sweepers; centralized control of Internet access. Under those circumstances, a blacklist will be a quaint means of proscription.

Finally, the United States is now the locus of cultural rather than political wars; political organized group warfare has been replaced by sociocultural battles: evangelicals vs. secular humanists; right-to-lifers vs. free-choicers; Second Amendment zealots vs. firearms regulators; nativists vs. universalists; localists vs. centralists; populists vs. elitists; gender orthodox vs. gender heterodox; alt-right vs. antifa; environmentalists vs. corporatists; vaxxers vs. nonvaxxers; red-staters vs. blue-staters; and the current heated debate over "The 1619 Project" and critical race theory.[12] Given the amorphousness of these groups and overlaps of these issues, and, again, their access to media platforms, blacklists are not a likely outcome.

In sum, even though the propensity to list and, thereby, proscribe, is a powerful undercurrent in the political culture of the United States, the classic blacklist seems a relic of the past. But one other element of the domestic Cold War has been resurrected in the newly enacted Texas abortion law—a snitching, or informing, subculture. Under the law, anyone who successfully sues an abortion provider could be awarded at least ten thousand dollars. And to prepare for that, Texas Right to Life has set up what it calls a "whistleblower" website where people can submit anonymous tips about anyone they believe to be violating the law. That includes anyone who helps a woman obtain an abortion (including those who give a woman a ride to a clinic or provide financial assistance to obtain an abortion). Private citizens who bring these suits don't need to show any connection to those they are suing. A number of other states will undoubtedly pass copycat versions.

The authors of the Federalist Papers insisted that perpetual vigilance was the key to protecting civil liberties. And yet, those who are attempting to limit those liberties are ferociously vigilant. But they support a strange mix of liberties, including gun-enforced vigilance against governments and informer-enforced vigilance against private decisions. The practice of tolerance, which once seemed to be the only sensible mode of maintaining a pluralistic society, has all but disappeared. In the United States today we have the curious phenomenon of raging intolerance and a cacophonous symphony of voices. The problem is not enjoying free speech; it is being heard (via speech or vote) and not being surveilled.

Acknowledgments

So many people have assisted my work in this field that I would need a book of equal length to mention them all. I have thanked many of them in my previous books, but here I would like to acknowledge those who have been the most helpful and who became, in the process, good friends.

Among the blacklistees and their families: Albert Maltz, Paul and Sylvia Jarrico, Alfred Lewis Levitt and Helen Slote Levitt, Edward and Sonia Biberman, Norma Barzman, Joe and Kate Lardner, Christopher and Mitzi Trumbo, Nancy Escher, and Lia Benedetti.

Dale Treleven, for employing me to handle the blacklist interviews for the UCLA Oral History Program.

Ellen Harrington, for engaging me to curate the blacklist exhibit for the Academy of Motion Picture Arts and Sciences and for her incredible efforts to make it work.

Ned Comstock (University of Southern California, Cinematic Arts Library) for his indispensable assistance on so many of my projects.

The journal editors who granted me access to their pages: Gary Crowdus and Richard Porton (*Cineaste*); David Culbert and James Chapman (*Historical Journal of Film, Radio and Television*); Richard Krafsur (*Emmy*); and Richard Koszarski (*Film History*).

The book editors who acquired and edited my previous manuscripts on this subject: Robert Hutchins, Leila Salisbury, and Anne Dean Dotson.

Steven Englund, with whom I started on this wonderful journey.

Paul Buhle and Brian Neve, my fellow toilers in the fields of Lord Blacklist.

Acknowledgments

This book is the third of my blacklist manuscripts that the University Press of Kentucky has published. Each project has been a rewarding one. My editor on this book, Ashley Runyon, has been wonderful. Her enthusiasm for the project has been unmatched in my experience. As usual, the staff of the Press has done a wonderful job. Sarah Olson provided excellent supervision of the editing process and Hayward Wilkirson designed a wonderful cover.

Notes

Preface

1. WGAW, *Newsletter,* April 1970, 10; *WGAW News,* May 1976, 21, 23.

1. Looking Back

1. Gordon Kahn, *Hollywood on Trial: The Story of the Ten Who Were Indicted* (New York: Boni and Gaer, 1948); Guy Endore, "Life on the Blacklist," *The Nation,* December 20, 1952, 568; Ring Lardner Jr., "My Life on the Blacklist," *Saturday Evening Post,* October 14, 1961, 38–44; Dalton Trumbo, *The Time of the Toad: A Study of Inquisition in America, by One of the Hollywood Ten* (Hollywood: Hollywood Ten, 1949), reprinted in *The Time of the Toad: A Study of Inquisition in America and Two Related Pamphlets* (New York: Perennial Library, 1972); Trumbo, "Blacklist-Black Market," *The Nation,* May 4, 1957, 383–87; Herbert Biberman, *Salt of the Earth: The Story of a Film* (1965; New York: Harbor Electronics Press, 2003); Elizabeth Poe, "The Hollywood Story," *Frontier,* 5 no. 7 (May 1954): 6–25.

2. Murray Kempton, *Part of Our Time: Some Ruins and Monuments of the Thirties* (New York: Simon and Schuster, 1955), 182, 183, 300; John Cogley, *Report on Blacklisting,* 2 vols. (New York: Fund for the Republic, 1956); Richard Corliss, "Dalton Trumbo: The Pen Is Mightier Than the Gun," *Village Voice,* September 2, 1971, 50 (reprinted in Corliss, *The Hollywood Screenwriters: A Film Comment Book* [New York: Avon, 1972]; and *Talking Pictures: Screenwriters in the American Cinema* [New York: Penguin, 1975]); Walter Goodman, *The Committee: The Extraordinary Career of the House Committee on Un-American Activities* (Baltimore: Penguin, 1969), 213, 214;

Stefan Kanfer, *A Journal of the Plague Years* (New York: Atheneum, 1973), 84; Hilton Kramer, "The Blacklist and the Cold War," *New York Times,* October 31, 1976, sec. 2, p. 16.

3. Howard Suber, "The Anti-Communist Blacklist in the Hollywood Motion Picture Industry" (Ph.D. diss., UCLA, 1968; Ann Arbor, MI: University Microfilms International, 1976); Robert Vaughn, *Only Victims: A Study of Show Business Blacklisting* (New York: Putnam's, 1972); *Hollywood on Trial,* prod. James C. Gutman; dir. David Halpern; written by Arnie Reisman; narrated by John Huston, black-and-white/color, 1976, 101 minutes (distributed by Corinth Films).

4. Larry Ceplair and Steven Englund, *The Inquisition in Hollywood: Politics in the Film Community, 1930–1960* (Garden City, NY: Anchor/ Doubleday, 1980); Nancy Lynn Schwartz, *The Hollywood Writers' Wars* (New York: Knopf, 1982); Victor S. Navasky, *Naming Names* (New York: Viking, 1980).

5. Robert Louis Benson and Michael Warner, eds., *Venona: Soviet Espionage and the American Response, 1939–1957* (Washington, DC: NSA/CIA, 1996). Among the Yale series of particular interest to students of the blacklist are Harvey Klehr, John Earl Haynes, and Fridrik Igorovich Firsov, *The Secret World of American Communism* (New Haven, CT: Yale University Press, 1996); Harvey Klehr, John Earl Haynes, and Kyrill Mikhailovich Anderson, eds., *The Soviet World of American Communism* (New Haven, CT: Yale University Press, 1998).

6. Kenneth Lloyd Billingsley, *Hollywood Party: How Communists Seduced the American Film Industry in the 1930s and 1940s* (Rocklin, CA: Forum, 1998). For more on Brewer, see Larry Ceplair, "Hollywood Unions and Hollywood Blacklists," in *The Wiley-Blackwell History of American Film,* vol. 2: *1929–1945,* ed. Cynthia Lucia, Roy Grundmann, and Art Simon (Malden, MA: Blackwell, 2012), 459–62.

7. Paul Buhle and Dave Wagner, *Radical Hollywood: The Untold Story behind America's Favorite Movies* (New York: New Press, 2002); *A Very Dangerous Citizen: Abraham Lincoln Polonsky and the Hollywood Left* (Berkeley: University of California Press, 2002); *Hide in Plain Sight: The Hollywood Blacklistees in Film and Television, 1950–2002* (New York: Palgrave Macmillan, 2003); *Blacklisted: The Film-Lover's Guide to the Hollywood Blacklist* (New York: Palgrave Macmillan, 2003).

8. Richard Schickel, "The Romance of American Communism," *Los Angeles Times Book Review,* May 12, 2002, 2.

9. Ronald and Allis Radosh, *Red Star over Hollywood: The Film Colony's Long Romance with the Left* (San Francisco: Encounter, 2005); Allan H. Ryskind, *Hollywood Traitors: Blacklisted Screenwriters, Agents of Stalin, Allies of Hitler* (Washington, DC: Regnery, 2015); Thomas Doherty, *Show Trial: Hollywood, HUAC, and the Birth of the Blacklist* (New York: Columbia University Press, 2018).

10. U. S. Code *§158* (a) (3).

11. See David K. Wiggins and Ryan A. Swanson, eds., *Separate Games: African American Sport behind the Walls of Segregation* (Fayetteville: University of Arkansas Press, 2016).

12. Anti-French (late 1790s); anti-Irish (1840s and 1850s); anti-Chinese (1880s); anti-Eastern European and Japanese (fin-de-siècle); anti–Eastern and –Southern European, anti-Asian (1920s); anti-Mexican (1950s); anti-Muslim and anti-Asian (2000s).

13. *United States Statutes at Large,* 40 Stat. 217.

14. Ibid., 40 Stat. 553.

15. California Penal Code §§ 11400 et seq.

16. U. S. C. § 2385.

17. Jon Weiner, "Radical Historians and the Crisis in American History, 1959–1980," in *Professors, Politics and Pop,* by Weiner (London: Verso, 1991), 180.

18. Suber, "The Anti-Communist Blacklist," 15.

19. See Sharon Waxman, "Hollywood's Raw Wound," *Washington Post,* November 23, 1997, https://www.washingtonpost.com/archive/lifestyle/style/1997/11/23/blacklist-hollywoods-raw-wound/cc9c55a5-e6b0–4622–8b2c-7fa38668205d/.

20. Ted Morgan, *Reds: McCarthyism in Twentieth-Century America* (New York: Penguin, 2004).

21. *Congressional Record,* 78th Cong., 1st sess. (February 1, 1943), 479.

22. *Variety,* May 5, 1947, 1, 8; May 16, 1947, 3; May 29, 1947, 7; Suber, "The Anti-Communist Blacklist," 21; US Congress, House of Representatives, Committee on Un-American Activities, 80th Cong., 1st sess., October 1947, *Hearings Regarding the Communist Infiltration of the Motion Picture Industry* (Washington, DC: US Government Printing Office, 1947), 312–13.

23. *Hearings Regarding the Communist Infiltration of the Motion Picture Industry,* 9–10.

24. Victor S. Navasky, "To Name or Not to Name," *New York Times,* March 25, 1973, sec. 6, 34; Suber, "The Anti-Communist Blacklist," 28.

25. Reprinted in Ceplair and Englund, *The Inquisition*, 445.

26. Suber, "The Anti-Communist Blacklist," 36–37.

27. Official Statement of the MPIC re Hearings of the House Un-American Activities Committee, March 12, 1951, Speeches on the Anti-Communist Fight in Hollywood folder, box 9, Joseph Roos Papers, Special Collections Library, University of Southern California.

28. Quoted in Larry Ceplair, "Blacklist? Never Heard of It," *The Nation*, January 31, 1981, 110.

29. For a full account of the role of the Screen Actors Guild in the blacklist era, see Larry Ceplair, "SAG and the Motion Picture Blacklist," *Screen Actor* 39, no. 3 (January 1998): 18–27.

30. Ceplair and Englund, *The Inquisition*, 394.

31. *Variety*, March 29, 1948, 1, 10; see Daniel J. Leab, "'The Iron Curtain' (1948): Hollywood's First Cold War Movie," *Historical Journal of Film, Radio and Television* 8, no. 2 (1988): 153–88.

32. See Daniel J. Leab, "How Red Was My Valley: Hollywood, the Cold War Film, and *I Married a Communist*," *Journal of Contemporary History* 19, no. 1 (January 1984): 59–88.

33. Dorothy B. Jones, "Communism and the Movies: A Study of Film Content," in Cogley, *Report on Blacklisting*, 218–21; Lillian Ross, "Onward and Upward with the Arts," *New Yorker*, February 21, 1948, 48; *Variety*, August 11, 1948, 5.

34. *Los Angeles Times*, March 6, 1980, quoted in Ceplair, "Blacklist? Never Heard of It," 109.

2. Jewish Anti-Communism in the United States and Hollywood

1. Larry Ceplair, *Anti-Communism in Twentieth-Century America: A Critical History* (Santa Barbara, CA: Praeger, 2011).

2. The vast majority of Jews were not Communists. Perhaps between 10 and 20 percent of Party members were Jews. For the various estimates, see Martin Dies, *Martin Dies' Story* (New York: Bookmailer, 1963), 98; Nathan Glazer, *The Social Basis of American Communism* (New York: Harcourt, Brace and World, 1961), 130, 133; Arthur Liebman, "The Ties That Bind: The Jewish Support for the Left in the United States," *American Jewish History Quarterly* 66, no. 2 (December 1976): 302–7; and Melech Epstein, *The*

Jew and Communism: The Story of Early Communist Victories and Ultimate Defeats in the Jewish Community, U. S. A. (New York: Trade Union Sponsoring Committee, 1959), 292.

3. The roots of Judeo-Bolshevism are well described by Paul Hanebrink, *A Specter Haunting Europe: The Myth of Judeo-Bolshevism* (Cambridge, MA: Belknap Press of Harvard University Press, 2018), 11–45.

4. David Nirenberg, *Anti-Judaism: The Western Tradition* (New York: Norton, 2013), 439.

5. Nathan Schachner, *The Price of Liberty: A History of the American Jewish Committee* (New York: American Jewish Committee, 1948), 75–77.

6. *New York Times,* February 15, 1919, 16.

7. Jeffrey Veidlinger, *In the Midst of Civilized Europe: The Pogroms of 1918–1921 and the Onset of the Holocaust* (New York: Metropolitan, 2021), 328.

8. Leonard Baker, *Brandeis and Frankfurter: A Dual Biography* (New York: Harper and Row, 1984), 160.

9. Stuart Svonkin, *Jews against Prejudice: American Jews and the Fight for Civil Liberties* (New York: Columbia University Press, 1997), 114.

10. Zachary Leader, *The Life of Saul Bellow: To Fame and Fortune, 1915–1964* (New York: Knopf, 2015), 171.

11. *New York Times,* February 17, 1934, 1.

12. Charles Herbert Stember et al., *Jews in the Mind of America* (New York: Basic, 1966), 157, 158.

13. Zosa Szajkowski, "A Note on the American-Jewish Struggle Against Nazism and Communism in the 1930's," *American Jewish Historical Quarterly* 59, no. 3 (March 1970): 274–75.

14. Gulie Ne'eman Arad, *America, Its Jews, and the Rise of Nazism* (Bloomington: Indiana University Press, 2000), 117.

15. Szajkowski, "A Note on the American-Jewish Struggle," 276.

16. Moshe Gottlieb, *American Anti-Nazi Resistance, 1933–41: An Historical Analysis* (New York: Ktav, 1982), 176–77.

17. Epstein, *The Jews and Communism,* 293, 300, 302.

18. "The Avukah," *Harvard Crimson,* February 18, 1941, www.thecrimson. com/article/1941/2/18/the-avukah-among-a-scholar-and/.

19. Nathan Glazer, "An Excerpt from *From Socialism to Sociology,*" www. pbs.org/arguing/nyintellectuals_glazer_2.html. For more on Avukah, see Robert F. Barsky, *Noam Chomsky: A Life of Dissent* (Cambridge, MA: MIT Press, 1997), 59–70.

20. Naomi W. Cohen, *Not Free to Desist: The American Jewish Committee, 1906-1966* (Philadelphia: Jewish Publication Society of America, 1972), 211-12.

21. Dies, *Martin Dies' Story*, 99.

22. Paul Jacobs, *Is Curly Jewish? A Political Self-Portrait Illuminating Three Turbulent Decades of Social Revolt, 1935-1965* (New York: Atheneum, 1965), 149.

23. Svonkin, *Jews against Prejudice*, 9.

24. Alexander Bittelman, *Program for Survival: The Communist Position on the Jewish Question* (New York: New Century, 1947), 7. The AJC's Library of Jewish Information issued a report analyzing this pamphlet and a subsequent article on the subject in *Political Affairs*, the Party's theoretical journal, claiming that they provided "convincing information as to the failure of the Communist appeal to Jews; they [Communists] have been by and large isolated from the bulk of the community" ("The National Committee of the Communist Party U. S. A. on Work among the Jews," Speeches on the Anti-Communist Fight in Hollywood folder, box 9, Joseph Roos Papers, Special Collections Library, University of Southern California; hereafter cited as Roos Papers).

25. Stephen H. Norwood, *Antisemitism and the American Far Left* (Cambridge: Cambridge University Press, 2013), 84, 97, 146-50.

26. Cohen, *Not Free to Desist*, 346-47.

27. Elliot Cohen, "An Act of Affirmation," *Commentary* 1, no. 1 (November 1945): 2. The Statement of Aims of the AJC, which had been written in October 1945, was not printed in the magazine until July 1948. It focused on the general aim of the AJC program: "to enlighten and clarify public opinion on problems of Jewish concern, to fight bigotry, and protect human rights, and to promote Jewish cultural interest and creative achievement in America" (*Commentary* 6, no. 1 [July 1948]: 7).

28. Nathan Glazer, "*Commentary*: The Early Years," in Commentary *in American Life*, ed. Murray Freedman (Philadelphia: Temple University Press, 2005), 46-47.

29. Svonkin, *Jews against Prejudice*, 271n33.

30. James Rorty and Winifred Raushenbush, "The Lessons of the Peekskill Riots: What Happened and Why," *Commentary* 10, no. 4 (October 1950): 320. As the 1950s wore on, however, *Commentary* took a much harder line on Communism and the Soviet Union. Cohen became, according to his

successor, Norman Podhoretz, maniacally determined to demonstrate that not all Jews were Communists (Podhoretz, *Making It* [New York: Random House, 1967], 134–35).

31. Svonkin, *Jews against Prejudice,* 142–43, 145.

32. Anti-Defamation League, *Anti-Semitism in the United States in 1947* (New York: Anti-Defamation League of B'nai Brith, 1947), 5.

33. Matthew Bernstein, *Walter Wanger: Hollywood Independent, 1934–1949* (Berkeley: University of California Press, 1987) 127.

34. Larry Ceplair and Steven Englund, *Inquisition in Hollywood: Politics in the Film Community, 1930–1960* (Garden City, NY: Anchor/Doubleday, 1980), 89–93; Louis Pizzitola, *Hearst over Hollywood: Power, Passion, and Propaganda in the Movies* (New York: Columbia University Press, 2002), 334–35; Greg Mitchell, *The Campaign of the Century: Upton Sinclair's Race for Governor of California and the Birth of Media Politics* (New York: Random House, 1992), passim; Giuliana Muscio, *Hollywood's New Deal* (Philadelphia: Temple University Press, 1997), 60; Jack L. Warner, *My First Hundred Years in Hollywood* (New York: Random House, 1964), 215–16; John Trumpbour, *Selling Hollywood to the World: U. S. and European Struggles for Mastery of the Global Film Industry, 1920–1950* (Cambridge: Cambridge University Press, 2002), 79.

35. Pizzitola, *Hearst over Hollywood,* 266–67.

36. Kevin Brownlow, *Behind the Mask of Innocence* (New York: Knopf, 1990), 443–53; *New York Times,* January 12, 1920, 28; Edward Wagenknecht, *The Movies in the Age of Innocence* (Norman: Oklahoma University Press, 1962), 129–30.

37. Paul Starr, *The Creation of the Media: Political Origins of Modern Communications* (New York: Basic, 2004), 296–326; Thomas Doherty, *Pre-Code Hollywood: Sex, Immorality, and Insurrection in American Cinema, 1930–1934* (New York: Columbia University Press, 1999); Raymond Moley, *The Hays Office* (Indianapolis, IN: Bobbs-Merrill, 1945); Thomas Doherty, *Hollywood's Censor: Joseph I. Breen and the Production Code Administration* (New York: Columbia University Press, 2007); "It Can't Happen Here" folder, MPPA/PCA Files, Margaret Herrick Library, Academy of Motion Picture Arts and Sciences; Larry Ceplair, "The Politics of Compromise in Hollywood: A Case Study," *Cineaste* 8, no. 4 (1978): 2–7. The MPPDA was renamed the Motion Picture Association of America in 1945.

38. Ring Lardner Jr., a member of the Hollywood branch of the Communist Party, estimated that well over 50 percent of Party members in Los

Angeles were Jewish (Neal Gabler, *An Empire of Their Own: How the Jews Invented Hollywood* [New York: Anchor, 1989], 331). Lardner was not Jewish.

39. Gabler, *An Empire of Their Own*, 319.

40. Michael E. Birdwell, *Celluloid Soldiers: Warner Bros.' Campaign against Nazism* (New York: New York University Press, 1999), 65.

41. Ibid., 29, 69.

42. Gabler, *An Empire of Their Own*, 353.

43. Ibid., 341.

44. Ben Hecht, *A Child of the Century* (New York: Simon and Schuster, 1954), 539.

45. Ibid., 343.

46. Ben Hecht, *A Guide for the Bedeviled* (New York: Scribner's, 1944), 205, 211. The studio bosses were not alone in this feeling. Harvard law professor Felix Frankfurter said he could not speak publicly about his opposition to President Franklin D. Roosevelt's court-packing plan because he would be heard and interpreted by the Hearst newspapers, *Chicago Tribune*, American Legion, Daughters of the American Revolution, and chambers of commerce "as the Jew, the 'red,' and the 'alien'" (Baker, *Brandeis and Frankfurter*, 327).

47. Quoted in Leonard Quart, "The Triumph of Assimilation: Ethnicity, Race and the Jewish Moguls," *Cineaste* 18, no. 4 (n.d.): 8–9.

48. Ben Urwand, *The Collaboration: Hollywood's Pact with Hitler* (Cambridge: Belknap Press of Harvard University Press, 2013), 173, 198–201.

49. Steven J. Ross, *Hitler in Los Angeles: How Jews Foiled Nazi Plots against Hollywood and America* (New York: Bloomsbury, 2017), 67–76, 118–19; *Jewish Daily Bulletin*, October 23, 1933, 2, http://pdfs.jta.org/1933/1933-10-23_2674.pdf?_ga=2.163094908.1929803413.1544732396-1328992177.1544732396.

50. Photocopy, n.d., in Research Americanism Committee folder, box 18, Roos Papers. *A Star Is Born* was released by Selznick International Pictures in 1937.

51. Joseph Breen to Robert Lord, December 5, 1937, quoted in Stephen Vaughn, *Ronald Reagan in Hollywood: Movies and Politics* (Cambridge: Cambridge University Press, 1994), 44. Most authors who mention Breen call him an anti-Semite. Thomas Doherty, however, who lists several of the anti-Jewish comments Breen made before becoming head of the PCA, dismisses them as typical of the "blunt slurs" of that time. Doherty states that

after 1934 Breen "is publicly and forthrightly *anti*-anti-Semitic" (*Hollywood's Censor: Joseph I. Breen and the Production Code Administration* [New York: Columbia University Press, 2007], 204). Breen also was an outspoken anti-Communist, and he suggested substituting Communists for Nazis in the film *The Three Comrades,* so that the impassioned speeches condemning Nazism could remain in the movie (Carr, *Hollywood and Anti-Semitism,* 158).

52. Gabler, *An Empire of Their Own,* 345.

53. Baker, *Brandeis and Frankfurter,* 391. Jewish congressman Samuel Dickstein (D-NY) had promoted such a committee to investigate pro-Nazi and profascist groups in the United States. Under the chairmanships of John McCormack (D-MA) and Martin Dies Jr. (D-TX), however, the Committee shifted its emphasis to the investigation of Communists. Dies was not an anti-Semite, but he was deaf and blind to the anti-Semitism of some of the Committee's witnesses (e.g., Walter Steele, George Van Horn Moseley, Fritz Kuhn) and two of its investigators (Edward Sullivan and J. B. Matthews). He, like the senators who investigated antiwar movies, see below, emboldened, amplified, and facilitated anti-Semites and refused to repudiate them.

54. Ceplair and Englund, *The Inquisition,* 109.

55. US Congress, House of Representatives, Special Committee on Un-American Activities, *Investigation of Un-American Propaganda Activities in the United States,* 75th Cong., 3rd sess., August 12, 1938, 1:540–41.

56. *Hollywood Reporter,* August 4, 1938, 1; November 26, 1938, 3; August Raymond Ogden, *The Dies Committee: A Study of the House Special Committee for the Investigation of Un-American Activities, 1938–1944* (Washington, DC: Catholic University of America Press, 1945), 56–57; Laura B. Rosenzweig, *Hollywood's Spies: The Undercover Surveillance of Nazis in Los Angeles* (New York: New York University Press, 2017), 158; Carr, *Hollywood and Anti-Semitism,* 171.

57. *Los Angeles Times,* March 27, 1939, 13; Ceplair and Englund, *The Inquisition, 1930–1960* (Garden City, NY: Anchor/Doubleday, 1980), 109, 156–57.

58. Thomas Doherty, *Show Trial: Hollywood, HUAC, and the Birth of the Blacklist* (New York: Columbia University Press, 2018), 20.

59. *Los Angeles Times,* February 16, 1940, 1, 22; Martin Dies, "The Reds in Hollywood," *Liberty,* February 17, 1940, 47–50; *Variety,* August 28, 1940, 4; Doherty, *Show Trial,* 21–23; Leo Rosten, *Hollywood, the Movie Colony, the Movie Makers* (New York: Harcourt Brace, 1941), 148.

60. Screenwriter Charles Bennett claimed that DeMille's office was used by the FBI and, later, war intelligence agencies to recruit studio workers to report on Nazi and Communist activity (Patrick McGilligan, ed., *Backstory: Interviews with Screenwriters of Hollywood's Golden Age* [Berkeley: University of California Press, 1986]).

61. Edward Dmytryk, *Odd Man Out: A Memoir of the Hollywood Ten* (Carbondale: Southern Illinois University Press, 1996), 95; Harry M. Warner, "United We Survive, Divided We Fall," folder 18, box 56, Jack L. Warner Collection, Cinema and Television Library, University of Southern California; Eugene Lyons, *The Red Decade: The Stalinist Penetration of America* (Indianapolis, IN: Bobbs-Merrill, 1941).

62. *Congressional Record,* 77th Cong., 1st sess., August 1, 1941, 87:141.

63. America First's John T. Flynn had authored Nye's resolution.

64. *St. Louis Globe-Democrat,* August 2, 1941, reprinted in Academy of Motion Picture Arts and Sciences, *Press Clippings File on the Senate Sub-Committee War Film Hearings,* ed. Donald Gledhill, vol. 1, August 1–October 15, 1941, "Build-Up," A.

65. "Sen. Nye and the Movies . . . ," *In Fact,* August 25, 1941, *Press Clippings File,* G.

66. James E. McMillan, "McFarland and the Movies: The 1941 Senate Motion Picture Hearings," *Journal of Arizona History* 29, no. 3 (Autumn 1988): 290.

67. *Congressional Record,* 77th Cong., 1st sess., September 9, 1941, 87:7627–30.

68. *Cleveland Plain Dealer,* September 12, 1941, *Press Clippings File,* "Third Day," G.

69. Quoted in Ruth Sarles, *A Story of America First: The Men and Women Who Opposed U. S. Intervention in World War II,* ed. Bill Kauffman (Westport, CT: Praeger, 2003), 53–55.

70. Ibid., 55.

71. "The Anti-Semitic Conspiracy," *New Republic,* September 22, 1941, *Press Clippings File,* "Seventh Day," I–J.

72. *Hollywood Reporter,* September 26, 1941, *Press Clippings File,* A.

73. *Congressional Record,* 77th Cong., 1st sess., October 7, 1941, in *Press Clippings File,* "Second Recess," kk.

74. ADL, *Anti-Semitism in the United States in 1947,* 55.

75. Reprinted in Robert Vaughn, *Only Victims: A Study of Show Business Blacklisting* (New York: Putnam's, 1972), 324–25. Ornitz's words were used

by the Freedom from Fear Committee, the Ten's defense group, in a leaflet titled "Today . . . Hollywood. Tomorrow . . . the Whole Country." Is what is happening in Hollywood, asked the leaflet, "Good for the Jews?" (folder 5, box 46, JFC Papers).

76. Gabler, *An Empire of Their Own*, 375.

77. *Los Angeles Examiner*, May 5, 1950, 2.

78. Roos was particularly instrumental in helping to clear the actor Edward G. Robinson (folder 21, box 92, JFC Papers).

79. Gang also chaired the Committee on Communism in the Jewish Community.

80. For more on the interrelationship of Wheeler, Gang, and Cohen, see Victor S. Navasky, *Naming Names* (New York: Viking, 1981).

81. Ceplair and Englund, *The Inquisition*, 391–92; Navasky, *Naming Names*, 100.

82. Navasky, *Naming Names*, 139–42.

83. Deborah Dash Moore, "Reconsidering the Rosenbergs: Symbol and Substance in Second Generation American Jewish Consciousness," *Journal of American Ethnic History* 8, no. 1 (Fall 1988): 26–27; Navasky, *Naming Names*, 114.

84. Navasky, *Naming Names*, 115.

85. Ibid., 117. Navasky's source cites the date of the memo as May 1951, but it had to have been written and sent one year later. The defense committee was established in January 1952.

86. Arnold Forster, *Square One: A Memoir* (New York: Fine, 1988), 127–28.

87. Quoted in Navasky, *Naming Names*, 112.

88. Phillip Deery, "'Never Losing Faith': An Analysis of the National Committee to Secure Justice in the Rosenberg Case, 1951–1953," *American Communist History* 12, no. 3 (2013): 26, 191, https://vuir.vu.edu.au/27783/1/Rosenberg%20Committee.pdf.

89. Ceplair and Englund, *The Inquisition in Hollywood*, 409. Navasky writes that Wilson told him that Huggins yelled, "Go back to Russia!" (*Naming Names*, 258).

90. John Wexley interview, in *Tender Comrades: A Backstory of the Hollywood Blacklist*. ed. Patrick McGilligan and Paul Buhle (New York: St. Martin's, 1997), 719, 720.

91. Malcolm P. Sharp, *Was Justice Done? The Rosenberg-Sobell Case* (New York: Monthly Review Press, 1956), xxxiv; Oliver Pilat, review of *The Judgment of Julius and Ethel Rosenberg* (New York: Cameron and Kahn, 1955),

Yale Law Journal 65, no. 3 (January 1956): 443, 444, https://digitalcommons. law.yale.edu/cgi/viewcontent.cgi?article=8451&context=ylj.

92. Irwin Ross, *The Communists: Friends or Foes of Civil Liberties?* (New York: AJC, 1950).

93. CRC Workbook on the Problem of Communism and Preservation of Civil Liberties (CRC, n.d. [March 1951], Anti-Communist folder, box 9, Roos Papers.

94. ADL leaders closely watched this investigation, troubled, as one wrote "that nearly every Fort Monmouth employee removed as a security risk by the Army or subpoenaed by the [Senate Permanent Investigations] subcommittee and publicly labeled a suspected communist is, judging from names, Jewish." Benjamin R. Epstein to Arnold Forster, November 16, 1953, in Arnold Forster and Benjamin R. Epstein, *Cross-Currents* (Garden City, NY: Doubleday, 1956), 70.

95. US Congress, House of Representatives, Committee on Un-American Activities, *The Ideological Fallacies of Communism: Staff Consultations with Rabbi S. Andhil Fineberg, Bishop Fulton J. Sheen, and Dr. Daniel A. Poling,* 85th Cong., 1st sess., September 4, September 25, October 18, 1957 (Washington, DC: United States Government Printing Office, 1958), 7.

96. Svonkin, *Jews against Prejudice,* 130–31.

3. A Debate over the Politics and Morality of Cooperative and Uncooperative Witnesses Who Testified before the House Committee on Un-American Activities, 1947–1953

Books reviewed in this essay: Victor S. Navasky, *Naming Names* (New York: Viking, 1980); Alan Casty, *Communism in Hollywood: The Moral Paradoxes of Testimony, Silence, and Betrayal* (Lanham, MD: Scarecrow, 2009).

1. Howard Suber, "The Anti-Communist Blacklist in the Hollywood Motion Picture Industry" (Ph.D. diss., 1968; Ann Arbor, MI: University Microfilms, 1976).

2. Betty Garrett, *Betty Garrett and Other Songs: A Life on Stage and Screen,* with Ron Rapoport (Lanham, MD: Madison, 1998), 137.

3. Quoted in Larry Ceplair and Steven Englund, *The Inquisition in Hollywood: Politics in the Film Community, 1930–1960* (Garden City, NY: Anchor/Doubleday, 1980), 380–81, 385.

4. WGAW, *Newsletter*, April 1970, 10; reprinted in Dalton Trumbo, *Additional Dialogue: Letters of Dalton Trumbo, 1942-1962*, ed. Helen Manfull (New York: M. Evans, 1970), 569-70.

5. Box 40, Dalton Trumbo Papers, Wisconsin Center for Film and Theater Research, cited in Larry Ceplair and Christopher Trumbo, *Dalton Trumbo: Blacklisted Hollywood Radical* (Lexington: University Press of Kentucky, 2015), 321-24.

4. Dashiell Hammett

I am indebted to Julie M. Rivett for reading and commenting on a draft of this chapter.

1. Jo Hammett, *Dashiell Hammett: A Daughter Remembers*, ed. Richard Layman and Julie M. Rivett (New York: Carroll and Graf, 2001), 104, 108.

2. Editors' commentary in *The Hunter and Other Stories*, ed. Richard Layman and Julie M. Rivett (New York: Mysterious, 2013), 66.

3. Richard T. Hammett, "Mystery Writer Was Enigmatic throughout Life," *Baltimore News-American*, August 19, 1973, in *Hardboiled Mystery Writers, Raymond Chandler, Dashiell Hammett, Ross Macdonald: A Literary Reference*, ed. Matthew J. Bruccoli and Richard Layman (New York: Carroll and Graf, 1989).

4. Dashiell Hammett, *Black Mask* 7 (November 1924): 128, reprinted in Bruccoli and Layman, *Hardboiled Mystery Writers*, 86.

5. Dalton Trumbo, *Johnny Got His Gun* (New York: Citadel, 2007), 114.

6. Hammett, "The Gutting of Couffignal" and "This King Business," in Dashiell Hammett, *The Big Book of the Continental Op*, ed. Richard Layman and Julie M. Rivett (New York: Vintage Crime/Black Lizard, 2017), 336, 441.

7. Trumbo, *Johnny Got His Gun*, 249.

8. Hammett to Blanche Knopf, March 28, 1928, in Dashiell Hammett, *Selected Letters*, ed. Richard Layman and Julie M. Rivett (Washington, DC: Counterpoint, 2001), 47.

9. Hammett, "Vamping Samson," *Editor* 69 (May 9, 1925), in Bruccoli and Layman, *Hardboiled Mystery Writers*, 100.

10. Hammett, "The Crime Wave," *New York Evening Post*, June 7 and July 3, 1930, 54 and 55, in Bruccoli and Layman, *Hardboiled Mystery Writers*, 125.

11. Hammett to editor of *Black Mask,* August 1942, in Hammett, *Selected Letters,* 26.

12. Hammett, "In Defence of the Sex Story," *Writer's Digest* 4 (June 1924): 17–18, in Bruccoli and Layman, *Hardboiled Mystery Writers,* 97.

13. Nathan Ward, *The Lost Detective: Becoming Dashiell Hammett* (London: Bloomsbury, 2015), 167.

14. Layman and Rivett, introduction to *The Big Book of the Continental Op,* x.

15. Dennis Dooley, *Dashiell Hammett* (New York: Felix Unger, 1984), quoted in Dashiell Hammett, *Lost Stories,* ed. Vince Emery (San Francisco: Vince Emery Productions, 2005), 134.

16. Sally Cline, *Dashiell Hammett: Man of Mystery* (New York: Arcade, 2016), 66, 115.

17. Hammett, introduction to *The Maltese Falcon* (New York: Modern Library, 1934), in Bruccoli and Layman, *Hardboiled Mystery Writers,* 117.

18. Hammett, *Black Mask,* 7, November 1924, 128, in Bruccoli and Layman, *Hardboiled Mystery Writers,* 86.

19. "Slippery Fingers," October 15, 1923; "It," November 1, 1923; "This King Business," January 1928; "The Cleansing of Poisonville," November 1927, all in *The Big Book of the Continental Op,* 34, 45, 454, 533.

20. "On the Way," *The Hunter,* 181.

21. Jo Hammett, *Dashiell Hammett,* 73, 79.

22. "Zigzags of Treachery," March 1, 1924, *The Hunter,* 88.

23. "The Girl with the Silver Eyes," March 1924, *The Hunter,* 146.

24. "The Cleansing of Poisonville," December 1927, *The Big Book of the Continental Op,* 565.

25. Ibid., 581.

26. Ibid., 601.

27. "Nelson Redline," unpublished manuscript, n.d., *The Hunter,* 118.

28. "The Sign of the Potent Pills," ca. 1927–1929, *The Hunter,* 28, 35.

29. "Magic," unpublished, n.d., *The Hunter,* 80.

30. "The Dain Curse," February 1929, *The Big Book of the Continental Op,* 715.

31. Joan Mellen, *Hellman and Hammett: The Legendary Passion of Lillian Hellman and Dashiell Hammett* (New York: HarperCollins, 1996), 104.

32. Hammett to Blanche Knopf, April 6, 1928 and June 25, 1928, in Hammett, *Selected Letters,* 47, 48.

33. Hammett to Josephine, May 31, 1927, in Hammett, *Selected Letters,* 38.

34. *The Hunter,* 141.

35. Hammett, "This Little Pig," *Collier's,* March 24, 1934, reprinted in Hammett, *Lost Stories,* 268–87.

36. David O. Selznick to B. P. Schulberg, July 18, 1930, reprinted in Bruccoli and Layman, *Hardboiled Mystery Writers,* 126.

37. Quoted in Alice Kessler-Harris, *A Difficult Woman: The Challenging Life and Times of Lillian Hellman* (New York: Bloomsbury, 2012), 89.

38. Editors' commentary in Hammett, *Selected Letters,* 59.

39. James Cooper, "Lean Years for the Thin Man," *Washington Daily News,* March 11, 1957, in Bruccoli and Layman, *Hardboiled Mystery Writers,* 225.

40. Hammett to Alfred A. Knopf, April 27, 1931, in Hammett, *Selected Letters,* 71.

41. Diane Johnson, *Dashiell Hammett: A Life* (New York: Random House, 1983), xix.

42. "Faith," unpublished, ca. 1926, *The Hunter,* 92.

43. "Nelson Redline," unpublished, n.d., *The Hunter,* 113.

44. Nancy Lynn Schwartz, *The Hollywood Writers' Wars* (New York: Knopf, 1982), 116.

45. Larry Ceplair and Steven Englund, *The Inquisition in Hollywood: Politics in the Film Community, 1930–1960* (Garden City, NY: Anchor/Doubleday, 1980), 56.

46. *Writers Take Sides: Letters about the War in Spain from 418 American Writers* (New York: League of American Writers, 1938), 28.

47. Hammett to Mary Hammett, September 11, 1936, in Hammett, *Selected Letters,* 109.

48. Hammett to Mary Hammett, September 17, 1936, in Hammett, *Selected Letters,* 11.

49. Hammett to Mary Hammett, February 21, 1936, in Hammett, *Selected Letters,* 99.

50. Mellen, *Hellman and Hammett,* 103.

51. Ibid., 314.

52. Julie M. Rivett, email to author, August 17, 2021.

53. Hammett to Mary Hammett, November 26, 1940, in Hammett, *Selected Letters,* 166.

54. Introduction to Dashiell Hammett, *The Big Knockover: Selected Stories and Short Novels,* ed. Lillian Hellman (New York: Vintage, 1989), xii.

55. Schwartz, *The Hollywood Writers' Wars,* 152.

56. Hammett to Mary Hammettt, November 25, 1938, in Hammett, *Selected Letters*, 143.

57. Hammett to Mary Hammett, September 11, 1936, in Hammett, *Selected Letters*, 107–8.

58. Hammett to Mary Hammett, November 25, 1938, in Hammett, *Selected Letters*, 141.

59. Richard Layman, *Shadow Man: The Life of Dashiell Hammett* (New York: Harcourt Brace Jovanovich/Bruccoli Clark, 1981), 173.

60. Hammett to Mary Hammett, September 27, 1938, in Hammett, *Selected Letters*, 137.

61. Hammett to Mary Hammett, October 13, 1938, in Hammett, *Selected Letters*, 139.

62. Hammett to Mary Hammett, December 19, 1938, and January 21, 1939, in Hammett, *Selected Letters*, 144, 145.

63. Quoted in Larry Ceplair, *Under the Shadow of War: Fascism, Anti-Fascism, and Marxists, 1918-1939* (New York: Columbia University Press, 1987), 201.

64. Mellen, *Hellman and Hammett*, 162.

65. The documents are reprinted in Hammett, *Selected Letters*, 155–59.

66. The document is reprinted in Hammett, *Selected Letters*, 165.

67. Mellen, *Hellman and Hammett*, 171–78.

68. Hammett to Mary Hammett, October 1, 1941, in Hammett, *Selected Letters*, 172.

69. Jo Hammett, *A Daughter Remembers*, 116.

70. E. E. Spitzer, "With Corporal Hammett on Adak," *Nation*, January 5, 1974, 6–9, in Bruccoli and Layman, *Hardboiled Mystery Writers*, 182.

71. Commentary by editors in Hammett, *Selected Letters*, 182.

72. Hammett, *Selected Letters*, 231n4.

73. Hammett to Josephine Dolan Hammett, January 15, 1945, in Hammett, *Selected Letters*, 404–5.

74. Jo Hammett, *A Daughter Remembers*, 123.

75. Bernard Kalb, "Remembering the Dashiell Hammett of 'Julia,'" *New York Times*, September 25, 1977, sec. D, pp. 15–16, in Bruccoli and Layman, *Hardboiled Mystery Writers*, 240.

76. Hammett to Hellman, May 15, 1944, in Hammett, *Selected Letters*, 327.

77. Hammett to Josephine Hammett, March 22, 1945, in Hammett, *Selected Letters*, 422.

78. Hammett, *Lost Stories,* 330.

79. Hammett to Josephine Hammett, July 27, 1944, in Hammett, *Selected Letters,* 351.

80. Hammett to Mary Hammett, April 7, 1945, in Hammett, *Selected Letters,* 427.

81. Hammett to Mary Hammett, October 2, 1946, in Hammett, *Selected Letters,* 481.

82. Public Letter, October 1947, in Hammett, *Selected Letters,* 493–94.

83. US Congress, House of Representatives, Committee on Un-American Activities, 80th Cong., 1st sess., *Report on Civil Rights Congress as a Communist Front Organization* (Washington, DC: US Government Printing Office, 1947). See also Gerald Horne, *Communist Front? The Civil Rights Congress, 1946-1956* (Rutherford, NJ: Fairleigh Dickinson University Press, 1987).

84. Reprinted in Johnson, *Dashiell Hammett,* 216.

85. Hammett, *The Big Knockover,* x.

86. Transcript reprinted in Bruccoli and Layman, *Hardboiled Mystery Writers,* 205.

87. Claudia Roth Pierpont, "Tough Guy: The Mystery of Dashiell Hammett," *New Yorker,* February 11, 2002, https://www.newyorker.com/magazine/2002/02/11/tough-guy.

88. Hammett, *Selected Letters,* 580–81; Victor S. Navasky, *Naming Names* (New York: Viking, 1980), 287–88.

89. US Congress, Senate, *Executive Sessions of the Senate Permanent Subcommittee on Investigations of the Committee on Government Operations,* 83rd Cong., 1st sess., March 24, 1953 (Washington, DC: US Government Printing Office, 2003), 2:945–46.

90. The full transcript is reprinted in Johnson, *Dashiell Hammett,* 265–72.

91. *Warner Bros. Pictures v. Columbia Broadcasting,* et al., 216 F.2d 945 (November 9, 1954).

92. Unidentified FBI report on Hammett's finances, March 26, 1957, in Bruccoli and Layman, *Hardboiled Mystery Writers,* 230–31.

93. Hammett, *The Big Knockover,* xxi.

94. James Cooper, "Lean Years for the Thin Man," *Washington Daily News,* March 11, 1957, in Bruccoli and Layman, *Hardboiled Mystery Writers,* 224.

95. FBI memo, January 17, 1961, in Bruccoli and Layman, *Hardboiled Mystery Writers,* 242.

5. Isobel Lennart and the Dynamics of Informing in Hollywood

1. *Hollywood Reporter,* March 8, 1951, 3; *Variety,* March 14, 1951, 1.

2. The transcript of the executive session indicates that Parks named twelve people. But Betty Garrett, his wife, wrote that he was given a list of names and that he read over the list with the Committee counsel. When he said the names of those who he knew to be members of the Communist Party, he was "not volunteering. He was reading" (US Congress, House of Representatives, Committee on Un-American Activities, *Investigation of Communist Activities in the Los Angeles Area*—Part 6, 1953, 2303–6, reprinted in Eric Bentley, ed., *Thirty Years of Treason: Excerpts from Hearings Before the House Committee on Un-American Activities, 1938–1968* (New York: Viking, 1971), 337–45; Betty Garrett, *Betty Garrett and Other Songs,* with Ron Rapoport (New York: Madison, 1998), 137.

3. *Los Angeles Times,* March 24, 1951, 1.

4. Howard Da Silva, interview in the radio documentary *Breaking the Blacklist,* WBAI-FM, New York, 1976. For a thorough analysis of the informing subculture, see Victor S. Navasky, *Naming Names* (New York: Viking, 1980).

5. Sterling Hayden, the first informer to offer a form of public repentance, did not specifically say that he regretted his decision to inform, but he did describe his act in self-loathing terms (Hayden, *Wanderer* [New York: Knopf, 1963], 390–92). Kazan, in his memoir, stated that what he had done was correct, but at first he was not sure that it was right. But, he added, "the truth is that within a year I stopped feeling guilty or even embarrassed about what I'd done" (Kazan, *A Life* [New York: Knopf, 1988], 465). Lennart made public her regret in 1970, when Robert Vaughn interviewed her. But in his book, *Only Victims: A Study of Show Business Blacklisting* (New York: Putnam's, 1972), Vaughn only mentioned Lennart's name as an informing witness; he did not include any portions of the interview. Large portions of the interview were reprinted in Navasky, *Naming Names.* Many of Lennart's scripts and some letters are housed at the American Heritage Center, University of Wyoming. Her daughter, Sarah Harding, possesses some scripts, letters, and pages from journals. In addition, there are some letters from her in the Lucy Kroll Papers, Library of Congress, and in the Jerome Robbins Papers, New York Public Library. I am deeply grateful to Sarah Harding for her assistance. In addition, I wish to acknowledge the contributions of Ned

Comstock (Cinema and Television Library, University of Southern California), Barbara Hall (Margaret Herrick Library, Academy of Motion Picture Arts and Sciences), Carol Bowers (American Heritage Center, University of Wyoming), Kurt Jensen, and David F. Miller (Twentieth Century-Fox Legal Department).

6. Lennart's journals are in the possession of Sarah Harding.

7. Lennart interview with Vaughn, in Navasky, *Naming Names*, 255.

8. US Congress, House of Representatives, Committee on Un-American Activities, *Communist Infiltration of the Hollywood Motion-Picture Industry—Part 8*, testimony of Isobel Lennart, May 20, 1952, 3516.

9. This script is in the possession of Sarah Harding.

10. *Communist Infiltration*—Part 8, 3514–15.

11. This group was a Communist front focused on mobilizing movie audiences to pressure the studios to improve working conditions of movie workers and the content of movies.

12. *Communist Infiltration*—Part 8, 3521.

13. SACLA to Director, November 9, 1944, file number 100–335744–1; SACLA to Director, January 9, 1945, file number 100–335774–2. (Freedom of Information files in possession of author). At the direction of Party head Earl Browder, the CP became the Communist Political Association in early 1944. This change was part of Browder's strategy to make Communism more American.

14. Sylvia Jarrico, interview by author, September 2, 2006.

15. *Communist Infiltration*—Part 8, 3520; *Hollywood Reporter*, May 20, 1942, 3. Coincidentally, their script, now titled *The Affairs of Martha*, was directed by Jules Dassin (also a Communist).

16. *Communist Infiltration*—Part 8, 3513.

17. *Hollywood Reporter*, November 15, 1943, 3, and July 18, 1945, 3; *Variety*, July 18, 1945, 3.

18. Of her twenty-eight screen credits, twenty were solo. Seven of the credits were for original stories, eight for adaptations, and thirteen for rewrites of scripts written by other writers.

19. Philip K. Scheuer, "First Play a Smash for Screenwriter," *Los Angeles Times*, May 5, 1964, D17.

20. Fay Kanin, speech at memorial for Isobel Lennart, *WGAW News*, March 1971, 4; Philip Dunne, *Take Two: A Life in Movies and Politics* (New York: McGraw-Hill, 1980), 98.

21. Lennart told an interviewer: "When we have a great year, we only lose $2,000" (Charles Champlin, "A Screenwriter Shares the Kudos," *Los Angeles Times*, October 11, 1967, C17).

22. *Communist Infiltration*—Part 8, 3522–23, 3528. She did not, however, cease all political activity. She signed the *amicus curiae* brief for the Hollywood Ten's appeal to the United States Supreme Court and a petition supporting the right of Albert Maltz, one of the Ten, to run for the board of directors of the Screen Writers Guild.

23. Isobel Lennart to Darryl F. Zanuck, February 4, 1952, Isobel Lennart File, Records of the Legal Department, Twentieth Century-Fox, Arts Special Collections Library, Charles E. Young Research Library, UCLA.

24. Lennart interview by Vaughn, in Navasky, *Naming Names*, 254–55; *Communist Infiltration*, Part 8, 3526–27; SACLA to Director, August 17, 1951, file number 100–335774-6.

25. SACLA to Director, December 20, 1951, file number 100–335774-7.

26. Lennart interview by Vaughn, in Navasky, *Naming Names*, 255; SACLA to Director, December 20, 1951, file number 100–335774-7.

27. Lennart interview by Vaughn, in Navasky, *Naming Names*, 254–55.

28. Ibid., 256.

29. Larry Ceplair and Steven Englund, *The Inquisition in Hollywood: Politics in the Film Community, 1930–1960* (Garden City, NY: Anchor/Doubleday, 1980), 447; and Navasky, *Naming* Names, 252, both credit her with naming twenty-one people. Actually, she named twenty-one people from the movie industry and two Communist Party functionaries.

30. *Communist Infiltration*, Part 8, 3527–28.

31. Lennart interview by Vaughn, in Navasky, *Naming Names*, 381–82.

32. Ibid., 257, 358. M-G-M executives had a similar relationship with Marguerite Roberts. When she invoked the Fifth Amendment in her testimony before the Committee, the studio bought out her contract, which was something no other studio did for an unfriendly witness.

33. Fuchs, in his two-page recollection of his work on *Love Me or Leave Me*, does not mention Lennart (*The Golden West: Hollywood Stories* [Lafayette, IN: Black Sparrow, 2005], 248–49).

34. Maurice Zinn to Milton Beecher, June 26, 1954, *Merry Andrew* folders, M-G-M Collection, Cinema-Television Library, University of Southern California.

35. Scheuer, "First Play"; Theodore Taylor, *Jule: The Story of Composer Jule Styne* (New York: Random House, 1979), 237; Lennart quoted in www.

barbra-archives.com/magazinearchives/streisand_look_magazine1968.
html.

36. Lucy Kroll to Isobel Lennart, May 21, 1964, box 473, Lucy Kroll
Papers, Library of Congress. I am grateful to Kurt Jensen, who located this
letter for me. Scheuer, "First Play"; Kanin, speech at memorial.

37. Isobel Lennart to Ray Stark, January 15, 1968, box 12, Isobel Lennart
Papers, American Heritage Center, University of Wyoming.

38. Dunne, *Take Two*, 244.

39. Lennart interview by Vaughn, in Navasky, *Naming Names*, 256–57.

40. Charles Champlin, "Isobel Lennart—In Memoriam," *Los Angeles
Times*, February 7, 1971, C30.

6. Ring Lardner Jr. and the Hollywood Blacklist

The author wishes to express his deep gratitude to the members of the Lardner family who read and commented on a draft of this chapter: Jim, Joe,
Kate, and Susan Lardner and Ann Waswo.

1. Ring Lardner Jr., "My Life on the Blacklist," *Saturday Evening Post*,
October 14, 1961, 43.

2. Lardner interview in *Tender Comrades: A Backstory of the Hollywood
Blacklist*, ed. Patrick McGilligan and Paul Buhle (New York: St. Martin's,
1997), 411.

3. Ring Lardner Jr., interview by author, September 22, 1976.

4. F. 466, Ring Lardner, Jr. Papers, Margaret Herrick Library; hereafter
cited as Lardner, Jr. Papers; reprinted in Robert Vaughn, *Only Victims: A
Study of Show Business Blacklisting* (New York: Putnam's, 1972), 332–33.

5. Eric Bentley, Ed. *Thirty Years of Treason: Excerpts from the Hearings
Before the House Committee on Un-American Activities, 1938–1968* (New
York: Viking, 1971), 184–88.

6. Interview by Bert Andrews, *New York Herald-Tribune*, January 7,
1948, f. 493, Lardner, Jr. Papers.

7. Ring Lardner Jr., "30 Years after the 'Hollywood Ten,'" *New York Times*,
March 18, 1978, 23.

8. Larry Ceplair and Christopher Trumbo, *Dalton Trumbo: Blacklisted
Hollywood Radical* (Lexington: University Press of Kentucky, 2015).

9. The first was written by Guy Endore, "Life on the Blacklist," *The Nation*,
December 20, 1952, 568.

10. Ring Lardner Jr., *The Lardners: My Family Remembered* (New York: Harper and Row, 1976), 124, 137, 214; unless otherwise noted, all biographical material is derived from this book. Ring Lardner Jr., "My Life on the Blacklist," *Saturday Evening Post*, October 14, 1961, 38–44; Ring Lardner Jr., *I'd Hate Myself in the Morning: A Memoir* (New York: Thunder's Mouth/ Nation, 2000); interview in *Tender Comrades*, 404–14; Kate Lardner, *Shut Up He Explained: The Memoir of a Blacklisted Kid* (New York: Ballantine, 2004); Barry Strugatz, "Interview with Ring Lardner, Jr.," *Film Comment* 24, no. 5 (September–October 1988): 52–71. For a review of Lardner's screenwriting career and a discussion of his credits, see Kenneth Geist, "The Films of Ring Lardner, Jr.," *Film Comment* 6, no. 4 (Winter 1970–71): 44–49.

11. Lardner to Ellis Lardner, n.d. (ca. Summer 1934), f. 288, Lardner, Jr. Papers.

12. Interviews with Joe Lardner, Kate Lardner, Nikola Trumbo, and Mitzi Trumbo.

13. Lardner, *The Lardners*, 256.

14. Lardner to Ellis Lardner, January 7, 1938, f. 288, Lardner, Jr. Papers.

15. Lardner to Ellis Lardner, May 10, 1938, f. 288, Lardner, Jr. Papers.

16. Lardner to Ellis Lardner, July 5, 1938, f. 288, Lardner, Jr. Papers.

17. Ff. 139 and 141, Lardner, Jr. Papers. Roberts's new company, Enterprise Productions, made three noir classics: *Body and Soul, Force of Evil,* and *He Ran All the Way.* Roberts was named, in September 1951, by Martin Berkeley, and he decamped for the United Kingdom to avoid a subpoena.

18. Howard Suber, "The Anti-Communist Blacklist in the Hollywood Motion Picture Industry" (Ph.D. diss., UCLA, 1968), 81.

19. F. 177, Lardner, Jr. Papers.

20. Ring Lardner Jr., interview by Bert Andrews, *New York Herald-Tribune*, January 7, 1948, f. 493, Lardner, Jr. Papers.

21. F. 468, Lardner, Jr. Papers.

22. Lardner, "My Life on the Blacklist," 39.

23. Craig Thompson, "The Tragedy of Ring Lardner, Jr.," *Coronet*, March 1951, 40, quoted in Bernard F. Dick, *Radical Innocence: A Critical Study of the Hollywood Ten* (Lexington: University Press of Kentucky, 1989), 166–67.

24. Lardner to John Lardner, September 1, 1950, f. 292, Lardner, Jr. Papers.

25. Lardner to Frances, September 11, 1950, f. 294, Lardner, Jr. Papers.

26. Lardner to Frances, January 26, 1951, f. 295, Lardner, Jr. Papers.

27. Lardner to Frances, March 4, 1951, f. 295, Lardner, Jr. Papers.

28. Lardner to Frances, March 4, 1951, f. 295, Lardner, Jr. Papers.

29. Lardner, *I'd Hate Myself*, 135–36. Several of the Ten used their prison time to work on novels. Trumbo started on what he conceived as his great war novel, but he did not return to it after he was released; Maltz, who had written several novels earlier, conceived the idea for *A Long Day in a Short Life* (New York: International, 1957), which he completed in Mexico; and Samuel Ornitz, also a published novelist, completed *Bride of the Sabbath* (New York: Rinehart, 1951).

30. After completing the movie, Losey left the country to avoid a subpoena from the Committee.

31. Lardner to Peter and Ann, n.d., f. 287, Lardner, Jr. Papers.

32. The files are in f. 321, Lardner, Jr. Papers.

33. Lardner to Ann, n.d., f. 285, Lardner, Jr. Papers.

34. Lardner, *The Ecstasy of Owen Muir* (New York: Cameron and Kahn, 1954), 112, 114.

35. Quoted in Martin Malia, *History's Locomotives: Revolutions and the Making of the Modern World*, ed. Terence Emmons (New Haven, CT: Yale University Press, 2006), 253.

36. For an in-depth, positive discussion of the novel and its place in 1950s culture, see Adam J. Sorkin, "Politics, Privatism and the Fifties: Ring Lardner Jr.'s *The Ecstasy of Owen Muir*," *Journal of American Culture* 8, no. 3 (Fall 1985): 59–73. It was republished by Seven Seas in 1966, New American Library in 1977, and Prometheus Books in 1997.

37. Lardner to Hannah Weinstein, December 7, 1956, f. 180, Ian McLellan Hunter Papers, Margaret Herrick Library (hereafter cited as Hunter Papers).

38. Similarly, Walter Bernstein brought in Abe Polonsky and Arnold Manoff to write scripts for *You Are There*, and Polonsky did the same for Paul Jarrico, Lardner, and Hunter for the Canadian series *Seaway*.

39. Albert Ruben, email to author, February 22, 2018.

40. Tise Vahimagi, "Weinstein, Hannah (1912–1984)," www.screenonline.org.uk/people/id/772169/index.html.

41. Agreement between Lardner and Hunter on profit sharing, f. 269, Lardner, Jr. Papers; Steve Neale, "Un-American Contributions to TV Costume Adventure Series in the 1950s," in *"Un-American" Hollywood: Politics and Film in the Blacklist Era*, ed. Frank Krutnik et al. (New Brunswick, NJ: Rutgers University Press, 2007), 198–209.

42. Lardner to Ann, January 15, 1956, f. 284, Lardner, Jr. Papers. The series was a huge hit and great commercial success (see Steve Neale, "Transatlantic Ventures and *Robin Hood*," in *ITV Cultures: Independent Television over Fifty Years*, ed. Catherine Johnson and Rob Turnock [Maidenhead, UK: Open University Press, 2005], 74).

43. Lardner, "My Life on the Blacklist," 42.

44. Lardner to Ann, January 15, 1958, f. 285, Lardner, Jr. Papers.

45. "Paris Blues," f. 165, Lardner, Jr. Papers.

46. "See No Evil," f. 171, Lardner, Jr. Papers.

47. The correspondence is found at f. 364, Lardner, Jr. Papers.

48. Lardner to Hunter, n.d., f. 274, Hunter Papers.

49. Lardner to Frances, August 13 and 14, 1959, f. 289, Lardner, Jr. Papers.

50. *A Breath of Scandal*, f. 2 and 4, Lardner Jr. Papers; Lardner to Ann, April 21, 1961, f. 286, Lardner, Jr. Papers.

51. Letters are in f. 345, Lardner, Jr. Papers.

52. Lardner, *Shut Up He Explained*, 188, 229.

53. Lardner to Gene Lichtenstein, April 2, 1972, f. 284, Lardner, Jr. Papers.

54. Lardner to Hunter, f. 274, Hunter Papers.

55. Lardner to William Abbott, August 27, 1961, f. 296, Lardner, Jr. Papers.

56. Lardner, "My Life on the Blacklist," 44.

57. The letters are in *Saturday Evening Post*, November 18, 1961, 4; November 25, 1961, 4 and 6; and January 13, 1962, 4. Walters's full letter is in *Congressional Record*, January 30, 1962, A676–80.

58. Roy M. Brewer, "The Truth about the 'Blacklist,'" *American Legion Magazine*, reprinted in Bentley, *Thirty Years of Treason*, 195–206.

59. Typescript, October 30, 1961, f. 339, Lardner, Jr. Papers.

60. Trumbo to Lardner, August 7, 1961, folder 3, box 221, Dalton Trumbo Papers, UCLA Special Collections.

61. F. 119, Lardner, Jr. Papers.

62. Joe Lardner, email to author, February 2, 2018.

63. Handwritten notes, n.d., f. 466, Lardner, Jr. Papers.

64. Lardner, "30 Years after the 'Hollywood Ten,'" 23.

65. *Congressional Record*, March 21, 1978, E1464–65.

66. "Hollywood Remembers the Blacklist," October 27, 1997, videocassette, Writers Guild of America, West Library, Los Angeles, CA.

7. Shedding Light on *Darkness at High Noon*

1. Written and directed by Lionel Chetwynd, narrated by Richard Crenna; voice of Carl Foreman, Richard McGonagle; aired on PBS, September 2002.

8. Looking Ahead

1. See Robert Kennedy Jr., *The Real Anthony Fauci: Bill Gates, Big Pharma, and the Global War on Democracy and Public Health* (New York: Skyhorse and Children's Health Defense, 2021), 212–18.

2. Michael Powell, "How a Famous Harvard Professor Became a Target over His Tweets," nytimes.com/2020/07/15/steven-pinker-harvard.html; Anne Applebaum, "The New Puritans," theatlantic.com/magazine/archives/2021/10 (originally published August 31, 2021); John McWhorter, "Academics Are Really, Really Worried about Their Freedom," *All*, September 1, 1920, 2020/09/academics-are-really-worried-about-their-freedom/615724/; John McWhorter, *Woke Racism: How a New Religion Has Betrayed Black America* (New York: Portfolio/Penguin, 2021). For a critical response to Applebaum, see Adam Gruri, "The Case Not Made: A Response to Anne Applebaum's 'The New Puritans,'" *Liberal Currents,* September 20, 2021, liberalcurrents.com/the-case-not-made-response-to-anne-applebaum's-the-new-puritans/. For a comparison of the Pinker episode to the McCarthy era, see Aaron Brown, "Pattern of Fears," *City Journal,* July 15, 2020, city-journal.org/steven-pinker-letter.

3. Https://schiff.house.gov/news/press-releases/schiff-sends-letter-to-google-facebook-regarding-anti-vaccine-misinformation.

4. Freedom to Dissent and the New Blacklist in America, July 1, 2019, https://www.nvic.org/nvic-vaccine-news/july-2019/freedom-to-dissent-and-new-blacklist-in-america.aspx#_edn63.

5. Jill Lepore, "The Forest for the Trees," *New Yorker,* December 6, 2021, 17.

6. "Kitchen Confessional: Food-World Star Alison Roman Lets All Hang Out," *New Yorker,* December 20, 2021, 48.

7. David Brooks, "The Terrifying Future of the American Right: What I Saw at the National Conservatism Conference," *The Atlantic,* November 18, 2021, https://www.theatlantic.com/ideas/archive/2021/11/scary-future-american-right-national-conservatism-conference/620746/.

8. Helen Lewis, "How Capitalism Drives Cancel Culture," *The Atlantic*, July 14, 2020, https://www.theatlantic.com/international/archive/2020/07/cancel-culture-and-problem-woke-capitalism/614086/.

9. Matt Stoller, *Goliath: The 100-Year War between Monopoly Power and Democracy* (New York: Simon and Schuster, 2019), 465.

10. Https://www.indeed.com/career-advice/career-development/do-not-hire-list.

11. Lewis, "How Capitalism Drives Cancel Culture."

12. Rashawn Ray and Alexandra Gibbons, "Why Are States Banning Critical Race Theory?," *Fixgov*, November 2021, https://www.brookings.edu/blog/fixgov/2021/07/02/why-are-states-banning-critical-race-theory/.

Annotated Films and Plays

Documentaries (in chronological order)

The Hollywood Ten, produced by Paul Jarrico; directed by John Berry; written by John Berry and the Hollywood Ten; starring the Hollywood Ten. Black-and-white, 15 minutes, 1950 (available on HBO).

An agitprop film made to convince the public that the Ten should not be imprisoned for contempt of Congress. The first half reviews the lives and works of the ten men; in the second half, they explain the reasons for their conviction and the consequences for the United States if they are imprisoned. Their warnings proved prescient, and listening to them predict what will happen is riveting.

Hollywood on Trial, produced by James C. Gutman; directed by David Halpern; written by Arnie Reisman; narrated by John Huston. Black-and-white/color, 101 minutes, 1976 (distributed by Corinth Films).

The first, and still the best, detailed look at the events leading up to the motion-picture blacklist. The roster of interviewees is extensive and impressive.

A Crime to Fit the Punishment, produced, written, and directed by Barbara Moss and Stephen Mack. Color, 46 minutes, 1982 (originally distributed by First Run Features, currently available at archive.org).

A major effort to cover the multifaceted nature of the making of *Salt of the Earth,* this documentary acquaints viewers with the outlines of the origins of the movie, the links between Hollywood and New Mexico, and the main characters in both. But it broaches few of the most interesting questions, including, surprisingly, those concerning the Communist Party.

Legacy of the Hollywood Blacklist, produced by Loren Stephens, Ellen Geiger, and Judy Chaikin; directed by Judy Chaikin; narrated by Burt Lancaster. Black-and-white/color, 60 minutes, 1987 (One Step Productions, available through Cinema Guild).

This film provides a historical context for the rise of radicalism in Hollywood (albeit it commits several rather embarrassing historical errors, notably in the dates) and a stirring montage of the Hollywood Ten's defense of their right not to be imprisoned simply for declining to answer the questions of a congressional committee about their membership affiliations. But its account of the blacklist's effect on the movie industry is a truncated, anachronistic mishmash of film clips, and the narrator does not ask hard questions of the subjects, all of whom are women. There is a soft, soppy glaze on the subject.

The Day the Cold War Came Home, produced by Tony Kahn, WCBV-TV Boston. Black-and-white, 21 minutes, 1988 (available through Cinema Guild).

This is, in effect, a home movie—an earnest, short, straightforward, sincere, and amateurish account of the blacklisted Gordon Kahn (one of the Hollywood Nineteen) and his family. We are told nothing about his pre-1950 screenwriting career or his politics or his post-1950 attempt to earn a living on the black market. We do learn about their lives in Mexico and New Hampshire, their financial difficulties, and the harassment they suffered.

Waldo Salt: A Screenwriter's Journey, produced by Robert Hillman and Eugene Corr; directed by Robert Hillman and Eugene Corr; written by Eugene Corr. Color, 45 minutes, 1990 (Eagle Rock Entertainment and WNET Channel 13, New York).

An excellent review of the life of a very intelligent and interesting writer. The arc of his career is well told, especially by Salt, and the blacklist is treated as one unfortunate episode in an otherwise full life.

Red Hollywood, produced, directed, and written by Thom Andersen and Noël Burch. Black-and-white/color, 118 minutes, 1996 (distributed by Cinema Guild).

This well-made documentary examines the films made by writers and directors who would later be blacklisted. Its main focus is film noir, but it introduces a new subgenre, film gris. Paul Jarrico, Ring Lardner Jr., Abraham Polonsky, and Alfred Levitt are interviewed.

Trumbo, produced by Will Battersby, Tory Tunnell, Alan Klingenstein, and David Viola; directed by Peter Askin; written by Christopher Trumbo. Color, 96 minutes, 2009 (Magnolia Home Entertainment).

A filmed version of Christopher Trumbo's play based on his father's letters. They are read by Joan Allen, Brian Dennehy, Michael Douglas, Paul Giamatti, Nathan Lane, Josh Lucas, Liam Neeson, David Strathairn, and Donald Sutherland.

Yoo-Hoo, Mrs. Goldberg, produced, directed, and written by Aviva Kempner. Color/black-and-white, 92 minutes, 2009 (Ciesla Foundation, distributed by International Film Circuit and National Center for Jewish Film).

Examines the broadcast career of Gertrude Berg and her radio and television serials *The Goldbergs.* Her shows had a very progressive point of view and ran into trouble with anti-Communists, who eventually forced the television program off the air. Its costar, Philip Loeb, was blacklisted and committed suicide.

Marsha Hunt's Sweet Adversity: A Life of Acting and Activism, produced by Richard Adkins, Joan Cohen, and Roger C. Memos; directed by Roger C. Memos; written by Richard Adkins. Black-and-white/color, 101 minutes, 2015 (Indie Rights).

Hunt, a liberal actress who supported many progressive causes, was blacklisted when she refused to explain or apologize for her actions. She remained active in many worthy causes and wrote a book on fashion.

Features (in chronological order)

Salt of the Earth, produced by Paul Jarrico; directed by Herbert Biberman; written by Michael Wilson; starring Rosaura Revueltas and Juan Chacon. Black-and-white, 94 minutes, 1954.

Made by a group of blacklisted Hollywood people, it re-creates, from a Marxist perspective, a fifteen-month miners' strike in New Mexico. The heart of the film is the exploitation of, and the prejudice toward, the Mexican American workers, and the rising consciousness of their wives. The activism and courage of the women, their ringing voices, are still inspiring.

The Way We Were, produced by Ray Stark; directed by Sidney Pollack; written by Arthur Laurents: starring Barbra Streisand, Robert Redford,

Bradford Dillman, and Lois Chiles. Color, 118 minutes, 1973 (Columbia Pictures).

Though it is mainly a love story between a radical (Streisand) and a liberal (Redford), it does briefly illustrate the fear and compromises caused by the 1947 hearings.

The Front, produced by Charles H. Joffe and Jack Rollins; directed by Martin Ritt; written by Walter Bernstein; starring Woody Allen, Zero Mostel, Herschel Bernardi, Michael Murphy, and Andrea Marcovicci. Color, 95 minutes, 1976 (Columbia Pictures).

An excellent look at the television black market, written and directed by two former blacklistees.

The House on Carroll Street, produced by Robert Benton; directed by Peter Yates; written by Walter Bernstein; starring Kelly McGillis, Jeff Daniels, and Mandy Patinkin. Color, 101 minutes, 1987 (Orion Pictures).

A blacklisted journalist (McGillis) teams with an FBI agent (Daniels) to thwart a scheme to smuggle ex-Nazis into the United States. The script is good on the conspiracies and hypocrisies of the early 1950s, and its eerie depiction of Ray Salwen (Patinkin), who is a perfectly realized screen version of Roy Cohn, the notorious counsel of Senator Joseph McCarthy. (Roy Cohn is also a central character in Tony Kushner's magisterial play *Angels in America* [1991].) An HBO version, directed by Mike Nichols and starring Al Pacino as Cohn, is available on DVD.

Fellow Traveller, produced by Colin Callender, Ben Gibson, and Jill Pack; directed by Philip Saville; written by Michael Eaton; starring Ron Silver, Hart Bochner, Imogen Stubbs, and Daniel J. Travanti. Color, 97 minutes, 1990 (available on BBC/HBO).

The only feature focused on an actual Communist, one who leaves the United States to avoid a subpoena from a congressional investigating committee. In the United Kingdom, he secures work on the television black market, writing for *The Adventures of Robin Hood.* When his close friend commits suicide, he is sure that it was caused by the witch hunt, and he enlists the friend's girlfriend to investigate. It is a simplistic look at the issues of the domestic Cold War, and the dialogue is stagy and contrived. But it captures well the paranoid atmosphere of the period and black-market television work in the United Kingdom.

Guilty by Suspicion, produced by Arnon Milchan; written and directed by Irwin Winkler; starring Robert De Niro, Annette Bening, and George Wendt; Warner Bros. Color, 105 minutes, 1991.

A liberal movie director returns to Hollywood from France in the midst of the 1951 House Committee on Un-American Activities hearings into Communist infiltration of the movie industry. He had attended a few Communist Party meetings and has been named by a friendly witness. When he refuses to comply with the studio's clearance program, job offers cease, his friends turn against him, and FBI agents follow and harass him. There are two basic problems with the main character: he is presented as if he were the only courageous person in Hollywood, and there is no basis in the character for his refusal to cooperate. By using a liberal rather than a Communist, Winkler has falsified the situation and ducked an examination of the real resisters, the Communists. (The original script had been written by Abraham Polonsky, who left the project when Winkler took over as director from Bertrand Tavernier.)

One of the Hollywood Ten, produced, written, and directed by Karl Francis; starring Jeff Goldblum and Greta Schacchi. Color, 149 minutes, 2000 (available through Vimeo).

This unreleased movie purports to recount the making of *Salt of the Earth* through the characters of Herbert Biberman, the director, and his actress wife, Gale Sondergaard. Francis has taken excessive liberties with the facts. (When Paul Jarrico, the producer of *Salt,* read the script, his reaction was *"oy vey."*) But the New Mexico scenes depicting the shoot are well done.

The Majestic, produced by Frank Darabont; directed by Frank Darabont; written by Michael Sloane; starring Jim Carrey, Martin Landau, and Bob Balaban. Color, 152 minutes, 2001 (Warner Bros.).

A somewhat convoluted approach to the subject, it again features an unremarkable non-Communist who rises to the occasion of being subpoenaed with a stirring speech.

Trumbo, produced by Kevin Kelly Brown; directed by Jay Roach; written by John McNamara; starring Bryan Cranston, Diane Lane, Helen Mirren, and Louis C. K. Color, 124 minutes, 2015 (Bleecker Street Films).

Although this film takes great liberties with the facts and invents many scenes, it does offer a reasonably accurate overview of Trumbo's life, from his subpoena to his winning an Academy Award for *The Brave One.*

Stage Plays

Eric Bentley, *Are You Now or Have You Ever Been?* (1972), in *Rallying Cry: Three Plays by Eric Bentley* (Washington, DC: New Republic Book Co., 1977).

Using transcripts of the 1950s House Committee hearings, Bentley dramatically presents the questions asked of and the answers given by Lionel Stander, Abe Burrows, Lillian Hellman, Larry Parks, Elia Kazan, Jerome Robbins, and Jose Ferrer.

Mark Kemble, *Names,* 1995.

Former members of the 1930s left-wing Group Theatre (Stella and Luther Adler, Lee Strasberg, Clifford Odets, Harold Clurman, and John Garfield, among others, gather, in 1952, to await the appearance of Elia Kazan and learn whether or not he cooperated with the House Committee on Un-American Activities.

Christopher Trumbo, *Trumbo: Red, White & Blacklisted* (New York: Playscripts, Inc., 2007). (Available on audio tape: L.A. Theatre Works, *Additional Dialogue: The Letters of Dalton Trumbo,* produced by Susan Albert Loewenberg; directed by Gordon Hunt; starring Harry Groener, Paul Winfield, Jeff Corey, and Christopher Trumbo. Audio Theatre Series, 87 minutes.)

Using his father's letters, Christopher Trumbo recaptures the fear and disruptions of the 1950s.

Radio Plays

Nat Segaloff, Daniel M. Kimmel, and Arnie Reisman, *The Waldorf Conference,* produced by Susan Albert Loewenberg; written by the above three; directed by John De Lancie; starring Edward Asner, Shelley Berman, Charles Durning, David Ellenstein, John Kapelos, George Murdock, and Richard Masur. 87 minutes, 1993 (Audible).

No transcript of the Waldorf Conference, at which the movie-industry heads decided to blacklist the Hollywood Ten, has come to light. The authors of this radio play have imaginatively re-created what likely was said there. The cast act the parts wonderfully.

Podcasts

The Blacklist Archive, June 21, 2016: "Tender Comrades: The Prehistory of the Blacklist"; "Crossfire: The Trials of the Hollywood Ten"; "Dorothy Parker"; "*The African Queen:* Humphrey Bogart, Katharine Hepburn and John Huston"; "The Strange Love of Barbara Stanwyck: Robert Taylor"; "He Ran All the Way: John Garfield"; "*Monsieur Verdoux:* Charlie Chaplin's Road to Exile"; "Storm Warning: Ronald Reagan, the FBI and HUAC"; "She: Richard Nixon + Helen Gahagan Douglas"; "*Salt of the Earth:* Howard Hughes + Paul Jarrico"; "*Born Yesterday:* Judy Holliday"; "Lena Horne + Paul Robeson"; "*On the Waterfront:* Elia Kazan"; "Frank Sinatra and Albert Maltz (Breaking the Blacklist, Part 1)"; "Kirk Douglas, Dalton Trumbo, and Otto Preminger (Breaking the Blacklist, Part 2)." Created, written, and hosted by Karina Longworth, http://www.youmustrememberthispodcast .com/episodes/2016/06/21/blacklistarchive.

The first in a series of podcasts in which Longworth tells "the secret and/or forgotten histories of Hollywood. . . . My goal," she says, "is to present the fairest picture of events that I can, based on my understanding of what I've read." It is well researched and well written, providing intriguing looks at some of the most interesting people and events.

Annotated Bibliography

Autobiographies and Memoirs (in alphabetical order by author)

Barzman, Norma. *The Red and the Blacklist: Intimate Memoir of a Hollywood Expatriate*. New York: Thunder's Mouth/Nation, 2003.

This is among the most detailed, and certainly the most entertaining, of blacklist memoirs. The Barzmans were among the first of the Hollywood émigrés to France, where they stayed for thirty years. She provides a lively account of those years—raising a family (seven children), helping her husband with his black-market work, engaging in several love affairs, building the blacklistees into a community, enjoying the friendships of Yves Montand, Simone Signoret, Pablo Picasso, and Sophia Loren. The book is filled with delicious anecdotes, and the reader is zipped along by the author's incredible zest for life.

Bernstein, Walter. *Inside Out: A Memoir of the Blacklist*. New York: Da Capo, 2000.

The screenwriter for *The Front*, the first, and still the best, cinematic depiction of the blacklist, as well as the excellent labor movie *The Molly Maguires* and many black-market television scripts, notably for *You Are There*, has written a deeply personal account of his life and career. Unlike many other blacklistees, he was not an established writer when he was listed in *Red Channels* and blacklisted, so he struggled before meeting Boris Karloff, who provided his entrée into television. He is refreshingly unrepentant about his membership in the Communist Party, and he bears no grudges.

Bessie, Alvah. *Inquisition in Eden*. New York: Macmillan, 1965.

The first of the Hollywood Ten memoirs, it is not among the best, and it is not always factually reliable. Bessie's Hollywood career started late in his life, was short, and his script output small. The most interesting parts of the book are his account of his years in Spain, fighting with the Abraham Lincoln Battalion to defeat the rebellion against Spain's Popular Front government, and his stories about surviving on the blacklist by working the lights at San Francisco's "hungry i" nightclub. (His *Men in Battle* is a fine account of the Spanish Civil War.)

Bessie, Dan. *Rare Birds: An American Family.* Lexington: University Press of Kentucky, 2001.

A lovely series of essays on interesting members of his family, including his father, Alvah Bessie, for whom he arrives at a new understanding.

Blair, Betsy. *Memory of All That: Love and Politics in New York, Hollywood, and Paris.* New York: Knopf, 2003.

Blair, a New York stage actress and dancer who had attended a Marxist study group, came to Hollywood via her marriage to Gene Kelly. She was active in many left-wing causes. She started acting in movies and television in 1947 and collected ten screen credits by 1951. She was not subpoenaed by the House Committee, but she was blacklisted. She broke through in 1955, with the help of Kelly, to secure a costarring role in *Marty.* They divorced in 1957, and she moved to Paris. She has many interesting stories to tell.

Bright, John. *Worms in the Winecup: A Memoir.* Lanham, MD: Scarecrow, 2002.

One of the most interesting, bitterest, and least known blacklistees. A reporter on the Chicago crime beat, Bright came to Hollywood and cowrote *Public Enemy* (1931). He followed with a long list of credits, cofounded the Screen Writers Guild, and joined the Communist Party. Named by nine informers, he was not subpoenaed, and his career ended. He had no success on the black market. This is a take-no-prisoners memoir.

Chaplin, Charles. *My Autobiography.* New York: Simon and Schuster, 1964.

His FBI file is a lengthy one, and he received a subpoena from the House Committee on Un-American Activities, but it was rescinded. Although he was not blacklisted, his left-leaning politics contributed to his forced exile from the United States.

Cole, Lester. *Hollywood Red: The Autobiography of Lester Cole.* Palo Alto, CA: Ramparts, 1981.

Cole was a cofounder of the Screen Writers Guild, one of the earliest members of the Communist Party in Hollywood, and a member of the

Hollywood Ten. He provides a detailed account of his vocation and the struggles of the Guild for recognition. He does not examine the complexities of being a Communist in the movie industry, and the book is marred by his mean-spiritedness, not only to those who informed but to former friends and allies who might have crossed him politically, personally, or professionally.

Dmytryk, Edward. *It's a Hell of a Life, but Not a Bad Living.* New York: Times Books, 1978; and *Odd Man Out: A Memoir of the Hollywood Ten.* Carbondale: Southern Illinois University Press, 1996.

Dmytryk, the only member of the Hollywood Ten to recant, reappear before the House Committee on Un-American Activities, and name names, recounts his screen career in the first of these books and his decision to recant in the second. His reasons for naming names should be critically examined.

Douglas, Kirk. *I Am Spartacus! Making a Film, Breaking the Blacklist.* New York: Open Road, 2012.

Both the subtitle and the book's main thesis are false. Douglas did not, because he could not, break the blacklist. He did hire the blacklisted screenwriter Dalton Trumbo at low, black-market rates, to write several scripts for Douglas's production company. But it was Eddie Lewis who brought Trumbo to Bryna Productions, and it was Lewis who provided the properties, mainly *Lonely Are the Brave* and *Spartacus,* on which Trumbo worked. And it was Lewis, not Douglas, who pushed the hardest for Trumbo to receive a screen credit. In addition, Douglas is unreliable about the facts, and Trumbo family members have challenged the credibility of many of his anecdotes about Trumbo. That said, the book does contain many interesting stories about the making of the film.

Dunne, Philip. *Take Two: A Life in Movies and Politics.* New York: McGraw Hill, 1980.

Dunne was one of the most active liberals in Hollywood during the 1930s and 1940s. He was also a cofounder of the Committee for the First Amendment. This very well-written memoir highlights both liberal values and liberal delusions.

Edwards, Anne. *Leaving Home: A Hollywood Blacklisted Writer's Years Abroad.* Lanham, MD: Scarecrow, 2012.

I have found no evidence that Edwards was blacklisted; her claim that she was does not ring true.

Gordon, Bernard. *Hollywood Exile, or How I Learned to Love the Blacklist.* Austin: University of Texas Press, 1999.

A very good account of his life on the black market, where Gordon wrote dozens of scripts and the characters he met along the way. When the Writers Guild began awarding screen credits to blacklisted writers, he amassed the most.

Grant, Lee. *I Said Yes to Everything: A Memoir.* New York: Blue Rider, 2014.

This is a candid and heartfelt account of an actress's life. Her account of her twelve years on the blacklist is especially compelling.

Hayden, Sterling. *Wanderer.* New York: Knopf, 1963.

A well-written account of his decision to leave his very successful movie career and become a world traveler. Previous to that, he had been a member of the Communist Party who, to save his career, met with FBI agents and became an informing witness. In this first public account of an informer, Hayden does not specifically say he that he regretted his decision, but he does describe his act in self-loathing terms.

Hellman, Lillian. *An Unfinished Woman: A Memoir.* Boston: Little, Brown, 1969; *Pentimento: A Book of Portraits.* Boston: Little, Brown, 1973; *Scoundrel Time.* Boston: Little, Brown, 1976; and *An Unfinished Woman: Reminiscences of Lillian Hellman.* New York: Barnes and Noble, 2001.

Very well-written works, but their veracity has been strongly questioned. She also inflates her manner of resistance to the House Committee on Un-American Activities, claiming that her "diminished Fifth Amendment" stance was original with her.

Hunt, Marsha. *The Way We Wore: Styles of the 1930 and '40s and Our World since Then.* Fallbrook, CA: Fallbrook, 1993.

Lovely photographs interspersed with her account of her political past and blacklisting.

Kazan, Elia. *Elia Kazan: A Life.* New York: Knopf, 1988.

A detailed account of the life of perhaps the most successful director of stage and screen and the most notorious of the informing witnesses. He writes that his decision was the correct one, though he is not sure if it was the right one, adding, "The truth is that within a year I stopped feeling guilty or even embarrassed by what I had done."

Koch, Howard. *As Time Goes By: Memories of a Writer*. New York: Harcourt Brace Jovanovich, 1979.
Though he was not a Communist, Koch, one of the Nineteen and perhaps its greatest talent, found himself blacklisted. He writes well about his great movie scripts (notably *Casablanca*), being coerced by Jack Warner into writing the movie that contributed to his blacklisting (*Mission to Moscow*), and his efforts to get off the blacklist.

Lardner, Kate. *Shut Up He Explained: The Memoir of a Blacklisted Kid*. New York: Ballantine, 2004.
After her father, David, died in World War II, her mother remarried David's brother, Ring Lardner Jr. Three years later Lardner was blacklisted, and three years after that imprisoned. Kate Lardner recounts her hazy childhood memories of those events, reproduces letters and clippings from Ring while he was in prison, and tells of her parents' distance from the children, her addictions, recovery, and reconciliation with them.

Lardner, Ring, Jr. *I'd Hate Myself in the Morning: A Memoir*. New York: Thunder's Mouth/Nation, 2000.
The son of the great writer Ring Lardner takes the reader through his early years, his decision to become a screenwriter and join the Communist Party, his blacklisting, and his work on the black market (he cowrote most of the scripts for the British television series *The Adventures of Robin Hood*). A meticulous historian, his account is the most trustworthy.

Laurents, Arthur. *Original Story By: A Memoir of Broadway and Hollywood*. New York: Knopf, 2000.
One of the best memoirs, in terms of writing and details.

Rapf, Maurice. *Back Lot: Growing up with the Movies*. Lanham, MD: Scarecrow, 1999.
The son of a prominent producer, the author traveled to the Soviet Union, joined the Communist Party, became a screenwriter, and was blacklisted.

Robinson, Edward G. *All My Yesterdays: An Autobiography*. With Leonard Spigelgass. New York: Hawthorn, 1973.

Robinson narrowly escaped the blacklist, talking several times with the FBI and appearing twice before the House Committee. He still regrets what he had to say—essentially that he, who had been a dedicated civil libertarian, had been duped. How, he wonders, did I let them push me around: "How could I? To this day I don't know."

Rouverol, Jean. *Refugees from Hollywood: A Journal of the Blacklist Years.* Albuquerque: University of New Mexico Press, 2000.

Her married name was Jean Butler; Rouverol was the name she used to write during the black market. Fearing a subpoena, she and her husband, screenwriter Hugo Butler, and their brood of children moved to Mexico in 1950, where they lived for several decades. Rouverol recounts well managing the family, her writing career, Hugo's films (a few with Luis Buñuel), and their harassment by the FBI.

Schulberg, Budd. *Moving Pictures: Memoirs of a Hollywood Prince.* New York: Stein and Day, 1989.

The son of a prominent studio executive, Schulberg traveled to the Soviet Union with Maurice Rapf, became a screenwriter and novelist, and joined the Communist Party. He became antagonistic toward the Party when its critics denigrated his novel *What Makes Sammy Run?* He became an informer and wrote the screenplay for *On the Waterfront,* a movie that approves of informing against mob-run labor unions.

Sigal, Clancy. *Black Sunset: Hollywood Sex, Lies, Glamour, Betrayal, and Raging Egos.* Berkeley, CA: Soft Skull, 2016.

This book is interesting because it is the only account by a soon-to-be-blacklisted Communist Party member cum Hollywood talent agent. Some readers may be put off by Sigal's egomania, and his writing style is an acquired taste.

Stewart, Donald Ogden. *By a Stroke of Luck.* New York: Paddington, 1975.

Stewart went from Yale to a successful career as a humorist (magazine articles and plays) to becoming one of the best screenwriters in Hollywood. Wanting to be more serious, he joined the Communist Party. To avoid a subpoena, he decamped for the United Kingdom, where he did mostly television work. He has written a witty and informative account of this hegira.

Trumbo, Dalton. *Additional Dialogue: Letters of Dalton Trumbo, 1942–1962.* Edited by Helen Manfull. New York: M. Evans, 1970.

An indispensable source, not only because Trumbo's letters are a virtual journal of the period, but because of the wit of the writer. Manfull did a masterful job of selecting and editing.

Biographies and Interviews (in alphabetical order by author or editor)

Alexander, Linda. *Reluctant Witness: Robert Taylor, Hollywood, and Communism.* Swansboro, NC: Tease, 2008.

A straightforward, clearly written, well-researched account of the actor's life and work. Alexander takes pains to clarify and contextualize Taylor's appearance as a friendly witness in 1947.

Bosworth, Patricia. *Anything Your Little Heart Desires: An American Family Story.* New York: Simon and Schuster, 1997.

Provides a very sympathetic account of her father, Bartley Crum, one of the attorneys for the Nineteen.

Buhle, Paul, and Dave Wagner. *A Very Dangerous Citizen: Abraham Lincoln Polonsky and the Hollywood Left.* Berkeley: University of California Press, 2002.

A very fine biography of one of the most brilliant minds and knowledgeable Marxists among the Hollywood Left. A labor organizer and novelist, Polonsky, before he was blacklisted, wrote *Body and Soul* and then wrote and directed *Force of Evil,* two of the best film noir movies. During the blacklist he wrote mainly for television, and, when he emerged, *Tell Them Willie Boy Is Here.*

Casty, Alan. *Robert Rossen: The Films and Politics of a Blacklisted Idealist.* Jefferson, NC: McFarland, 2013.

A very good commentary on the blacklisted director, who decided to inform to regain his career. Casty sees him as a moral hero.

Caute, David. *Joseph Losey: A Revenge on Life.* New York: Oxford University Press, 1994.

Losey left Hollywood to avoid appearing before the House Committee, and he lived and worked in the United Kingdom thereafter, enjoying a highly successful career there. Caute does not like his subject, but he provides a detailed account of Losey's life and work.

Ceplair, Larry. *The Marxist and the Movies: A Biography of Paul Jarrico.* Lexington: University Press of Kentucky, 2007.

Jarrico was not in the front rank of screenwriters, but he is notable for his production of *Salt of the Earth* and his valiant campaign to get the Writers Guild of America to restore screen credits to those who wrote on the black market during the 1950s. He was also a stalwart member of the Communist Party, who maintained a vast archive on its activities in the movie industry.

Ceplair, Larry, and Christopher Trumbo. *Dalton Trumbo: Blacklisted Hollywood Radical.* Lexington: University Press of Kentucky, 2015.

A detailed discussion of the life of one of Hollywood's most successful screenwriters and his successful effort to break through the blacklist.

Cook, Bruce. *Dalton Trumbo: A Biography of the Oscar-Winning Screenwriter Who Broke the Blacklist.* New York: Scribner's, 1977.

Written with the full cooperation of Dalton Trumbo and containing interviews with many of his contemporaries and family members.

Corliss, Richard. *Talking Pictures: Screenwriters in the American Cinema.* New York: Penguin, 1975.

This compilation includes five blacklisted writers: Sidney Buchman, Dalton Trumbo, Howard Koch, Abraham Polonsky, and Ring Lardner Jr.

Fariello, Griffin. *Red Scare: Memories of the American Inquisition.* New York: Norton, 1995.

Eighty-two interviews with a wide variety of participants, willing and unwilling, in the domestic Cold War, including nine motion-picture blacklistees, Roy Brewer, and Christopher Trumbo.

Hanson, Peter. *Dalton Trumbo, Hollywood Rebel: A Critical Survey and Filmography.* Jefferson, NC: McFarland, 2001.

A thorough and first-rate examination of the movies written by Dalton Trumbo, both above- and belowground.

Horne, Gerald. *The Final Victim of the Blacklist: John Howard Lawson, Dean of the Hollywood Ten.* Berkeley: University of California Press, 2006.

A well-researched and factually informative account of the most recognizable Communist screenwriter of the 1930s and 1940s. Lawson had been a successful playwright for the left theater in New York, cofounded the Screen Writers Guild, dominated the movie branches of the Communist

Party, and wrote several books on play- and screenwriting. But this biography lacks depth of analysis, and Horne fails to explain Lawson's personal motivations, his aesthetic theories, or his politics.

Kessler-Harris, Alice. *A Difficult Woman: The Challenging Life and Times of Lillian Hellman.* New York: Bloomsbury, 2012.

There are dozens of books on Hellman, the hugely successful playwright of the 1930s, and 1940s, who rose to postblacklist fame via her four memoir-type books but was then attacked for fabricating most of them. This book is an excellent starting point, following, sympathetically and critically, the twists and turns and contexts of this controversial woman. [See also Peter S. Feibleman, *Reminiscences of Lillian Hellman* (New York: Avon, 1990); Carl Rollyson, *Lillian Hellman: Her Legend and Her Legacy* (San Jose, CA: ToExcel, 1999); William Wright, *Lillian Hellman, the Image, the Woman* (New York: Simon and Schuster, 2000); Deborah Martinson, *Lillian Hellman: A Life with Foxes and Scoundrels* (New York: Counterpoint, 2005); Alice Griffin and Geraldine Thorsten, *Understanding Lillian Hellman* (Columbia: University of South Carolina Press, 2009); Jackson R. Bryer, ed., *Conversations with Lillian Hellman* (Jackson: University Press of Mississippi, 2009); Dorothy Gallagher, *Lillian Hellman: An Imperious Life* (New Haven, CT: Yale University Press, 2014).]

Langdon, Jennifer. *Caught in the Crossfire: Adrian Scott and the Politics of Americanism in 1940s Hollywood.* New York: Columbia University Press, 2009.

An excellent deep study of the making of *Crossfire* (RKO, 1947), an anti-anti-Semitic film that likely led to the subpoenaing and eventual blacklisting of Adrian Scott, its producer, and Edward Dmytryk, its director.

Losey, Joseph. *Losey on Losey.* Edited by Tom Milne. Garden City, NY: Doubleday, 1968.

In this set of interviews, the blacklisted director discusses his pre-émigré Hollywood films (*The Boy with Green Hair* and *The Prowler*), his decision to emigrate, his major European films, and his work with Bertolt Brecht on *Galileo.*

MacAdam, Henry, Duncan Cooper, Abraham Polonsky, and Fiona Radford. *The Gladiators vs. Spartacus.* 2 vols. Newcastle-upon-Tyne: Cambridge Scholars, 2020.

Volume 1—*Dueling Productions in Blacklist Hollywood: The Race to the Screen*—tells the story of the competing projects, both involving blacklisted writers, to produce a movie about Spartacus. Volume 2—*Abraham Polonsky's Screenplay*—provides the wherewithal to compare the winner and the loser.

McGilligan, Patrick, ed. *Backstory 2: Interviews with Screenwriters of the 1940s and 1950s*. Berkeley: University of California Press, 1997.
This collection includes three blacklisted writers: Arthur Laurents, Ben Maddow, and Daniel Mainwaring.

John Meroney, "Rehearsals for a Lead Role: Ronald Reagan in the Hollywood Wars."
Should this book ever be published (Meroney has been working on it for more than two decades), it promises to be the definitive anti-Communist take on the blacklist.

Neve, Brian. *The Many Lives of Cy Endfield: Film Noir, the Blacklist, and Zulu*. Madison: University of Wisconsin Press, 2015
Neve has researched well the life and work of this director, who emigrated to England to escape the blacklist but was eventually forced to name names to regain his career.

Schickel, Richard. *Elia Kazan: A Biography*. New York: HarperCollins, 2005.
A detailed and sympathetic account of the life of a hugely successful stage and screen director, who chose to be a friendly witness. [Other worthy books on Kazan: Michel Ciment, ed., *Kazan on Kazan* (New York: Viking, 1974); Thomas H. Pauly, *An American Odyssey: Elia Kazan and American Culture* (Philadelphia: Temple University Press, 1983); Elia Kazan and Michel Ciment, *An American Odyssey* (New York: St. Martin's, 1989); Jeff Young, ed., *Kazan on Kazan* (London: Faber and Faber, 1999); Brian Neve, *Elia Kazan: The Cinema of an American Outsider* (London: I. B. Tauris, 2009).]

Slide, Anthony. *Actors on Red Alert: Career Interviews with Five Actors and Actresses Affected by the Blacklist*. Lanham, MD: Scarecrow, 1999.
Slide interviewed Phil Brown, Rose Hobart, Marsha Hunt, Marc Lawrence, and Doris Nolan. Of the five, only Lawrence testified before the House Committee and cooperated. Hobart was named by another witness but did not appear.

Swindell, Larry. *Body and Soul: The Story of John Garfield*. New York: Morrow, 1975.

A fine biography of one of the subpoenaed actors whose untimely death was caused by his inability to resolve his fierce desire to keep his career and his equally fierce desire not to be a "stool pigeon."

General Histories and Monographs
(in alphabetical order by author)

Barranger, Milly S. *Unfriendly Witnesses: Gender, Theater, and Film in the McCarthy Era.* Carbondale: Southern Illinois University Press, 2008.

Barranger examines the experiences of seven prominent women of stage and screen whose lives and careers were damaged during the blacklist era. It is thoroughly researched, but she does not venture far from her close examination of her subjects' personalities and struggles.

Barson, Michael. *Better Dead Than Red: A Nostalgic Look at the Golden Years of Russiaphobia, Red-Baiting, and Other Commie Madness.* New York: Hyperion, 1992.

In this mainly visual (photographs, cartoons, and headlines) look at the Red Scare years, Barson adopts a tongue-in-cheek, "nostalgic" look back at the period.

Bentley, Eric, ed. *Thirty Years of Treason: Excerpts of Hearings Before the House Committee on Un-American Activities, 1938–1968.* New York: Viking, 1971.

Included in this massive tome are sections on the Hollywood hearings of 1947, 1951, and 1952, featuring the testimonies of eleven "friendly" and "unfriendly" witnesses in 1947; and eleven informing and Fifth Amendment witnesses in 1951 and 1952.

Billingsley, Kenneth Lloyd. *Hollywood Party: How Communists Seduced the American Film Industry in the 1930s and 1940s.* Rocklin, CA: Forum, 1998.

This book is skewed to the viewpoint of Roy Brewer, who was the most zealous anti-Communist in Hollywood.

Birdnow, Brian E. *The Subversive Screen.* Santa Barbara, CA: Praeger, 2019.

This book wears its ideological heart on its cover: a hammer and sickle. The author advertises it as an exploration of "the ties between Soviet agents, CPUSA leaders, American Communists" and a variety of Hollywood personnel, but it actually indicts the American Communist Party for its effort to take control of the motion-picture industry. Birdnow presents a factually accurate discussion of the Comintern's international media network and its connections to Hollywood; the formation of the Hollywood branches of the Party; and the activities of Hollywood Communists. However, he analyzes only three films (the infamous pro-Soviet movies of World War II). His two main conclusions are silly: The pro-Soviet movies led to the 1947 hearings, which, in turn, played a leading role in the demise of Hollywood's "Golden Age"; and the Hollywood Communists "sought nothing less than the defeat and destruction of the United States and its reconstruction along Stalinist lines."

Booker, M. Keith. *Film and the American Left: A Research Guide.* Westport, CT: Greenwood, 1999.

This very useful reference work thoroughly explores leftist elements in American films through the 1990s. The author critically examines the political content and implications of hundreds of films.

Brianton, Kevin. *Hollywood Divided: The 1950 Screen Directors Guild Meeting and the Impact of the Blacklist.* Lexington: University Press of Kentucky, 2016.

What began as a meeting to contest the institution of a loyalty oath and the takeover of the Guild by Cecil B. DeMille escalated into a hot debate between zealous anti-Communists and wishy-washy liberals. Brianton does an excellent job undermining the mythical elements of this meeting, but he fails to make the reader see why this meeting was so important. By 1950, Hollywood was not "divided": all the Guilds had either adopted loyalty oaths or made it clear they would not protect any of their blacklisted or subpoenaed members who were members of the Communist Party. This book is, then, a footnote, well-researched and clearly written.

Brimner, Larry Dane. *Blacklisted!: Hollywood, the Cold War, and the First Amendment.* Honesdale, PA: Calkins Creek, 2018.

This book, written for young adults, is a fine introduction to the subject. It is a concise, clearly written account of the 1947 hearings. The many illustrations, documents, and photographs are very well chosen.

Buhle, Paul, and Dave Wagner. *Blacklisted: The Film-Lover's Guide to the Hollywood Blacklist.* New York: Palgrave Macmillan, 2003.

An essential research tool, this tome is a massive compilation of films and biographies (with more than two thousand entries).

Buhle, Paul, and Dave Wagner. *Hide in Plain Sight: The Hollywood Blacklistees in Film and Television, 1950–2002.* New York: Palgrave Macmillan, 2003.
The follow-up to *Radical Hollywood,* carrying the story forward into the television era, the decline of the studio system, and the work of the Hollywood exiles. In both books, the authors celebrate (and overvalue) the success of the Left in changing movies.

Buhle, Paul, and Dave Wagner. *Radical Hollywood: The Untold Story behind America's Favorite Movies.* New York: New Press, 2002.
An exhaustive analysis of the movies influenced by left-wing employees of the motion-picture industry, from the silent era to the coming of television. The authors tend to overextend the term "left" and to overestimate its influence.

Carr, Robert K. *The House Committee on Un-American Activities, 1945–1950.* Ithaca, NY: Cornell University Press, 1952.
Narrower in chronological expanse than Goodman (see below), it is well-researched and judicious.

Casty, Alan. *Communism in Hollywood: The Moral Paradoxes of Testimony, Silence, and Betrayal.* Lanham, MD: Scarecrow, 2009.
A critique of "the romanticized version of the Hollywood blacklist." His aim is to right the moral balance between House Committee informers and unfriendly witnesses. Casty argues that the unfriendly witnesses, by their silence, protected a criminal regime, were morally complicit in the consequences of what they defended or supported, weakened the liberal Left, and strengthened the conservative Right, whereas, in his estimation, the informers told the "truth." (See chapter 3 for an in-depth review.)

Ceplair, Larry. *Anti-Communism in Twentieth-Century America: A Critical History.* Santa Barbara, CA: Praeger, 2011.
A detailed examination of the varieties of anti-Communism in the United States, including the de facto variety of the motion picture industry.

Ceplair, Larry, and Steven Englund. *The Inquisition in Hollywood: Politics in the Film Community, 1930–1960.* Garden City, NY: Anchor/Doubleday, 1980; paperback editions by University of California Press (1983) and University of Illinois Press (2003).
The first detailed study of the background and context of the motion picture blacklist and still the best book on the subject.

Cogley, John. *Report on Blacklisting*. 2 vols. New York: Fund for the Republic, 1956.

The first in-depth examination of the blacklist in film and television. Cogley and one of his main researchers, Paul Jacobs, were fervent anti-Communists, and it colors their analysis. There is little sympathy here for the unfriendly and Fifth Amendment witnesses. Several of the chapters are based on the research of Elizabeth Poe Kerby, but Cogley has substantially altered her conclusions. For example, he fully accepts the bottomless claim of anti-Communists that they were blacklisted by Communists in the 1930s and 1940s.

Critchlow, Donald T. *When Hollywood Was Right: How Movie Stars, Studio Moguls, and Big Business Remade American Politics*. Cambridge: Cambridge University Press, 2013.

A biased argument that the Republicans in Hollywood were the good guys. Critchlow is particularly enamored of Ronald Reagan, but he covers all the usual suspects, from 1930 to 1980, including George Murphy, Richard Nixon, John Wayne, and others. He is much better on the intricacies of politics than film history. He commits many factual errors in his recounting of films and filmmakers.

Dick, Bernard F. *Radical Innocence: A Critical Study of the Hollywood Ten*. Lexington: University Press of Kentucky, 1988.

Dick has provided the reader with a detailed assessment of the Ten's creative output. He has thoroughly mined all their artistic work, from page to screen. Although his critical comments are occasionally too academic, his evaluations are reasonable. He includes a chronology, bibliography, and filmography for each man.

Dick, Bernard F. *The Screen Is Red: Hollywood, Communism, and the Cold War*. Jackson: University Press of Mississippi, 2016.

In this book, Dick surveys but does not critically examine a wide range of politically tinged films, some of them neither red nor pink. It consists of twenty-one short essays concerning a wispily connected body of films and two television shows, 1930 to the present.

Doherty, Thomas. *Show Trial: Hollywood, HUAC, and the Birth of the Blacklist*. New York: Columbia University Press, 2018.

Doherty focuses on the 1947 hearings. Relying mainly on an impressive use of primary sources, he provides sections on all the House Committee's witnesses, while steering clear of partisanship, polemics, and intemperance. He begins with an overview of the 1930s and World War I, and concludes with a what-happened-to-them chapter.

Dowdy, Andrew. *"Movies Are Better than Ever"—Wide-Screen Memories of the Fifties*. New York: Morrow, 1973.
Contains a very good chapter on seven anti-Communist films.

Faulk, John Henry. *Fear on Trial*. New York: Simon and Schuster, 1964.
An excellent account of Faulk's fall from grace and his winning battle in the courts against the publication that smeared him.

Frankel, Glenn. *Shooting Midnight Cowboy: Art, Sex, Loneliness, Liberation and the Making of a Dark Classic*. New York: Farrar, Straus and Giroux, 2021.
The previously blacklisted writer Waldo Salt wrote the script and won an Academy Award.

Frankel, Glenn. *High Noon: The Hollywood Blacklist and the Making of an American Classic*. New York: Bloomsbury, 2017.
A fine, deep study of the classic Western cum allegory of the fear induced by anti-Communism, and an examination of how a subpoena from the House Committee on Un-American Activities ended the friendship and business relationship of the film's writer, Carl Foreman, and its producer, Stanley Kramer. (For my take on the matter, see chapter 7.)

Freedland, Michael. *Hollywood on Trial: McCarthyism's War against the Movies*. With Barbara Paskin. London: Robson, 2007.
The authors argue that anti-Semitism was the main catalyst for the House Committee's investigation of Hollywood. They do not make a convincing case.

Friedrich, Otto. *City of Nets: A Portrait of Hollywood in the 1940s*. New York: Harper and Row, 1986.
Though the 1947 House Committee hearings are not the central portion of this fine book, it is worth reading for the context it provides.

Gladchuck, J. Joseph. *Hollywood and Anti-Communism: HUAC and the Evolution of the Red Menace, 1935–1950*. New York: Routledge, 2007.
His thesis is unremarkable: The Red Scares of 1939 and the postwar years were cultivated by anti-Communists. Their efforts combined with the

unchecked mandate of the House Committee on Un-American Activities to condemn the Hollywood Ten, ushered in the motion-picture blacklist. It is well researched.

Goodman, Walter. *The Committee*. New York: Farrar, Straus and Giroux, 1968.
Still the best look at the House Committee on Un-American Activities.

Hendershot, Cyndy. *Anti-Communism and Popular Culture in Mid-Century America*. Jefferson, NC: McFarland, 2003.
Looks at anti-Communist content in a wide range of media: films, television, books, journalism, among others.

Hoberman, J. *An Army of Phantoms: Movies and the Making of the Cold War*. New York: New Press, 2011.
The most detailed year-by-year look at Hollywood during the first decade of the Cold War. Hoberman looks at dozens of films and sets them in their larger political context, and he profiles the confrontations between politicians and moviemakers during that era. Though the book lacks a sustained analytical theme, it provides a fascinating chronological examination of Cold War films and politics.

Hogan, David J., ed. *Invasion USA: Essays on Anti-Communist Movies of the 1950s and 1960s*. Jefferson, NC: McFarland, 2017.
Twenty-one essays covering forty films.

Horne, Gerald. *Class Struggle in Hollywood, 1930–1950: Moguls, Mobsters, Stars, Reds, and Trade Unionists*. Austin: University of Texas Press, 2001.
An in-depth examination of the most significant labor battle in Hollywood, pitting the studio bosses and International Alliance of Theatrical Stage Employees (IATSE) against a democratic union, the Conference of Studio Unions (CSU). Employing a red-baiting strategy, blacklisting, and thugs and goons, the IATSE broke the back of the CSU and dealt a death blow to the Left in Hollywood. Horne also demonstrates that organized crime played a key role in the IATSE and the ranks of studio management.

Humphries, Reynold. *Hollywood's Blacklists: A Political and Cultural History*. Edinburgh: Edinburgh University Press, 2008.
This book does not add much to the subject. It lacks a central thesis and a coherent, unifying theme. Most of the chapters are conglomerates of

illogically arranged topics. Nor is it a cultural history. Those who wish to know the historical and political background to the blacklist (1930s and 1940s) will not find it here.

Kahn, Gordon. *Hollywood on Trial: The Story of the Ten Who Were Indicted.* New York: Bonia and Gaer, 1948; New York: Arno Press and New York Times, 1972.
The first book on the Ten, which makes no pretense at objectivity but does present a factually correct account of the unfriendly Nineteen and their strategy. Kahn was one of the nineteen unfriendly witnesses, and the Ten asked him to write this book as part of their effort to avoid prison and blacklisting.

Kanfer, Stefan. *A Journal of the Plague Years.* New York: Atheneum, 1973.
A well-written account of the post-1947 lives of film and broadcast blacklistees. He provides a very sketchy overview of the pre-1947 years, and there are no references.

Kempton, Murray. *Part of Our Time.* New York: Simon and Schuster, 1955.
His chapter on the Hollywood Ten is intended to be ironic, but it comes off as supercilious. Without knowing or talking to these men, he thinks he can analyze their motives; without reading anything they have written, he believes he can downgrade them as artists. His essay on them is a perfect example of liberal anti-Communism and condescension. (He recanted, to some degree, in 1968.)

Krutnik, Frank, Steve Neale, Brian Neve, and Peter Stanfield, eds. *"Un-American" Hollywood: Politics and Film in the Blacklist Era.* New Brunswick, NJ: Rutgers University Press, 2007.
An excellent collection of articles, covering all facets of the blacklist era.

Lawson, John Howard. *Film in the Battle of Ideas.* New York: Masses and Mainstream, 1953.
Lawson, one of the Hollywood Ten who had written extensively on playwriting, here parrots the Party line that Communists cannot have any effect on screen content and should, instead, organize unions, guilds, and audiences to create pressure for progressive films.

McGilligan, Patrick, and Paul Buhle. *Tender Comrades: A Backstory of the Hollywood Blacklist.* New York: St. Martin's, 1997.

An anthology of in-depth interviews with thirty-six former blacklistees. An indispensable source.

Mayhew, Robert. *Ayn Rand and* Song of Russia: *Communism and Anti-Communism in 1940s Hollywood.* Lanham, MD: Scarecrow, 2005.
Mayhew, an acolyte of Rand's, presents a skewed analysis of the film and its makers.

Miller, Merle. *The Judges and the Judged: Report on Black-listing in Radio and Television for the American Civil Liberties Union.* New York: Doubleday, 1952.
The first detailed look at blacklisting in the broadcast industries. It caused a split in the ACLU's board when one board member criticized Miller for not giving equal time to the blacklisting by the Left.

Navasky, Victor S. *Naming Names.* New York: Viking, 1980.
An intensive examination of the informers and those they named. Navasky interviewed many of the key friendly and unfriendly witnesses, and he tells their stories well. He concludes by posing the questions of forgiveness, obedience, and candor. (For an in-depth review, see chapter 3.)

Neve, Brian. *Film and Politics in American Society: A Social Tradition.* New York: Routledge, 1992.
Neve focuses on seven directors, five of whom were either blacklisted or informed, and shows how they negotiated their roles in relation to the studio system, and how their film work reflected the broader industrial, bureaucratic, social, and political developments of the period 1935–1970.

Nizer, Louis. *The Jury Returns.* Garden City, NY: Doubleday, 1966.
Nizer recounts how he won the libel suit of John Henry Faulk and exposed the nastiness of those who blacklisted him.

Nielsen, Mike, and Gene Mailes. *Hollywood's Other Blacklist: Union Struggles in the Studio System.* London: BFI, 1995.
Gene Mailes's personal account of his fight to impose democratic unionism and local autonomy on the IATSE is complemented by Nielsen's context and commentary.

Prime, Rebecca. *Hollywood Exiles in Europe: The Blacklist and Cold War Film Culture.* New Brunswick, NJ: Rutgers University Press, 2014.

This book covers the emergence of a left-wing core of movie artists during the 1930s and 1940s, the early years of the blacklist, runaway productions, the work of the film émigrés in Europe, and noir films. The author shows how blacklisted émigrés played a significant role in creating an international black market and weakening the blacklist. Her focus, however, is not on all the exiles; it is on four directors: Jules Dassin, Joseph Losey, John Berry, and Cy Endfield. She virtually ignores blacklisted writers, even though they outnumbered directors two to one.

Radosh, Ronald, and Allis Radosh. *Red Star over Hollywood: The Film Colony's Long Romance with the Left.* San Francisco: Encounter, 2005.

Laboring under the delusion that the truth about Communism in Hollywood has been forever obscured by the revisionist histories of the New Left, the authors, both fervent anti-Communists, zealously track, mislabel, and misinterpret the activities of the Communists and fellow-travelers in the movie industry. Whatever "truth" they thought they found is hidden by the polemics.

Ross, Steven J. *Hollywood Left and Right: How Movie Stars Shaped American Politics.* New York: Oxford University Press, 2011.

Ross examines the careers of ten Hollywood people, five on the right (including Louis B. Mayer and Ronald Reagan) and five on the left (Charlie Chaplin and Edward G. Robinson among them), to illustrate that the impact of Hollywood activists on US politics has been long, deep, and varied. He concludes that conservatives have enjoyed much more success than the Left.

Ryskind, Allan H. *Hollywood Traitors: Blacklisted Screenwriters, Agents of Stalin, Allies of Hitler.* Washington: Regnery, 2015.

The title of this book alone informs the reader of the writer's bias. Ryskind, the son of a zealous Hollywood anti-Communist and friendly witness, plays fast and loose with facts and definitions to make his points.

Ryskind, Morrie. *I Shot an Elephant in My Pajamas.* With John H. Roberts. Lafayette, LA: Huntington House, 1994.

A fierce anti-Communist and one of the friendly witnesses at the 1947 hearings, he tells here the story of his odyssey from Russia to Broadway to Hollywood as well as his conversion to conservative politics.

Salo, Matti. *Hiljaiset Sankerit* [The brave ones]. Helsinki: Painatuskekus/ Suomen, 1992.

This book has not been translated, and it is probably difficult to find, but it is an incredibly detailed examination of the careers and scripts of fifty-three blacklisted screenwriters. Salo was an indefatigable researcher.

Sbardellati, John. *J. Edgar Hoover Goes to the Movies: The FBI and the Origins of Hollywood's Cold War*. Ithaca, NY: Cornell University Press, 2012.
An excellent, probing study of the role played by the FBI in identifying, compiling dossiers, and exposing "subversives" in Hollywood.

Schwartz, Nancy Lynn. *The Hollywood Writers' Wars*. Completed by Sheila Schwartz. New York: Knopf, 1982.
Though she died before she had completed writing this book, the author had conducted a formidable number of interviews with blacklisted writers. Since they are all now deceased, this book remains an essential reference source. There is, however, an unfinished quality to the book; it is lacking in critical analysis of the personalities and events.

Shaw, Tony. *Hollywood's Cold War*. Amherst: University of Massachusetts Press, 2007.
A fine analysis of Hollywood's treatment of Soviet-US relations, 1917–1989, using selected films to illustrate his main themes.

Sherman, Fraser A. *Screen Enemies of the American Way: Political Paranoia about Nazis, Communists, Saboteurs, Terrorists, and Body-Snatching Aliens in Film and Television*. Jefferson, NC: McFarland, 2011.
This work contains one chapter on the Red Scare in Hollywood.

Shindler, Colin. *Hollywood Goes to War: Film and American Society*. London: Routledge and Kegan Paul, 1979.
A good introduction to the relation between the politics of a time period and the movies made during it.

Smith, Jeff. *Film Criticism, the Cold War, and the Blacklist*. Berkeley: University of California Press, 2014.
An examination of the meaning imposed on films by scholars and critics. Conceptual nomenclatures abound, but few, especially "meaning" and "interpretation," are clearly explicated. Lengthy, well-researched and well-presented discussions of significant Cold War movies comprise the meat of the book, but they are in the form of conventional movie criticism. Smith does not systematically employ his own criteria.

Stabile, Carol A. *The Broadcast 41: Women and the Anti-Communist Blacklist*. London: Goldsmiths, 2018.

A dark look at the early days of television broadcasting, when anti-Communism dominated decision-making. It returns to the discussion women, forty-one of whom paid a steep price for their progressive ideas and activities. It is well researched and argued, albeit Stabile tends to overstate her main themes.

Suber, Howard. "The Anti-Communist Blacklist in the Hollywood Motion Picture Industry." Ph.D. diss., UCLA, 1968; Ann Arbor, MI: University Microfilms International, 1976.

A dissertation that should have been published. It is a deeply researched monograph on the mechanics of the blacklist. Suber was the first author since Elizabeth Poe to actually speak to the blacklisted people. It also contains a very helpful roster of all the witnesses, their films, and, in the case of the blacklistees, those who named them.

Vaughn, Robert. *Only Victims: A Study of Show Business Blacklisting*. New York: Putnam's, 1972.

A dissertation that was published. He also interviewed some of the blacklisted people. His account is also one of the earliest sympathetic ones. It includes the statements the Ten attempted to deliver to the House Committee on Un-American Activities.

Vaughn, Stephen. *Ronald Reagan in Hollywood: Movies and Politics*. Cambridge: Cambridge University Press, 1994.

Using Reagan's life story, his movie career, and his presidency of the Screen Actors Guild as lenses, Vaughan provides a well-researched examination of the origins and institutionalization of the blacklist in Hollywood.

Writers Guild of America West. *Written By* 19, no. 5 (September–October 2015).

An excellent collection of articles about, and interviews with, blacklisted writers.

Salt of the Earth

Baker, Ellen R. *On Strike and on Film: Mexican American Families and Blacklisted Filmmakers in Cold War America*. Chapel Hill: University of North Carolina Press, 2007.

Using Rosenfelt's book (see below) as a template, Baker has added more details and sociological nomenclature. She has not added much to Silverton's account or that of James J. Lorence. She is best when recounting the history of mining and miners in Grant County, the history of the unions, the roles of the Communist Party and of the women. Her account of the making of the movie has several errors of fact, and she does not provide a critique of the film or explain how this movie incorporated the Marxist viewpoints of its makers, particularly Michael Wilson.

UCLA Oral History Program: Roy Brewer, John Bright, Jeff Corey, Mary Davenport, Guy Endore, Paul Jarrico, Sylvia Jarrico, Robert W. Kenny, Elizabeth Poe Kerby, Alfred Lewis Levitt, Helen Slote Levitt, Eddie Lewis, Albert Maltz, Ben Margolis, Michael Wilson, Zelma Wilson.

Novels

Since these are not sources, and I am not a literary critic, I will forbear offering annotations.

Epstein, Leslie. *San Remo Drive.* New York: Other Press, 2003.

Goldstein, Paul. *Errors and Omissions.* New York: Doubleday, 2006.

Gores, Joe. *Hammett: A Novel.* New York: Putnam's, 1975.

Toperoff, Sam. *Lillian and Dash: A Novel.* New York: Other Press, 2013.

Blacklist Articles and Reviews by the Author

Articles (in chronological order)

"The Politics of Compromise in Hollywood." *Cineaste* 8, no. 4 (ca. 1978): 2–7.

A study of the making of *Blockade*, a film about the Spanish Civil War, written by future blacklisted writer John Howard Lawson.

"Hollywood Blacklist." *Emmy,* Summer 1981, 30–32, 52.

An examination of the television blacklist.

"Great Shows: *You Are There.*" *Emmy,* January/February 1982, 43–47.

Written by three blacklisted writers: Abraham Polonsky, Walter Bernstein, and Arnold Manoff.

"The Writers Guild Redeems Its Past." *Emmy,* January/February 1983, 6, 44.

The story behind the decision to award pensions to blacklisted writers.

"*The House on Carroll Street.*" *Cineaste* 16, no. 4 (1988): 46–47.

"A Communist Labor Organizer in Hollywood: Jeff Kibre Challenges the IATSE, 1937–1939." *The Velvet Light Trap,* no. 23 (Spring 1989): 64–74.

Kibre tried and failed to break the grip of the corrupt International Alliance of Theatrical Stage Employees on the studio labor force.

"Hollywood Left." In *Encyclopedia of the American Left,* edited by Mari Jo Buhle et al., 339–42. New York: Garland, 1990.

A study of the progressive forces in Hollywood.

"Who Wrote What? A Tale of a Blacklisted Screenwriter and His Front." *Cineaste* 18, no. 2 (1991): 18–21.

The story of the script for *Broken Arrow*, written by the blacklisted Albert Maltz and fronted by his friend Michael Blankfort. The two became estranged following Blankfort's friendly testimony to the House Committee on Un-American Activities.

"The Communist Party in Hollywood," "The Hollywood Blacklist," "Elia Kazan," "Albert Maltz," "Abraham Polonsky," "The Unfriendly Hollywood Nineteen," and "Michael Wilson." In *The Political Companion to American Film*, edited by Gary Crowdus. Boston: Lakeview, 1994.

Short articles on various topics and people of the blacklist era.

"SAG and the Motion Picture Blacklist. *Screen Actor* 39, no. 8 (January 1998): 18–26.

Written as part of the Guild's commemoration of the fiftieth anniversary of the start of the motion-picture blacklist.

"Shedding Light on *Darkness at High Noon*." *Cineaste* 27, no. 4 (Fall 2002): 20–23.

A critique of a documentary about the estrangement between Stanley Kramer and Carl Foreman during the making of *High Noon*. See chapter 7.

"The Many Fiftieth Anniversaries of *Salt of the Earth*." *Cineaste* 29, no. 2 (Spring 2004): 8–9.

A discussion of the film and its importance.

"Righting a Wrong: Paul Jarrico and Correction of Blacklist-Era Screen Credits," *Cineaste* 32, no. 4 (Fall 2007): 30–33.

Details Jarrico's yeoman-like effort to restore credits to writers who wrote on the black market.

"Albert Maltz, Philip Stevenson, and 'Art Is a Weapon.'" *minnesota review*, no. 69 (2007): 153–62.

The two blacklisted writers' challenge to Communist Party orthodoxy.

"Isobel Lennart and the Dynamics of Informing in Hollywood." *Historical Journal of Film, Radio and Television* 27, no. 4 (October 2007): 513–30. See chapter 5.

"Reporting the Blacklist: Anti-Communist Challenges to Elizabeth Poe Kerby." *Historical Journal of Film, Radio and Television* 28, no. 2 (June 2008): 135–45.

Kerby wrote the first detailed exposé of the motion-picture blacklist and became, as a result, a target of anti-Communists.

"The Base-Superstructure Debate in the Hollywood Communist Party." *Science & Society* 72, no. 3 (July 2008): 319–48.
  A detailed look at a key issue among Marxist filmmakers, highlighted by a clash between John Howard Lawson and Michael Wilson.

"The Film Industry's Battle against Left-Wing Influences, from the Russian Revolution to the Blacklist." *Film History* 20, no. 4 (2008): 399–411.
  An account of the unstinting efforts of motion-picture executives to protect their product from their left-wing employees.

"Julian Blaustein: An Unusual Movie Producer in Cold-War Hollywood." *Film History* 21, no. 3 (2009): 257–75.
  Blaustein, in the face of the domestic Cold War, produced three movies that went against the tide: *Broken Arrow, The Day the Earth Stood Still,* and *Storm Center.*

"Hollywood Unions and Hollywood Blacklists." In *Blackwell's History of American Films,* edited by Cynthia A. Lucia et al. Oxford, UK: Blackwell, 2012.

"A History of the Hollywood Unions and Guilds and Their Involvement with Blacklisting: Kirk Douglas, *Spartacus,* and the Blacklist." *Cineaste* 38, no. 1 (Winter 2012): 11–13.
  A review of the misstatements and falsehoods in Douglas's memoir, *I am Spartacus!*

"A Marxist in Hollywood: The Screenwriting Career of Michael Wilson (1914–1978)." *Historical Journal of Film, Radio and Television* 34, no. 2 (June 2014): 187–207.
  An analysis of Wilson's efforts to infuse his scripts with his Marxist outlook on writing.

"The United States Government (in the form of the Federal Bureau of Investigation, the Immigration and Naturalization Service, and the House Committee on Un-American Activities) versus Three Aliens (Charlie Chaplin, Bertolt Brecht and Hanns Eisler)." *Historical Journal of Film, Radio and Television* 38, no. 1 (2018): 20–53.
  The unrelenting, and ultimately successful, effort of the United States government to rid the country of these "subversive" artists.

"Ring Lardner, Jr. and the Hollywood Blacklist." *Historical Journal of Film, Radio and Television* 39, no. 1 (2019): 75–95.
  See chapter 6.

"The Broadcast 41: *Women and the Anti-Communist Blacklist.*" *Cineaste* 45, no. 2 (Spring 2019): 73–74.

Book Reviews (in chronological order)

"*Hollywood Red* and *The Hollywood Writers' Wars.*" *Cineaste* 12, no. 2 (1982): 54–56.

Books by Lester Cole and Nancy Lynn Schwartz.

"*Running Time.*" *Cineaste* 12, no. 3 (1983): 48–49.

Cold War movies, written by Nora Sayre.

"*Radical Innocence: A Critical Study of the Hollywood Ten.*" *Film Quarterly* (Summer 1989): 33–34.

Review of a book by Bernard F. Dick.

"*Backstory: Interviews with Screenwriters of Hollywood's Golden Age* by Pat McGilligan"; "*Backstory 2: Interviews with Screenwriters of the 1940s and 1950s* by Pat McGilligan"; "*Writers in Hollywood, 1915–1951* by Ian Hamilton.*" *Cineaste* 18, no. 4 (1991): 53–55.

Review of two collections of interviews with Hollywood screenwriters and a history of writers in Hollywood.

"*The Final Victim of the Blacklist.*" *Cineaste* 32, no. 1 (Winter 2006): 74–75.

Review of a biography of John Howard Lawson.

"*On Strike and on Film.*" *Cineaste* 32, no. 3 (Summer 2007): 96–97.

Review of an account of the making of *Salt of the Earth*, by Ellen Baker.

"McCarthyism Revisited." *Historical Journal of Film, Radio and Television* 28, no. 3 (August 2008): 405–14.

A book review essay of the McCarthy phenomenon.

"*Hollywood's Blacklists.*" *Cineaste* 35, no. 2 (Spring 2010): 83–84.

Review of Reynold Humphries's political and cultural history of the blacklist.

"*The Writers.*" *Cineaste* 40, no. 3 (Summer 2015): 78.

Review of a history of the Screen Writers Guild and the Writers Guild of America written by Miranda J. Banks.

"*Film Criticism, the Cold War, and the Blacklist.*" *Cineaste* 40, no. 4 (Fall 2015): 75–77.

Review of the development and influence of film criticism during the Cold War, by Jeff Smith.

"*The Screen Is Red: Hollywood, Communism, and the Cold War.*" *Cineaste* 41, no. 1 (Winter 2015), Web exclusive.

Review of Bernard F. Dick's analysis of films made during the Cold War.

"*Hollywood Exiles in Europe: The Blacklist and Cold War Film Culture.*" *Science and Society* 80, no. 3 (July 2016): 429–31.

> A review of Rebecca Prime's book on the film work of blacklisted exiles and its influence on the culture of the Cold War.

"*Hollywood Divided.*" *Cineaste* 42, no. 3 (Summer 2017): 75–76.

> An account of how the campaign for a loyalty oath provoked a major divide in the Directors Guild of America, written by Kevin Brianton.

Film Reviews (in chronological order)

"A Crime to Fit the Punishment." *Cineaste* 13, no. 3 (1984): 26–27.

> A documentary on *Salt of the Earth.*

"The Squishiness of Current Blacklist Documentaries." *Cineaste* 16, no. 4 (2008): 26–27.

> Critique of blacklist documentaries.

"*Guilty by Suspicion.*" *Cineaste* 18, no. 3 (1991): 46–47.

"*Trumbo* (the Movie) Versus Trumbo (the Life)." *Cineaste* 41, no. 2 (Spring 2016): 20–23.

"*Silver Lode:* A Western Parable about McCarthyism." *Cineaste,* https://www.cineaste.com/winter2020/silver-lode-western-parable-about-mccarthyism.

Index

Index

Index

Index

Fort Monmouth, NJ, 47, 84, 170n94
Forum, 68
Fosse, Bob, 114
Fox Film Corporation, 73
Fox, William, 30, 73
France, 14, 31, 67, 81
Frankfurter, Felix, 166n46
Freedom from Fear Committee, 169n75
Freeman, Y. Frank, 37
friendly witnesses, x, 2, 15, 20, 22, 49–55, 63–65, 120
Front, The, 23
Frontier, 133
Fuchs, Daniel, 112, 178n33

Galvan, Pedro, 135
Gang, Martin, 43, 47, 53, 54, 169n79
Garfield, John, 125
Garrett, Betty, 52, 176n2
Geisel, Theodore, 152
Genius, 140
Gentleman's Agreement, 40
George King Productions, 134
German Communist Party, 78
Germany, 6, 14, 17, 78, 81, 124
GI Joe, 127
Girls High School (NYC), 100
Girosi, Marcel 135
GI Willie, 127
Glass, George, 146
Glazer, Nathan, 27, 29
Glenn, Charles, 79
Goebbels, Josef, 78
Gold, Harry 44
Gold, Lee, 104
Goldwyn, Samuel, 17, 18, 30, 40, 42
Good Housekeeping, 112
Goodman, Walter, 1
Goodyear Television Playhouse, 23
Google, 152, 154
Göring, Hermann, 78
Grant, Cary, 125
graylist, 10, 11, 47, 97
Grayson, Katherine, 106

Great Britain. *See* United Kingdom
Green, Johnny, 21
Greene, Marjorie Taylor, 151
Greenglass, David, 44
Griffith, D. W., 32

Hachette, 152
Hall, Barbara, 176–77n5
Hammett, Dashiell, ix; blacklisted, 89; and congressional investigating committees, 90–92; and Continental Op, 69–72; early years, 68–69; enlistment in army, 67, 83–85: and imprisonment, 88–89; joins Communist Party, 76–77; last years, 92–93; and Lillian Hellman, 75, 82, 83, 84, 87, 88, 92, 93; political activism, 76–83, 86–88; writing career, 69–76
—MAGAZINE ARTICLES AND STORIES: "After School," 74; "The Cleansing of Poisonville," 73; "From the Memoirs of a Private Detective," 69; "Nelson Redline," 76; "Night Shade," 90; "On the Way," 74; "This Little Pig," 74
—MOVIE CREDITS: *Watch on the Rhine,* 75
—MOVIES BASED ON HIS BOOKS: *City Streets,* 74; *The Glass Key,* 75; *The Maltese Falcon,* 74, 92; *Mister Dynamite,* 74; *Roundhouse Nights,* 73; *Secret Agent X-9,* 75; *The Thin Man,* 74, 75; *Woman in the Dark,* 74
—NONFICTION BOOKS: *The Battle of the Aleutians,* 84
—NOVELS: *The Dane Curse,* 72, 73; *The Glass Key,* 70, 73; *The Maltese Falcon,* 70, 73; *Red Harvest,* 67, 71, 73, 76; *The Thin Man,* 70–73
—UNPUBLISHED NOVELS: "Tulip," 92
Hammett, Josephine (née Dolan), 67

225

Index

Index

Index